THE
Herb
BIBLE

p

THE Herb BIBLE

A Complete Guide to Growing and Using Herbs

JENNIE HARDING

This is a Parragon Publishing Book
This edition published in 2005

Parragon Publishing
Queen Street House
4 Queen Street
Bath BA1 1HE, UK

Produced by THE BRIDGEWATER BOOK COMPANY

• ISBN 1-40546-036-9

Printed in Indonesia

Notes for the Reader

Herbs contain natural substances that are used
in medicine and they must always be treated with respect.
This book is intended as a source of information; it is
not intended to be used as a medical textbook. If you
are undergoing medical treatment, do not take herbal
remedies without first consulting your physician. It is
also advised that any long-term treatment should be
administered under the guidance of a medicinal herbalist.
Please follow the safety advice contained in the book.
However, the use of a herb for any purpose is at the
reader's own risk and the publisher cannot be held
responsible for any adverse reactions that may result from
the use of a herb or its derivative contained in this book.

The Recipes:

• This book uses imperial, metric or US cup
  measurements. Follow the same units of measurement
  throughout; do not mix imperial and metric.

• All spoon measurements are level: teaspoons are
  assumed to be 5 ml, and tablespoons are assumed to
  be 15 ml.

• Unless otherwise stated, milk is assumed to be whole,
  eggs and individual vegetables such as carrots are
  medium, and pepper is freshly ground black pepper.

• Recipes using raw eggs should be avoided by infants,
  the elderly, pregnant women, convalescents, and anyone
  suffering from an illness.

• Do not use a larger quantity of herbs than is
  recommended in the recipes.

Contents

the world of
herbs

Introduction

Welcome to the Herb Bible, a detailed manual that will show you how to grow and use herbs in your daily life. In our modern world, there is a growing wish to be connected to nature as an antidote to stress and pressure. Many of us would like to live in healthier and simpler ways, rediscovering the knowledge and understanding of the natural world used by our ancestors, such as cultivating and using our own herbs for cooking and medicine. In times past, the practice of simple herbalism was common knowledge, and although the day-to-day use of it declined in the last century, the principles can easily be rediscovered, as you will see. Growing herbs and using them in the kitchen and as medicines can make a real and satisfying contribution to your life, helping to support your health and improve your connection to the Earth.

In this book you will discover how herbs can make a real difference to your well-being as well as your environment and your diet. Humankind has used plants for their beneficial effects since the dawn of civilization, and many herbal traditions have grown up worldwide linked to particular plants that grow locally, whose benefits have been appreciated for centuries. In many cases, science is now offering detailed explanations as to why those herbs actually work, supporting the traditional use of the plant as a medicinal aid.

In the Herb Bible you will find four sections. First, there is detailed information about growing your own herbs, then a selection of simple and delicious recipes that use herbs to enhance flavors. This is followed by a section looking at herbs medicinally, for self-help and general well-being. Finally, you will find a directory with 70 common herbs shown in detail, so you can refer to that section if you are looking for a particular herb. Each herb's botanical information and uses are clearly shown so you can see how it could be used to help you.

It is important to say at the outset that herbal traditions, including herbal medicine itself, are to be taken seriously. Herbs can be very beneficial if used correctly; however, they must also be respected as powerful agents. If you have a recognized medical condition or if you are unsure about using herbs in your particular circumstance, you should always consult your physician or a registered herbal practitioner.

right Grinding herbs and spices in a pestle and mortar releases their pungent flavors when added to food.

below: left Blue-flowered borage and fresh green mint make an attractive and colorful display in your garden.

below Basil is a particularly aromatic plant that grows well in the sun. It can also be kept on a windowsill or in a conservatory.

below: right Feverfew (left) and lavender (right) are both used effectively to ease headaches and migraines.

Examples of herbal tradition

In Western herbal medicine, extract of **horse chestnut** (*Aesculus hippocastanum*) has been used traditionally as an ointment to help varicose veins or hemorrhoids. Scientific investigation has shown that horse chestnut contains a combination of active ingredients called aescin. This combination strengthens the vein walls, stopping leakage, as well as reducing swelling, heaviness in the legs, and itching. Horse chestnut extract can now be obtained as a natural supplement.

Garlic (*Allium sativum*) is now scientifically recognized as having immune-stimulating and antiviral properties, as well as helping to reduce cholesterol. In the 17th century, Nicholas Culpeper, one of the most well-known Western herbalists, said "... [garlic] voids tough phlegm, purges the head ... is a good preservative against and remedy for any plague, sore or foul ulcer."

9

The world of **herbs**

Entering the world of herbs is like coming into a garden whose delights
you have yet to discover. Before you start on the journey, it helps to have
some answers to common questions—this can guide you into a better
understanding of what herbs are all about. You may then feel your
appetite has been stimulated—which is one of the main effects
of using herbs—to find out more!

What is a herb?

All herbs are plants, but not all plants are herbs.
The usual way of defining a herb is as a plant that
may be *useful*, either as a food, as a flavoring, or
as a medicinal agent with a therapeutic effect. A
herb is a special type of plant, with the potential
to bring about changes in the body. This can
happen either through eating it with food or using
it medicinally. Actually, many herbs are used for
both flavor and medicine! Herbs are often aromatic
as well, with special fragrances that have mentally
uplifting or physical effects. Rosemary
(*Rosmarinus officinalis*), for example, is an
excellent flavoring for lamb; as a medicinal herb, it
is helpful for poor circulation; and as a powerful,
fresh fragrance, it helps poor concentration.

What about spices?

Spices, such as ginger (*Zingiber officinale*) or
black pepper (*Piper nigrum*), are the seeds,
berries, or roots of particular plants. They are used
in cooking, especially in Eastern countries, to give
a fiery flavor full of zesty warmth; they are
also very important in traditional approaches to
medicine such as Ayurveda, the natural medicine
of India. Medicinally they are often used to help
digestive problems and support the immune
system. Spices have been part of the Western
European medical tradition since Roman times,
when they were brought to the West via ancient
trade routes.

right Yellow-
flowered
dandelion is
a powerful
cleansing and
diuretic herb—
much more than
a simple weed!

below Pungent
spicy ginger
improves the
circulation as
well as adding
zest to food.

Dandelion

left Herbs are useful plants whose properties have been appreciated over centuries of cultivation and harvesting.

below left Black peppercorns are a powerful immune-boosting spice, especially helpful for chesty coughs.

below Exotic dishes flavored with spices stimulate the digestive system to break down and absorb nutrients efficiently.

Black pepper is described in Culpeper's 17th-century *Herbal* as a spice that "dissolves wind in the bowels ... helps the cough and other chest diseases and stirs up the appetite." In Indian Ayurvedic medicine, fiery black pepper is regarded as one of the best defenses against colds, coughs, or other "damp" conditions of the body. Modern herbal medicine uses black pepper as a digestive stimulant and also an antibacterial remedy.

Aren't a lot of herbs just weeds?

Many useful plants that you might call weeds are actually healing herbs. Some common examples are nettle (*Urtica dioica*), one of the first spring green herbs, which was often made into a nourishing soup; dandelion (*Taraxacum officinale*), the scourge of the suburban lawn, which is in fact a source of cleansing, bitter-green leaves and a root that, if roasted and ground, tastes rather like coffee; and the common daisy (*Bellis perennis*), with leaves that soothe bruises and cuts, and flowers that calm digestive troubles. All these native plants are found in herbals, proving their ancient uses; these were the simple ingredients that people picked from fields and hedgerows and used as natural medicine.

Herbs in history

The use of herbs by humankind is estimated to go back some 60,000 years in history. Early proof of the use of herbs includes archeological evidence from an ancient site in Iraq. There, in ancient caves, the remains of a Neanderthal man were found, together with a wreath containing several herbs, all of which still grow in the region and some of which are still used in medicine. Herbs have been constantly used in rituals, medicine, cosmetics, and healing in different cultures across the globe, and many of these traditions still continue today.

Coriander

China

Here, the use of herbs is recorded in a famous text, *The Yellow Emperor's Book of Internal Medicine*, which is over 4,000 years old. In it, remedies such as ginger are recorded as helping the digestion, and opium as relieving pain. Traditional Chinese Medicine makes use of thousands of herbal ingredients, often combined into powders to be mixed with water and drunk. Clinics of Traditional Chinese Medicine are now found all over the world and are often able to help with stubborn chronic problems such as eczema.

India

The Indian tradition of using herbs and spices goes back approximately 4,000 years to the Vedic texts, which form the basis for Ayurvedic medicine. Aromatic ingredients such as cinnamon, ginger, coriander, and sandalwood were used as fragrant medicines to bring balance internally to the whole system. Ayurvedic medicine still makes use of these and many other ingredients in healing and in food to restore vitality.

The Arab civilization

In early medieval times, the Arab civilization was renowned for its healing skills. The Arab physician Abu Ibn Sina (980–1037), or Avicenna, wrote *The Canon of Medicine*, a text that details many ingredients in common use at the time. He was familiar with ingredients like camphor, camomile, and lavender, and many of his remedies were plants from as far away as Tibet and China.

left Camomile is used in Western herbal medicine to reduce fever and as a soothing treatment for skin inflammation.

below left Lavender fields are an expanse of attractive purple—large quantities of the flowers are needed to extract essential oil for perfumery and aromatherapy.

The West

Western herbal medicine owes a great deal to the Ancient Greeks, who in turn learned from the Ancient Egyptians. Hippocrates, born in Greece around 460 BC, used herbs such as opium as a narcotic, lungwort for lung infections, and pomegranate to stop bleeding. Another Greek physician, Dioscorides, cataloged all the plants and spices available at this time and his text *De Materia Medica*, published in AD 78, was a standard source in Western herbalism for several centuries.

The 16th and 17th centuries in England produced some of the most famous Western herbalists: John Gerard (1545–1611), who grew an incredible collection of herbs in his own garden in Holborn, London; Nicholas Culpeper (1616–54), whose famous *Herbal* of 1649 made information on herbs and healing widely available; and the diarist John Evelyn (1620–1706), whose *Discourse of Sallets* encouraged people to use herbs in their diet for health. Despite the rise of interest in chemical drugs during the 18th and 19th centuries, and the dominance of drug companies in the 20th century, herbalism has survived and is enjoying renewed popularity.

13

growing
herbs

Why **grow your own** herbs?

It's very easy these days to buy either fresh or dried herbs from supermarkets; in fact, this may be the only way many people come across them. However, learning about these plants by growing them yourself is a unique experience, because it immediately changes the relationship you have with them. You begin to appreciate herbs in new ways because growing them is a natural step to using them, and therefore you start to become much more involved with your own environment. Here are some other reasons for getting started.

A healthy tonic tea

Pick two or three fresh sage leaves and a 2-in/5-cm sprig of myrtle. Wash the leaves and place in a cup; pour over $\frac{2}{3}$ cup boiling water. Put a saucer over the top of the cup and let infuse for 15 minutes. Lift out the leaves, then add a teaspoon of honey to the tea and sip slowly.

below Growing herbs on a windowsill is very easy and using them fresh adds delicious flavors to your food.

FOENICULUM VULGARE

It's easy!

Growing herbs can be as simple as planting a few seeds in a pot and standing it on your windowsill. Many aromatic herbs love the sunlight, so the warmer it is, the better they grow and the more fragrant they become. A pot of basil sitting there will release a wonderful fresh, green, and slightly spicy aroma into the air, and the leaves can easily find their way into salads or into tomato-based dishes with a Mediterranean feel. Many herbs are also low-maintenance plants and actually do better if you don't fiddle with them too much!

It's satisfying

Planting your own herb area lets you experiment with color, shape, and fragrance, so that your senses of sight, taste, and smell are really enhanced. On a warm, summer's evening, it can be very pleasant to walk around the herbs, plucking a leaf or two here and there, smelling and tasting the results of your work. Simple tasks like gathering herbs for your own tea or choosing flavorings for your cooking take on a new meaning when the herbs are your own. Every day, even in the winter, you can find leaves or flowers to use. The aroma of food you cook with your own herbs certainly stimulates your appetite!

It's good for your health

When you grow your own herbs, you know exactly how you have done it—how the plants have been watered, fed (if necessary), and harvested. Such organically grown herbs are wonderful to use, full of flavor and vitality, and an extremely useful tool for maintaining health. You can be confident that the plants will have a useful therapeutic value because they have been grown exactly as they should, without any unnecessary pesticides or chemical fertilizers. Only a few generations ago, these plants were the basis of medicine, and people collected and used them regularly to support their health; your herb collection can be used in a similar way.

CHAMOMILLA RECUTITA

SALVIA OFFICINALIS

SELINUM CRISPUM

ALLIUM SATIVUM

Start with the soil

Before you even think about starting to plant your garden or how it might look, it is really important to know about the soil in which you are going to plant your herbs. There are many types of soil, influenced by the geographical location of where you live as well as environmental factors like moisture. Different herbs do well in different types of soil, so you will not get good results if you put in plants that do not match your environment.

What is soil?

If you pick up a handful of soil and look at it closely, you will see it is a collection of different kinds of particles, some large, some small. It actually has a very complex structure, made up of stones, minerals, salts, microbes, pieces of decomposing plant matter, and tiny insects. If you get the chance to look at a soil sample under a microscope, it can look like a miniature zoo! Soil is a living thing, and in order for anything to grow successfully the balance of all the elements in it must be nurtured and maintained. For the gardener, this means the regular addition of good organic matter—compost—to keep the soil full of nutrients.

Soil types

If you take a fork and dig a hole down to about 12 inches/30 cm, you will start to see some of its characteristics. Is it dark and crumbly (loam), or is it light and sandy? Is it sticky and heavy (clay), or very wet (marshy)? If there are any plants growing near by, do their roots go deep or are they near the surface? Darker soils, where the plants root deeply, are good for general herb cultivation; lighter-colored or wetter, heavier soils will suit particular types of herbs.

Soil tests

You can buy soil testing kits from your local supplier. These will help you analyze your soil type, and identify whether your soil is acid or alkaline. Try testing different areas in your garden—you may find variations in acidity or alkalinity even in a small plot.

Soil types

Chalky If you live in a chalk area, the soil will be light and well drained. Good herbs to choose are hyssop, juniper, rosemary, summer savory, and sweet marjoram.

Light, sandy Sand makes the soil very dry and water drains away quickly. It is very good for Mediterranean herbs like lavender, thyme, and tarragon, which need dry conditions.

Loam This dark soil is full of nutrients and is light and crumbly; it allows lots of air to the roots and helps plants stay healthy and strong. Good herbs to choose here are basil, chervil, coriander, dill, lovage, or sage.

Clay Clay soil tends to be full of heavy, sticky clods. Herbs with strong, deep roots are needed here, such as comfrey, sorrel, lemon balm, and mint.

Marshy If you live in an area that is poorly drained, you will need to consider herbs that thrive in a wet environment such as angelica or valerian.

habitat

Identifying soil types

Take an empty screw-top jar and fill it up halfway with soil from your garden. Top up the jar with water, then screw on the lid and shake it. Let the soil settle; you will find layers of light sand and heavier stones and clay particles. These give you a good idea of the balance of your soil.

Sandy and clay soils tend to be more acid, and therefore good for plants like sorrel, juniper, dandelion, and heather. Neutral or rich loamy soils tend to be more alkaline and good for plants like elder, rose, yarrow, or thyme species. Acid soil is generally harder to manage—it needs lime and good quality organic matter to make it more alkaline and suitable for a wider variety of plants.

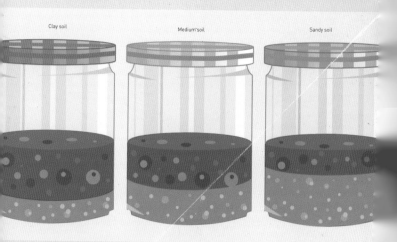

Clay soil   Medium soil   Sandy soil

Your space: microclimates

When beginning to plan a herb garden, it is important to consider how your actual garden space works in terms of "microclimates." These are pockets of light and shade, warmth and cool, dry and damp, and they all provide different environments, enabling you to plan your planting for maximum effect. Any garden will have several key zones. The first step is to use a compass to plot north accurately, and to enter this on a simple sketch of the garden. This quickly shows the way the sun travels over the area—i.e. the angle of east to west. Areas facing south are the warmest, areas facing north are the coolest.

below Designing a herb garden can be a very satisfying project, enabling you to create a beautiful aromatic space to enjoy and use.

Map your space

Draw a simple sketch of your garden, showing areas of open ground, lawn, paths, trees, and large shrubs. Use a compass to show north and add this to the sketch. Then note the east-to-west angle, the way the sun crosses the garden, and the south, where it is warmest. It helps to know and sketch the position of the hottest place in the garden during the summer, which is when most herbs are at their best—this will be the best place for aromatic herbs like lavender or rosemary. They produce more essential oils in their leaves if they re situated in full hot sunshine. The coolest, darkest places are good for herbs that like moist nd shade, like comfrey. Mapping these areas will elp you to decide where you would like to create herb beds and borders, or simply where to plant herbs alongside existing plants. If you want a seat in your herb garden to enjoy the sights and aromas, put it in the sunniest area and plant aromatic herbs near it.

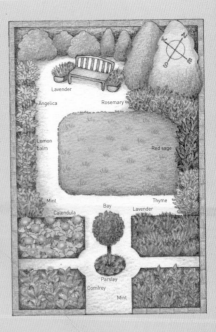

Lavender
Angelica
Rosemary
Lemon balm
Red sage
Mint
Bay
Thyme
Calendula
Lavender
Parsley
Comfrey
Mint

Other key microclimates

South-facing walls

These retain the heat and protect tender plants from frost; they can enable you to grow Mediterranean-type herbs, like thyme or sage, in generally cooler climates.

Ponds or water features

These will promote more damp in the soil around them, so they will be good sites for moisture-loving herbs like angelica.

Paved areas

If these are in sunny positions, the pavers will hold the heat, and these are excellent sites for pots of aromatic herbs.

Fences

These provide shelter from wind as well as patches of shade at particular times of day, which suits herbs like lemon balm that do not like too much sun.

Other things to notice about your garden are the areas you instinctively like to visit, the places where you tend to sit, and the way you usually walk around it. All your useful herbs need to be planted in areas you go to often; that way you will pick them and use them!

left Plant herbs in pots or let them grow naturally between pavers—you can try many different attractive combinations.

Using small spaces

Tarragon

You do not have to live in an idyllic country house in order to plant and use herbs successfully. In fact, because many herbs are very compact plants, they lend themselves very well to being planted in smaller spaces where they can very easily create an attractive and aromatic display. In an urban setting, it is easy to find ways of planting herbs close to buildings or walls, where they instantly improve the environment. As ever, it is important to plan your herb planting in such a way as to make using them easy and accessible.

Balconies

These work very well as herb-growing spaces, particularly if the sun gets to them for at least part of the day. One thing you will have to do is water your herbs more often than if they were planted in the ground. Small pots of herbs work best if they stand in a saucer and you water them from beneath; large pots need to be kept moist but not too wet. You can fix a trellis to a side wall and use it to train a vine in a pot, or you can buy simple sets of shelves for a varied display of different herbs. Try growing your own cherry tomatoes in a pot with some fresh basil to accompany them!

Windowsills

In southern European countries, these small spaces are often packed with pots or trays of herbs like parsley, thyme, or sweet marjoram, to be cut fresh for cooking. Warmer climates mean these herbs can be grown outside. In cooler, northern climates, pots of herbs need to be on a sunny window ledge indoors, protected from cold winds. Remember not to overwater these herbs—just keep them moist. Chives work well in a pot, as do herbs like tarragon or summer savory—used fresh, they add fine flavors to dishes.

Porches

These are often overlooked, but if they are sheltered they make excellent protective spaces for tender plants, and can almost work like mini-conservatories. Aromatic fragrant herbs like lavender, scented geraniums, or bay trees are very attractive outside your front door, and all of these work well in pots or tubs. The front porch is also an excellent space where you can move some pots from the garden in the fall to protect them through the winter.

Courtyards

In southern Europe again, stone-walled courtyards are often homes for a whole array of pots and climbing plants like vines. The walls offer protection and create a suntrap, which is ideal for aromatic herbs; the space also becomes an attractive place to relax and unwind. Town houses with no garden but a small patio can create one, quite simply, by choosing a varied collection of aromatic shrubs like myrtle or bay for large tubs, or large pots of rosemary, hyssop, and fennel to create aroma and attractive colors.

opposite Pots of aromatic herbs like lavender, scented geraniums, or rosemary grow well on sunny balconies and steps.

ng herbs for sun and shade

you have decided where the zones of sun or shade are in your
den or space, it then helps to know what types of herbs are suited
these areas. This will help you plan your garden in more detail
nd choose plants that will grow successfully for you. Herbs were
riginally wild plants, growing in particular environments such as
eep within woodland or on the edges of meadows, on hillsides or
lose to water. To get the best results, you need to choose a spot for
our plant that mirrors the kind of location it would choose in the
vild. The three groups of plants shown below need different levels of
unlight or shade; they can easily be cultivated in an average garden,
vhich will have these kinds of spaces.

Rosemary

opposite A
woodland garden
is a haven for
plants that thrive
in part or full
shade under
a protective
canopy of trees.

Herbs for full sun

Many of these (marked*) are aromatic herbs, which
have special cells within their leaf structure containing
essential oils—highly concentrated fragrances.
The more sun these plants enjoy, the stronger their
fragrances. In the Mediterranean region, where
these plants originate, their aroma travels some
distance. Some of these aromatic plants have their
essential oils extracted by distillation and are used in
aromatherapy (see pages 138–141); this is a special
way to use these natural fragrances for health
and well-being.

Yarrow, dill*, tarragon*, borage,
calendula, fennel*, hyssop*, bay,
lavender*, lovage*, horehound,
garlic*, oregano*, coriander*,
basil*, sweet marjoram*,
rosemary*, sage* (common),
sage* (clary), fenugreek,
sunflower, myrtle*,
nasturtium, red clover,
raspberry, savory,
horsetail.

Herbs for part-sun, part-shade

These are herbs that grow best in dappled sunlight,
out of the glare of full sun. In the wild, their natural
habitat was often at the edges of woodlands, where
the canopy of trees was less dense but still offered
some protection. They can be planted under the shade
of trees or shrubs to simulate this environment.

Angelica, chervil, camomile, lemon balm,
peppermint, parsley, sorrel, comfrey,
lady's-mantle, wild strawberry,
juniper, echinacea, eyebright, nettle.

Angelica

Fennel

Aromatic steam

To experience the intensity of the aroma in lavender flowers, try this exercise: place 2 tbsp fresh or dried blooms in a heatproof glass dish. Pour over generous ¾ cup of boiling water and immediately smell the fragrant steam, in which tiny aromatic molecules of essential oil are floating. Inhaling the steam for about 10 minutes really helps chesty coughs, because the essential oil in the lavender soothes the respiratory passages and helps you cough up mucus. The sweet floral aroma is very soothing.

Lavender

Herbs for full shade

In the depths of woodlands and forests, where the light penetrates least, are found some of the most potent of all herbs, such as belladonna (deadly nightshade) and mandragora (mandrake), whose roots and bulbs contain poisonous ingredients called alkaloids. Fortunately there are some gentler, easy-to-grow herbs that are beneficial and also love a shady environment. They tend to have rich-green leaves and do well in the darker corners of the garden.

St.-John's-wort, evening primrose, lungwort, valerian, sweet violet.

St. John's wort

Herbs for **extreme climates**

Growing herbs is easy in most types of soil, but
there are some areas where climatic conditions
pose more of a challenge when planning a
garden. Here you need to think not just about the
soil and its condition, but also of other features
that you can build, to protect and shelter your
herbs. You may also be surprised at the number
and type of plants you can actually choose from.
One way to find out what may do well is to have
a look at the types of plants you find growing
wild locally to where you live.

Coastal regions

If you live near a beach or a river estuary, or
near cliffs, the sea will tend to have certain effects
on your garden. Exposure to salt in the air and
extreme winds can damage many plants. The soil
may be thin or rocky, and you may have to deal
with steep slopes in your garden. However, you
can begin to change the microclimate, by planting
a hedge as a windbreak, using tough plants like
privet; then behind the hedge you can plant useful
shrubs like elder (*Sambucus nigra*), juniper
(*Juniperus communis*), or rosemary (*Rosmarinus
officinalis*) in its tall-growing species 'Miss Jessup's
Upright', which can grow up to 6 ft/2 m tall. Other
herbs that will do well once there is more shelter
are Mediterranean herbs like fennel (*Foeniculum
vulgare*) or lavender (*Lavandula* species), which
thrive in dry, poor soils. If you have a very
sloping garden, many of the low-growing herbs
like marjoram (*Origanum majorana*) or thyme
(*Thymus* species) grow into aromatic mats, which
look beautiful in a rockery.

Hot dry regions

If you live in a very arid area, there are aromatic
shrubs, trees, and other plants that are very good at
sending long roots into the earth to find water. One
such tree is eucalyptus (*Eucalyptus globulus* and other
species), which in the fiery outback of Australia, its
native habitat, can grow up to 200 ft/60 m in height.
Its aromatic, pale-green leaves are a source of
essential oil. In the Mediterranean, shrubs like myrtle
(*Myrtus communis*) or bay (*Laurus nobilis*) are a
source of fragrant green leaves all year round, again
rich in essential oils. Also, any of the Mediterranean
herbs will do well in this type of climate. Make use of
walls to provide some shade for plants like chives
(*Allium schoenoprasum*) or lemon balm (*Melissa
officinalis*) as a protection from full sun.

above A coastal garden can still be planted with herbs—try using fences or windbreaks to protect your plants.

Peppermint

Cool wet regions

In these types of regions you need to choose the varieties of herbs and medicinal plants that do well in water, or close to it. Moist areas are often home to a huge variety of lush plants, and herbs like all the mints (*Mentha* species), horsetail fern (*Equisetum arvense*), angelica (*Angelica archangelica*), valerian (*Valeriana officinalis*), or comfrey (*Symphytum officinale*) will thrive where there is plenty of water, as will tasty salad ingredients such as watercress (*Nasturtium officinale*).

Herbs for color

A herb garden can be a delight to look at, particularly because of the wonderful variety of colors and shapes of the flowers, as well as particular types of leaf. It will have a different appearance to an ornamental garden, where the colors tend to be very strong and dramatic; the appearance of herbs together tends to create a more muted effect, yet is still beautiful and vibrant. Here are groups of herbs and flowers shown together according to their colors; you may decide you want to plant areas featuring just one color for a particular effect, or choose colors that contrast with each other to please your eye.

Marjoram

Rose

Herbs grouped by colors

Red-pink flowers Roses (*Rosa gallica, damascena,* or *centifolia* species).

Blue flowers Borage (*Borago officinalis*), rosemary (*Rosmarinus officinalis*).

Blue-purple flowers Hyssop (*Hyssopus officinalis*), lavenders (*Lavandula* species), comfrey (*Symphytum officinale*), thyme (*Thymus vulgaris*), sweet violet (*Viola odorata*).

Purple Echinacea (flowers) (*Echinacea purpurea*), black peppermint (leaves) (*Mentha x piperita*), purple-ruffled basil (leaves) (*Ocimum basilicum*), purple sage (leaves) (*Salvia officinalis*).

Pink-purple flowers Chives (*Allium schoenoprasum*), marjoram (*Origanum majorana*), oregano (*Origanum vulgare*), clary sage (*Salvia sclarea*).

Yellow-green leaves Lady's-mantle (*Alchemilla vulgaris*), dill (*Anethum graveolens*), fennel (*Foeniculum vulgare*), lovage (*Levisticum officinale*).

Yellow flowers Witch hazel (*Hamamelis virginiana*), sunflower (*Helianthus annuus*), St.-John's-wort (*Hypericum perforatum*), evening primrose (*Oenothera biennis*), cotton lavender (*Santolina chamaecyparissus*), dandelion (*Taraxacum officinale*), curry plant (*Helichrysum angustifolium*).

White and cream flowers Myrtle (*Myrtus communis*), elder (*Sambucus nigra*), white comfrey (*Symphytum officinale*), Roman camomile (*Anthemis nobilis*), sweet cicely (*Myrrhis odorata*), feverfew (*Tanacetum parthenium*), valerian (*Valeriana officinalis*).

Orange flowers Calendula (*Calendula officinalis*), nasturtium (*Tropaeolum majus*).

Variegated foliage (green and cream leaves) Lemon balm (*Melissa officinalis*), pineapple mint (*Mentha suaveolens*), ginger mint (*Mentha x gentilis*), lemon thyme (*Thymus citriodora*).

Silver leaves Curry plant (*Helichrysum angustifolia*), lavenders (*Lavandula* species), horehound (*Marrubium vulgare*), sage (*Salvia officinalis*), eucalyptus (*Eucalyptus globulus* and other species).

The color wheel

This rainbow wheel shows you the range of colors in the spectrum. Where colors are side by side, you will find they sit well together; if they are on opposite sides of the wheel, they will be a contrast to each other.

Green is a universally harmonizing shade—as green leaves show well! Green is very restful to the eyes and helps you to relax. Reds, oranges, and yellows have a warm vibration and a cheering effect. Blues and purples are soothing to the eye, as you find if you view a field of lavender flowers,

for example, a sea of purple that immediately calms your vision. Creamy white flowers are moving from yellow to paler shades still, and have a soothing effect; if the color wheel is spun quickly enough, all the colors merge to become white, a universal shade.

These ideas can help you to plan the type of color scheme you would like to have in your herb garden if you are starting from scratch, or decide where to put plants if your garden is already established.

Herbs to **attract** beneficial insects

Planting herbs in your garden is an excellent
way to encourage beneficial insects to visit your
space. Many of these insects are losing their
natural habitat because of intensive farming
methods, which destroy the hedgerows and
meadows where they would normally be found.
As well as being wonderful to look at, many of
these insects act as pollinators—particularly
useful if you are also growing fruit. They also
help to keep your garden naturally free from
pests like aphids, which attack in large numbers.
Attracting beneficial insects is a way of helping
your garden without the use of pesticides. These
insects are drawn to the aromas of the herbs, in
particular when they are in flower; they are also
very attracted to paler-colored flowers, which
they can see well. These beneficial insects arrive
in large numbers when your herbs are in full
flower, usually between the months of June
and August.

Fruit trees

Hover flies

These yellow-and-black striped insects really are the
organic gardener's friend. They are attracted to many
herbs, such as yarrow, dill, camomile, coriander,
fennel, lavender, feverfew, or thyme, and when they
come to the garden they also feed on larvae and adult
aphids, and whitefly. Planting the types of herbs listed
here near vegetables, for example, will encourage the
hover flies to come and help reduce the pest
population in your garden.

Butterflies

People who plant flowers to attract butterflies are also
helping with conservation—many species of butterfly
are increasingly being seen in town gardens. They are
very sensitive to aromas. Red admirals, tortoiseshells,
painted ladies, and common blues are stunning to
watch and they are attracted to the fragrances
of herbs like lavender, or flowers like rose or myrtle.
If you grow cabbage and you want to discourage
cabbage butterflies, whose caterpillars love the green
leaves, try an old country trick—plant hyssop next to
your cabbage and the aroma will confuse
the butterflies, attracting them away!

Bee hives

Roses

Bees and bumble bees

These do not play a part in pest control, but they are excellent pollinators. The sound of bees in your herbs is very much a part of a summer's day, and if you have enough space for a hive, excellent honey can be made if the bees visit fragrant herbs like lavender or rosemary. Bumble bees are endangered, again because of the use of chemicals in farming and loss of natural habitat; if you plant herbs, you are providing them with food. Watching them dive into your herbs with almost reckless energy is a joy, especially when they fly away literally dusted with pollen.

Ladybugs

These familiar red-and-black-winged beetles are also excellent at pest control; they are particularly fond of fennel, coriander, and dill, which are all members of the same botanical family of plants, the *umbelliferae*. Planting these herbs in your garden will ensure a good number of ladybugs—and they are very fond of aphids which so often attack roses.

31

A **healing garden:** a place of retreat

It is a very good idea to visit one or two established herb gardens to give you ideas as you decide what kind of space to create. Many country houses or botanical gardens have extensive collections of herbs in their grounds, illustrating different styles and layouts. It is also interesting to notice how you feel in these spaces. Very often you will notice a sense of tranquility, calm, peace, and warmth. If so, stop and observe where you are, and try and decide why you feel that way. A herb garden is often a very healing space, for different reasons.

Layout

Look at the way the herb garden is arranged. Herb plots laid out in regular, raised beds are typical of monastic-style medicinal gardens, where all the plots are surrounded by paths. These encourage you to walk all around the beds, and give you very easy access to what is planted. This design makes harvesting the herbs very easy. Herb gardens where plots of herbs are surrounded by box hedging are very attractive and may have a lovely fragrance; however, the emphasis there is on looks rather than usefulness—an ornamental approach.

Walls

The traditional medieval herb garden had walls all around it. Originally this was because the gardens were actually within the walls of castles, but walled gardens continued to be built even after castles fell out of use. It was quickly discovered that enclosing the garden within walls had great advantages—raising the temperature, protecting plants from wind and harsh weather, and creating a suntrap. A walled space can feel very safe, very contained and is often quiet, too, because the stone adds a level of sound-proofing. It can be a calm and attractive place to relax and unwind.

Landscaping

Sometimes herb gardens have a sunken area, a level that is lower than the ground level. This works very well in cooler or coastal climates, again to keep the wind at bay and the temperature warm. Very tender herbs can be planted on the lower level to protect them from frost. The Queen's Garden behind Kew Palace at Kew Gardens in London is designed exactly like this, and on a hot summer's day the aroma of all the herbs in the lower level is intense as the power of the sun is concentrated there.

Special features

Sometimes, the quiet and peace of a herb garden is concentrated around a particular feature. One example might be an ornamental seat, an arch, or an arbor placed to take full advantage of the sun as well as aromatic flowers like roses or honeysuckle nearby. Another might be a camomile lawn, which releases its apple-like fragrance as you walk over it. A sundial placed in the center of a round herb plot gives it balance and focus, like the hub of a wheel. Any of these ideas can be incorporated into your own garden. In the past, features like these encouraged people to walk around the space, enjoy it, and interact with the plants there.

top left Gravel paths among herb beds bring you very close to plants and encourage you to touch and smell them.

top right Designing a herb garden around a central feature focuses your eyes and gives a sense of balance and harmony.

bottom Placing a seat among aromatic beds creates a restful and meditative space, where the perfumes of herbs and flowers soothe the senses.

Simple **herb garden** design

To help you plan your herb garden, here is an exercise to try so you can design a garden according to your needs. First, complete the sketch of your available space (see pages 20–21) showing areas of light and shade, and the north–south axis. Then make notes, using the following questions:

Why do you want to plant a herb garden?

For cooking

Do you want to use fresh herbs in cooking, and grow enough to dry or preserve for the winter months?

Herbs to consider: basil, thyme, fennel, marjoram, sage, garlic, rosemary, and tarragon; because these herbs are all useful and tasty flavorings and seasonings.

For medicine

Do you want to grow herbs to use for health, to make teas and other preparations?

Herbs to consider: feverfew, eyebright, lady's-mantle, echinacea, and St.-John's-wort; because these herbs all help common ailments and improve well-being.

For cosmetic use

Do you want to use herbs to take care of your skin?

Herbs to consider: lavender, horsetail fern, red clover, and comfrey; because these herbs all have soothing anti-inflammatory and skin-improving effects.

For aromas

Do you want a particularly fragrant garden?

Herbs/flowers to consider: peppermint, rose, Roman camomile, sage, thyme, basil, and oregano; because these plants have highly fragranced leaves and flowers due to their essential oil content.

For looks

Are you interested in a particular type of layout? What herbs would suit a formal garden layout?

Herbs/shrubs to consider: bay, myrtle, rosemary, and lavender; because these plants can be clipped into geometric or stylized shapes, which suit a more formal garden design.

above You can use herbs you grow yourself to make your own natural skincare preparations.

left Medicinal herb teas taste more delicious when prepared with fresh, organically grown herbs.

Answering these questions will help you to decide on the kind of use you think you will make of your herbs. You may find all the reasons are true to a degree, so try to get a feel for what your main interests would be. It is also useful to think about the following questions:

Is your garden already established, in which case herbs need to fit into its existing layout?
If so, you need to note carefully where the spaces are, and whether they are in light or shade.

Are you starting a new garden or a new part of your garden?
If so, you will need to check the soil—it may be necessary to dig in some compost to revive the soil and provide more nutrients.

Are you working in a small, confined space?
If so, what kind—a courtyard, a balcony, or a very small garden? Depending on this, you may need to plant in pots—see pages 42–43.

Once you have the answers to these questions, look at pages 36–47 to find a whole range of different herb garden designs. These range from small spaces to more complex designs like herb wheels, from more ornamental layouts to practical plots for kitchen and medicinal use. You can use these pages to help you decide on your layout. It is then best to try and sketch your proposed garden to scale, along with areas you plan to plant up. There is a sample sketch of a garden below to help you get started.

As you work, remember that in the past, herb gardens were places of beauty as well as utility. This is your chance to create your own haven of peace and tranquillity, as well as plants to use for your health and well-being.

above Fresh herbs make delightfully tasty garnishes in soups and other dishes.

below Make a sketch of your available space, showing areas of light and shade and existing features.

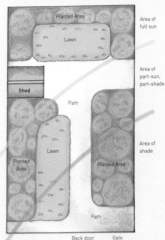

Planted Area

Lawn

Area of full sun

Shed

Path

Area of part-sun, part-shade

Planted Area

Lawn

Planted Area

Area of shade

Path

Back door   Gate

35

The herb wheel: a simple layout

This is a very simple herb plot to plan and create, particularly if you want all your herbs to be concentrated in one area of your garden. The design originated in the 19th century, when people used large cartwheels laid in the ground and planted different herbs between the spokes. As these are less plentiful these days, the shape of a wheel can be easily created using stones or bricks to make a framework. The advantage of the "compartments" is that they keep the herbs contained and neat; using bricks or small, flat stones to mark out the wheel also creates small paths, which makes visiting the beds very easy. This means you can harvest your herbs, clip bushes, and tend to the garden's needs with good access to all areas.

Dill

right A herb wheel is a simple and effective way to grow herbs in a small space and be able to pick them easily.

Choosing the site of the herb wheel needs care; you need to find a level location in your garden, sheltered and preferably in full sun, particularly if you want to plant herbs you will use in the kitchen. You also need to be able to get to the herb wheel easily and quickly—if it is at the bottom of your plot, you might not be so keen to fetch those herbs when it's cold and raining! This may mean adding a path to it if you don't already have one.

The size of the wheel is up to you. It is easy to mark out a circle by sinking a strong cane into the ground and tying a long piece of string to it. At the other end of the string tie another sharp stick, which you can use to trace your circle on the ground, placing stones as you go to show the edge. A circle of approximately 6 ft/2 m in diameter can then be divided into four, six, or eight segments, as you wish. The edges of the segments can be marked with flat stones or bricks sunk into shallow trenches in the ground. Fill in the gaps between the bricks with coarse sand, or use mortar if you want a solid finish.

The soil in the segments needs a mixture of one-third each of garden sand, compost, and topsoil. This ensures good drainage, a light, crumbly texture, and good levels of nutrients. This mixture is good for common kitchen herbs you may wish to consider, such as:

Dill	*Anethum graveolens*
Marjoram	*Origanum majorana*
Thyme	*Thymus vulgaris*
Sage	*Salvia officinalis*
Rosemary	*Rosmarinus officinalis*
Summer savory	*Satureja hortensis*
Peppermint	*Mentha x piperita*
Parsley	*Petroselinum sativum*

In an eight-segment wheel you could plant up one herb per segment, or in a four-segment wheel you could combine two per area. Bear in mind your herbs will spread, so allow space for them to grow healthily.

Marjoram

Mint

36

Medicinal herbs to consider

Yarrow	*Achillea millefolium*
Roman camomile	*Anthemis nobilis*
St.-John's-wort	*Hypericum perforatum*
Borage	*Borago officinalis*
Clary sage	*Salvia sclarea*
Feverfew	*Tanacetum parthenium*

Culinary herbs to consider

Garlic	*Allium sativum*
Chives	*Allium schoenoprasum*
Lovage	*Levisticum officinale*
Parsley	*Petroselinum crispum*
Basil	*Ocimum basilicum*
Oregano	*Origanum vulgare*

Herb beds: a monastic layout

This type of herb garden is much larger and more complex, and would suit a new, empty plot, particularly if you can start from scratch. Its design is based on ideas taken from the monastic tradition of herb-growing. As far back as the 10th and 11th centuries, monasteries and convents were the first hospitals, providing remedies grown and prepared from their extensively laid-out gardens to treat local people and travelers. During the time of the Crusades, many exotic plant species found their way into these gardens, such as the opium poppy (*Papaver somniferum*), whose seeds yield a juice from which modern drugs such as morphine are derived. Ancient monastic herb gardens also allowed for the cultivation of vegetables alongside the medicinal plants, such as onions, leeks, beets, beans, garlic, and parsnips, which were part of the monks' staple diet, as well as flowers like roses or lilies. Many beautiful manuscripts from medieval times show illustrations of the kinds of plants the monks grew.

For this layout, you may wish to choose a plot with some shade available, or plant some larger shrubs such as elder (*Sambucus nigra*) or trees like apple (*Malus domestica*) to create a variety of microclimates. Shady areas will enable you to grow herbs like comfrey (*Symphytum officinale*) or valerian (*Valeriana officinalis*). The design features oblong-shaped raised beds bordered with either bricks or heavy wooden planks, set out with wide paths between them. Keeping the paths wide lets you move a wheelbarrow in between the beds, which helps when you are composting the plot. Ideally, the whole garden would be enclosed within walls so that very tender herbs could be positioned in sheltered places or aromatic climbing roses positioned to create a beautiful, fragrant, and colorful display—they need warmth and sun. A centerpiece such as a sundial or a statue makes a striking feature, or you could choose a bay tree and keep it well clipped to create a living sculpture.

Individual beds do not need to be more than 3 ft/1 m wide, so access is easy, and can be around 8 ft/2.5 m in length. Raising the beds slightly by surrounding them with bricks or boards gives good drainage and makes the adding of compost each spring an easy task. When planning your planting, you could choose to include beds for more medicinal herbs and beds for culinary herbs, or you could plant members of the same botanical family in the same bed, such as fennel, coriander, and angelica—all members of the *umbelliferae* plant family. Remember to take into account the amount of sun or shade your plants will enjoy when planning where to put them. When you buy your plants to set in place, just put them down in their pots first, in position according to your layout, and check that they are in the best position. Eventually you will have a garden which is quite structured in its layout but which gives you easy access to all your herbs for simple enjoyment as well as harvesting.

above St.-John's-wort has very attractive yellow flowers and dark foliage, and was used in medieval times to treat wounds.

left A monastic herb garden is surrounded by walls and contains beds laid out in a geometric pattern with wide paths for easy access.

A kitchen herb border

This is a herb plot that is intended primarily to be used in conjunction with cooking. In the 18th century, country houses had very extensive kitchen gardens for producing the large amounts of fruits and vegetables needed to supply whole households. Part of the kitchen garden would be an area devoted to the herbs and spices used for flavoring food. As well as flavoring fresh dishes, herbs and spices would also be used in pickling, salting, and preserving processes, which kept the household going through the wintertime, as well as in the making of candies, such as young angelica stems (*Angelica archangelica*) boiled in sugar.

below Angelica stems have a sweet and slightly spicy taste when boiled in sugar.

As many herbs have untidy or sometimes invasive habits when they are growing, it is a good idea to incorporate some kind of hedge or divider into the kitchen plot to keep things in order. One idea would be to plant low-growing small hedges of box (*Buxus sempervirens*) in diamond shapes to create small beds. Another would be to divide up the border with paths made of pavers, which also have the advantage of giving you really easy access to all the herbs for harvesting, clipping, and collecting seeds.

Some herbs, such as sage or rosemary, are "perennial," meaning they grow back in the spring without replanting. Other herbs, such as calendula or basil, are "annual," and these need to be sown or planted each year. When you plan the kitchen border, it helps to put perennials in a prominent position where they will stay, and fill in the gaps with annuals, which you will plant each spring. Many of the perennial herbs are evergreen, such as myrtle, bay, rosemary, and thyme, and these will give you a show of leaves throughout the wintertime—as well as kitchen flavors!

Ideally, the best orientation for the kitchen herb border is south-facing, and it works best against a wall, but of course it also needs to be close to your back door or within easy access of your kitchen. When you plan your planting, check the height and spread of the plants (given on pages 178–251 of this book, and also on pot labels in garden centers). Then make sure the taller plants, like fennel, are toward the back of the plot, and the low-growing plants, like thyme, are at the front or close to the paths.

Herbs for a basic kitchen border

Perennials

Tarragon	*Artemisia dracunculus*
Peppermint	*Mentha x piperita*
Thyme	*Thymus vulgaris*
Fennel	*Foeniculum vulgare*
Chives	*Allium schoenoprasum*
Lovage	*Levisticum officinale*
Rosemary	*Rosmarinus officinalis*
Sage	*Salvia officinalis*
Myrtle	*Myrtus communis*
Juniper	*Juniperus communis*

Annuals

Basil	*Ocimum basilicum*
Chervil	*Anthriscus cerefolium*
Coriander	*Coriandrum sativum*
Garlic	*Allium sativum*
Summer savory	*Satureja hortensis*
Marjoram	*Origanum majorana*
Dill	*Anethum graveolens*

Some herbs, like marjoram, can be obtained in golden-leaved varieties, creating a beautiful display of colorful and useful foliage.

left A kitchen border can supply you with fresh herbs all year round to add to your cooking and use for your health.

41

Growing herbs in pots

A collection of herbs in different-size pots can make a very attractive display anywhere, particularly if you do not have much space. A container with a single herb or flower, such as lavender, really creates an impact on the eyes and concentrates the aroma. Pots can also be used in the garden itself; for example, invasive herbs, which send out vigorous roots called runners, can be contained by being planted in a pot with the base taken out, and set deep in the ground so water can drain away. Provided they are not too heavy, pots can also be moved from one part of the garden to another to take advantage of different levels of sun and warmth. If you live in a climatic region that makes growing herbs in the garden more difficult, then pots may well be the answer for you.

right A container is a very compact and tidy way to grow a selection of useful herbs.

Types of container

Many herbs have compact attractive shapes, and they do well in a whole range of different pots and containers. Different-size terra-cotta pots, wooden half-barrels, and old sinks or troughs can all be used for planting. Plastic pots can also be used, but may not be frost-resistant. Make sure you plant your herb in a pot large enough for its roots to spread well, particularly if you want a perennial to grow steadily for a few years.

below Try using different types and designs of pots to create an attractive display in your space.

Choices of herbs

Invasive herbs like mint (*Mentha* species) or comfrey (*Symphytum officinale*) do best when planted alone in a pot because they are contained. Herbs with attractive foliage, like variegated lemon balm (*Melissa officinalis*), or bright, dramatic flowers like butterfly lavender (*Lavandula stoechas*) also look more attractive in concentration. Tall herbs like angelica (*Angelica archangelica*) need very large pots but can add a sculptured look to a more formal herb plot. Mixtures of annual herbs like calendula (*Calendula officinalis*) and nasturtium (*Tropaeolum majus*) can create splashes of color; an extremely aromatic pot can be made out of several species of basil (*Ocimum basilicum*), such as 'Purple Ruffles' with a spicy aroma, the highly fragrant 'Genovese', the little Greek basil 'Minimum', and the lemon-scented 'Citriodora'.

Preparing and maintaining pots

After you have chosen your pot, you need to put a layer of stones or broken pieces of pot in the base for proper drainage and to allow air to the roots of your plants. Then fill up the pot with a balanced, soil-based potting compost from the garden center, or try mixing your own with one-third topsoil, one-third compost, and one-third coarse sand. The soil mixture does need to be richer than normal soil, as the herbs will exhaust the limited supply of nutrients more quickly than in garden conditions. You will need to give them some liquid feed every six weeks or so in the growing season (see pages 52–53 for how to make your own plant food). You will also need to water your pots, but not too much. Small pots can stand in a saucer and be watered from below; with larger pots, test the surface and make sure the compost is dry before you add more water.

43

Using your **conservatory**

Many ordinary houses now have conservatories added on to them, creating wonderful spaces in which to grow unusual aromatic plants that would not normally survive in cooler climates. The idea of a conservatory is nothing new—back in the 17th century, ingenious plantsmen were creating ideas for artificially warmed glasshouses to grow exotic fruit like melons; later these special areas became known as "orangeries" because they were used to grow citrus fruit. Often with underfloor heating, these buildings were the first large-scale greenhouses, and today many of them can still be seen in the grounds of large country mansions. Extensive botanical collections of exotic plants became extremely popular in the 19th century, and the Temperate House at Kew Gardens in London is a fine example of a graceful glass-and-metal conservatory from that period.

Chili peppers

A conservatory on the back of a house lets in more than average amounts of sunlight and has a consistently warm average temperature, especially if it can be heated during the winter months. Provided there is enough moisture available, it is possible to grow some very interesting aromatic plants, adding interest to the traditional palms on display.

Examples of plants for the conservatory

Ginger (*Zingiber officinale*) This has lush green leaves and the root is highly aromatic.

Turmeric (*Curcuma longa*) This is a member of the same botanical family as ginger and has similarly-shaped leaves, as well as a yellow root.

Lemongrass (*Cymbopogon citratus*) This is an attractive, tall, lemon-scented grass, very popular in Indian and Thai cooking.

Citrus trees Sweet orange (*Citrus sinensis*), bitter orange (*Citrus aurantium*), mandarin (*Citrus reticulata*), lemon (*Citrus limonum*). All aromatic citrus trees have attractive, shiny, dark-green aromatic leaves as well as brightly colored, tasty

fruit. Most northern climates are too cold for these trees, which will not tolerate frost, so the conservatory is an ideal place for them. Modern compact, low-growing cultivars are available from garden centers and are easy to grow in large pots. The scent of citrus flowers, particularly creamy white, bitter orange blooms, is exquisitely soft and floral; it is the source of a fine essential oil used in aromatherapy for stress and anxiety.

Scented pelargoniums These are tropical geranium species with extremely beautiful aromatic leaves, such as *Pelargonium graveolens*, which has a strong rosy fragrance, used in aromatherapy, or *Pelargonium citriodora* with lemon-scented leaves. They must be kept indoors in cooler climates, though in regions with hot summers they could be taken outdoors in pots.

Peppers (*Capsicum* species) Sweet peppers and hot chili peppers grow well in conservatories.

Care of your exotic species involves careful watering and regular feeding, as well as spraying with a fine water-vapor mist to stop the leaves from drying out too much.

right: top A conservatory can become a beautiful environment with a tropical feel, especially if you choose unusual plants.

right: bottom left There are hundreds of geranium species, but those with scented leaves tend to require special protection from cold conditions.

right: bottom right Orange trees are delightful in a conservatory—fruit and flowers appear together and orange blossoms have an exquisite fragrance.

Forest gardening: a nature-friendly approach

Nasturtium

So far, the ideas for herb garden layouts have been quite structured, even formal. However, your planting does not have to be that way. Since many herbs are found growing naturally deep in woodland or on the outskirts of groups of trees, it makes sense to consider ways of planting them that echo the natural environment where they would choose to grow themselves. The idea of a "forest garden" has been pioneered in Britain by Robert Hart, who has planted and nurtured his own land for many years to provide him with food in a natural setting. He has modeled his garden on the structure of woodland that is native to Britain, but there are examples of forest gardens all over the world, including Africa, India and Australia, where those natural environments have been the focus for design. The unique advantage of the forest garden system is that it can suit any environment, size of plot, and choice of plants. In appearance it can look "untidy"— that is, totally unlike a formal or organized garden. Yet its secret is that all the plants support each other.

right Elderflowers make a deliciously tasty tea, which helps the immune system.

below In a woodland garden, there are three key layers: trees, bushes, and low-growing plants.

A forest garden has two or three "layers"—either trees, shrubs, and herbaceous plants, or just shrubs and low-growing plants. A very edible garden can be designed with fruit and nut trees in the top layer, soft-fruit shrubs in the middle layer, and perennial vegetables and herbs lower down. This type of garden is unique, in that everything is grown together and not separated into beds. What happens is that in early spring, the vegetable layer comes into leaf first, then comes the middle layer, and finally the trees, exactly as in woodland, so everything in turn gets the right conditions for new growth.

You can introduce some simple principles of forest gardening quite easily without redesigning your whole plot. If you already have an established garden and want to include some herbs and interesting salads in your diet, you can adapt your space by observing where the spaces are, and planting your herbs and shrubs where they will get the right kind of light and warmth.

Perennials like the mints (*Mentha* species), sweet cicely (*Myrrhis odorata*), and so-called weeds like dandelion (*Taraxacum officinale*) and nettles (*Urtica dioica*), all have interesting-tasting leaves, which add new flavors to salads, especially when their leaves are tender in the early spring. Sunny patches in your garden can be used to plant nasturtium (*Tropaeolum majus*) for edible flowers and leaves, which add color and taste to salads. A larger space could be made available for an elder tree, which provides wonderful flowers for herbal tea, as well as berries that can be made into a tasty syrup for winter coughs. If you grow your own peas and beans, planting calendula flowers nearby can improve your yields and provide a herb to use in infusions and skin lotions. Placing these useful plants between your ornamentals brings a new dimension to your garden.

47

Growing unusual salad herbs

These days, the emphasis in healthy eating is geared towards salad, and most of the salads we buy in the supermarket are mass-produced and rather tasteless. It is good to know that many unusual salad herbs are easy to grow. Back in the 17th century, John Evelyn wrote a document called *A Discourse of Sallets*, in which he encouraged people to eat green leaves for the nutrients and health-giving properties they contained; his advice holds good today. Instead of the bland salads on offer in the supermarkets, try growing these plants in your garden—their leaves are pungent, peppery, and stronger-tasting, and they make exciting and interesting taste combinations when mixed with milder leaves. Their powerful flavors also improve your digestion by increasing the flow of digestive juices.

Good King Henry
(*Chenopodium bonus-henricus*)

This is actually a type of spinach, which has been grown all over Europe since medieval times. It needs a fairly sunny site but will tolerate some shade. Seeds can be bought from herb suppliers, and once it is established in the garden it will remain a perennial source of leaves. The mature leaves have a webbed shape and are slightly smaller than spinach. Young leaves and flowers can be added to salads, and more mature leaves cooked in stews, where they add a pungent flavor. It grows to a maximum height of 3 ft/1 m, and plants should be set about 12 inches/30 cm apart. It grows well in most soils.

Sorrel (*Rumex acetosa*)

This is related to the common dock leaf, but it has a leaf shape more like an arrow. Its sharp taste is due to high levels of oxalic acid, which should not be eaten in very large amounts, as it can affect uptake of iron and calcium. A few sorrel leaves scattered in a salad provides a pleasant occasional taste. The leaves can also be added to soups or cooked, mixed green vegetables. The plant tolerates shade, and is very easy to grow; each plant needs approximately 1 sq ft/30 sq cm of room.

right and below
Sorrel leaves add
a piquant and
sharp taste to
a green salad
mixture, giving an
unusual flavor.

far right Salad
burnet is very
easy to grow
because it self-
seeds and gives
a constant supply
of leaves.

Corn salad
(*Valerianella locusta*)

This is mild-tasting but delicious. It is an annual,
but will seed itself once established. It has the
advantage of being available in late winter and
early spring, having grown slowly all through the
cold months. Because it is so low-growing—rarely
above 4 inches/10 cm tall—it does well as a
ground-cover plant, and it also tolerates shade.
It can be harvested continually once it appears,
providing a generous supply of leaves. If you
let a few plants flower, the blooms are a gentle
pale blue.

Salad burnet (*Sanguisorba minor*)

This is an attractive plant that blooms all year
round and has small russet flowers and double
rows of delicate leaflets. It tastes very much like
cucumber, a mild flavor. It works well in a green
salad mixture, and also adds a mild flavor to
potato salad. The young leaves are best for eating.
It grows to about 12 inches/30 cm in height and it
self-seeds. It does well in drier soils.

Companion planting

Many herbs are extremely beneficial to the garden itself, improving the soil and environment, as well as attracting the beneficial insects to preserve your precious plants. Over thousands of years of trial and observation, gardeners all over the world noticed improvements in size, health, and yields when certain plants were cultivated close together. By observing nature, seeing what worked, and copying what they saw, they found that these effects could be reproduced.

right The wild herb borage is usually found in woods or on waste ground.

One famous example is the fact that garlic plants under rose bushes really do deter aphids and other predatory insects. Certain types of calendula (marigold), called tagetes, actually give out secretions from their roots, which help keep weeds at bay—which is particularly good near vegetables. Farmers in past times would plant nasturtiums under their apple trees; not only would these keep away aphids, but they would then be plowed back into the soil as a "green manure" to enrich the earth with nutrients and feed the growing tree. Aromatic herbs give out such strong aromas they attract bees, so growing them near your orchard would improve the pollination of your fruit trees.

Good companion plants

This chart shows how common herbs can help other plants to grow when they are planted nearby.

Basil	Helps apples, asparagus, grapevines, and tomatoes and works well planted close to parsley and summer savory.
Borage	Helps fava beans, cucumbers, grapevines, large zucchini/squash, tomatoes, and strawberries.
Calendula	Helps artichokes, all beans, peas, and potatoes.
Camomile	(Roman or German) Helps broccoli, Brussels sprouts, cauliflower, kohlrabi, peas, and tomatoes.
Chives	Help apples, cabbage, carrots, grapevines, leeks, roses, and tomatoes.
Clover	Helps apples, Brussels sprouts, cabbage, and pears.
Coriander	Helps radishes and spinach.
Dill	Helps Brussels sprouts, cabbage, carrots, cauliflower, celery, kohlrabi, and leeks.
Fennel	Helps cabbage, squash, leeks, and large zucchini.
Garlic	Helps apples, string beans, lettuce, peaches, pears, plums, and roses.

Red sage

Calendula

Special companion herbs

Borage, with its lovely blue flowers, encourages the growth of strawberries so the fruit is healthy and tasty, and the leaves resist fungi and other diseases.

The **camomiles** are such all-rounders that they are considered to be the "plant physicians" and can be planted anywhere to encourage healthy growth.

Hyssop	Helps broccoli, cabbage, grapevines, and kohlrabi.
Lavender	Helps cabbage, citrus fruit, and tomatoes.
Lemon balm	Helps potatoes and tomatoes.
Sweet marjoram	Helps beans, broccoli, cabbage, and potatoes.
Mint	Helps broccoli, cauliflower, kohlrabi, peas, and tomatoes.
Nasturtium	Helps apples, apricots, cucumbers, and zucchini.
Parsley	Helps artichokes, asparagus, lettuce, and potatoes.
Rosemary	Helps beans, broccoli, Brussels sprouts, carrots, cauliflower, and tomatoes.
Sage	Helps carrots, cauliflower, grapevines, kohlrabi, and tomatoes.
Summer savory	Helps all beans, onions and potatoes.
Thyme	Helps beans, cauliflower, eggplants, and lettuce.
Yarrow	Helps corn and raspberries.

Using herbs like this is a totally organic way to enhance your whole garden, as well as providing you with herbs for cooking and medicine. The more you work with plants, the more you may discover relationships between them that are unique to your particular garden and climate.

General maintenance of the herb garden

Most herbs are quite happy if left relatively alone, as they are plants that originally came from the wild and are used to surviving unaided. However, when you plant them for specific reasons you will want to ensure that they have the best possible conditions and therefore produce the best results for you. Here are three key ways to care for your herb plot.

Watering

If you have a lot of herbs in pots, watering will be particularly necessary, especially if the weather is very sunny (see pages 42–43). In the garden, moisture-loving herbs like angelica or the mints will need extra water in very hot conditions, but with average rainfall they will thrive happily. Remember, many herbs from Mediterranean climates, like thyme, rosemary, or lavender, do better when it is extremely hot and dry, producing even more essential oil in their leaves and flowers and therefore a stronger aroma.

Feeding

Here, there are two aspects that can help your herbs. Compost (well-rotted plant material) is important because it improves the fertility of the soil, providing nutrients to growing plants, particularly seedlings as they become established. Of course, compost can be bought from garden suppliers, but it is also a good thing to make yourself. You may be lucky enough to be supplied with free bins in your area. Compost bins are mostly made of plastic or wood. The best way to make compost is to fill the bin in layers; you can put grass cuttings in there, but alternate with vegetable peelings from the kitchen, or clippings of leaves and twigs from the rest of the garden, making sure these are chopped up into small pieces. The secret to decomposing the material is to use what is called an "activator"; one of the

simplest and most efficient is to add comfrey leaves. Keep the heap moist and the comfrey will encourage the breakdown of the material. The compost is ready when it is dark brown and crumbly, which can take up to six months over the winter, or up to three months between spring and summer.

Comfrey leaves are also supremely useful as a liquid plant food, which is very easy to make and use—it is called "green manure." Just half-fill a bucket with comfrey leaves, then cover them with water and let it stand at the bottom of the garden for two to three weeks. In that time, the leaves will decompose to a pungent-smelling nitrogen-rich liquid, which is excellent food for herbs in pots as well as fruit and vegetables. Use one part liquid to three parts water when using the brew.

Mulching

This is protecting the ground close to your herbs with a thick covering up to 6 in/15 cm deep, to keep weeds at bay and also to help maintain the temperature when it gets cool. Different materials can be used, and mostly they decompose slowly over time and add to the soil. Leaf mold, bark chippings, mushroom compost, or thick layers of your own compost will do the trick. For the Mediterranean herbs such as thyme or sage, a layer of fine gravel between plants improves drainage.

Comfrey

right Watering is particularly necessary if weather conditions get very dry but remember—not too much.

far right: top Making your own compost is quite easy and an environmentally friendly way to dispose of kitchen vegetable waste.

far right: bottom Healthy herbs show vigorous growth, thanks to the right balance of water and nutrients.

Jobs for the **spring** and **summer**

One of the joys of the herb garden is the variety of tasks throughout the seasons. Annuals will, of course, go through their cycle in a year from seedling back to seed, but the perennials also have their times of optimum leaves and flowers. Each season brings new things to discover. As you work, you will need to take the climatic conditions around you into consideration. Spring, for instance, starts at different times in different latitudes, and late frosts can damage tender plants.

Jobs for the spring

Once the ground has started to warm up, it is good to prepare the soil by digging in compost, particularly if your soil is very heavy. Early springtime is also the best time to plant seeds of herbs like calendula, borage, nasturtium, parsley, or summer savory in trays, then keep them in the greenhouse or conservatory to germinate. You can also leave annuals like nasturtium until late spring, once you are past the last frost, and then sow seeds directly into the open. Basil likes warmth, and will do well either in a pot or sown outside once the general temperature has risen. Herbs like coriander or dill can also be sown straight into

the ground at this time. Seedlings sown in the greenhouse can be brought outside in the late spring and planted out. Early springtime is not a good time to do too much clipping or pruning because of the chance of late frosts. Wait until the weather has really warmed up before you cut the perennials, like sage, right back to new shoots. This encourages new leaf growth and gives the bush a good shape. Rosemary will flower early, and once it has finished blooming you can cut the bush back to encourage leaf production. Finally, check your pots—you may need to trim the plants, repot any herbs that show signs of being cramped, add compost, or give them a liquid feed.

below When filling your pots, mix together compost, coarse sand, and garden soil to get a light and airy consistency.

below Trimming and pruning is best done with a sharp pair of shears; wear gloves when dealing with roses.

right Summer is the time when you will be harvesting herbs, flowers, and seeds for use in the kitchen and through the winter.

Jobs for the summer

This is the time when the herbs are at their peak—full of fragrance and vitality—and you will start to harvest the plants for their leaves, flowers, or seeds. Poppy, calendula, nasturtium, sunflower, fennel, dill, and lovage seeds can be collected, dried, and stored. The best way to keep your seeds is in paper envelopes marked clearly with what they are. Keep a general eye on moisture, bearing in mind not to overwater. In the summertime, most of the kitchen herbs are producing abundant aromatic leaves, which make delicious flavorings—vibrant green basil leaves with fresh tomatoes has to be one of the most wonderful summer combinations. As well as using fresh herbs as much as possible for simple medicines like herbal teas and also in cooking, you will be harvesting and preserving herbs for use during the winter months. Cutting back lemon balm and other herbs, like the mints, as they flower encourages them to produce more leaves, so you have a good harvest.

Jobs for the **fall** and **winter**

Later in the season is when the herb garden can start to look dried out and exhausted as most of the annuals reach the end of the growth cycle. It is a time when tidying up is needed on a large scale to ensure good overwintering for your plants during their more dormant cycle. The good news, if you have aromatic shrubs like rosemary or myrtle in the garden, is that they are evergreen and will continue to provide color and structure to your plot as well as useful leaves throughout the colder months.

below In the colder months, the herb garden is dormant, but evergreens still provide aromatic leaves and touches of color in a winter landscape.

Jobs for the fall

It is important to cut back and tidy your herbs as much as possible; herbs like lemon balm or the mints now have tough straggly stems, which can be cut away. In the springtime they will regenerate from the soil level. All annuals that have died back, such as summer savory, borage, or calendula, can be dug up and put into the compost bin to be recycled into plant food. Large clumps of perennial plants like tarragon can be dug up and replanted in pots to keep them going over the winter, and in the spring they can be divided into new plants. Fall is when the first frosts appear, so any pots of tender plants or trees like bay need to come into a cool greenhouse or conservatory for protection. Also you can protect plants in the ground with coverings such as plant fleece or plastic, or put straw between plants to keep the ground warmer.

Jobs for the winter

The ancient Celts regarded All Saints' Day (1 November) as the beginning of their New Year. This was the time when it was darkest, moving toward the winter solstice on 21 December; in plant terms, a time of hibernation, but in human terms it is a time of planning for the coming year. Wintertime can be profitably used to decide how you want to work with your herbs in the spring, based on what has worked and what has not. This is a good time to plan new layouts for the new season. It is also a time for ordering seed catalogs and thinking about other varieties of herbs you might like to try growing. As far as the garden goes, keep your valuable plants protected from severe cold, either with fleece or plastic coverings. Outdoor containers may be too heavy to bring in; if they are made of terra-cotta, it is a good idea to wrap them in fleece or sacking to stop them from cracking in the frost. Pots kept indoors should not be fed any more, and just given the minimum of water to see them through. If you pot up plants like tarragon, mint, or chives in the fall and keep them in a warm greenhouse or conservatory, they will provide you with fresh leaves throughout the winter.

top left Recycling material you have cut back from your herb garden will help to make rich compost for next spring, so nothing is wasted.

bottom left Any plants in terra-cotta pots either need protecting with plant fleece or they need to be brought into a greenhouse or conservatory to protect them from frost.

Propagation methods

Propagation increases your plant stock using different methods, such as saving seeds and growing them the following year. Of course, you can buy plants from garden suppliers or markets, and this is particularly useful when you are setting up your herb plot. However, once your garden is established you may wish to keep it going using propagation techniques; this is more economical than buying new plants all the time.

Soil

There are four key ways of propagating herbs. Some plants can be propagated using more than one method.

1. Growing from seed

Sowing seeds in greenhouse conditions in early spring is much more successful than planting them straight outdoors, because seeds are less likely to be eaten and tender seedlings will be protected from frost. You need seedling trays and a good commercial seed compost to fill the individual compartments. Moisten the compost, then scatter two or three seeds into each space, and strain a fine layer of compost over the top. To ventilate, you can put a loose plastic bag over the tray to hold in the moisture. Put the tray somewhere warm but out of the light until the seedlings show; then remove the cover and put the tray into the light as the seedlings become stronger. They can then be transferred to larger pots or planted outside as the weather permits. This method suits herbs like basil, chervil, dill, sweet marjoram, summer savory, and sunflower.

Later in the spring you can plant the following seeds straight outdoors: borage, calendula, camomiles (German and Roman), coriander, evening primrose, fennel, feverfew, fenugreek, horehound, lemon balm, and parsley.

2. Dividing roots

This is a method for the late spring or fall. The plant is dug up and separated into several clumps or the roots are actually carefully prised apart. The separated sections are then individually replanted. This method suits herbs like peppermint, chives, comfrey, fennel, lady's-mantle, lovage, or sweet cicely in the late spring; in the fall, separate clumps of thyme, sweet marjoram, or tarragon.

3. Layering

This works well for shrubs like rosemary or sage, which can become very leggy and woody. You simply use a peg or a piece of wire to hold down a long stem still attached to the parent plant, and pile earth on top of it. In two months, roots will have formed, and the new plant can be cut away from the original bush, dug up and carefully replanted.

4. Taking softwood cuttings

Softwood cuttings are taken in the late spring or early summer, from aromatic shrubs like lavender, rosemary or sage. You simply select a nonflowering side shoot and pull it gently off the plant; it leaves a small "heel" of bark, which is important for root development. Press the cutting into potting compost—three or four can be placed in one pot. Keep the compost moist, and when new leaves have formed the plants have rooted. Plant them into larger pots or outdoors.

far left Seeds should be harvested and stored in dry conditions, in paper envelopes marked with the plant species.

left Seedlings need light, warmth, enough moisture, and good nutrition to mature into strong and healthy plants for your garden.

below Pull off side shoots, leaving a little "heel" of bark, then press into compost at the edge of your pot to encourage root formation.

Harvesting herbs

Although there are specific seasons when herbs can be harvested, some herbs are available all year round. Evergreens like rosemary will survive the winter and provide fresh leaves, but the flavor and effect will be much less intense in the colder months than in the summer, when the aromatic oils are at their peak. Harvesting herbs is all about choosing the optimum time for maximum aromatic and therapeutic effect.

Bay leaves

The best time to pick aromatic herbs like basil is just before they come into flower, when the fragrance is concentrated in the leaves; to encourage leaf production, it is best to cut off the flowering stems. Many medicinal herbs such as yarrow or St.-John's-wort are collected when they are actually in flower, so leaves and blooms are used. Calendula or camomile flowers should be carefully picked for drying when they are just freshly opened. When collecting seeds, the best way is to pick the whole flowering head of the plant, such as fennel, then tie a brown paper bag over the flowers and hang them upside down. The seeds will drop into the bag when they are ripe. Roots like dandelion are generally best harvested in the fall when they are plump with food for the winter.

All herbs and flowers are best harvested on a dry day, ideally in the morning before the sun has affected the plant. Cut the herbs with a sharp knife, scissors, or shears, choosing one species at a time, and gently lay them flat in a basket. Carefully sort out any weeds, then pick out any diseased or damaged leaves and ensure the stems are dry before tying them into bunches for drying, or other methods of preserving (see pages 62–63). If you do not have much space, pick only a small amount at one time; if you leave piles of fresh herbs unattended, they will wilt and lose their potency.

A tasty, fresh herbal tea

Pick 5 fresh camomile flowers and 5 fresh mint leaves, and place in an infuser; pour over generous ¾ cup boiling water and let infuse for 15 minutes. Strain out the leaves and flowers, then add a teaspoon of honey and a slice of lemon, and enjoy. This tea helps calm the digestion and soothes the nerves.

Dried calendula

Dried lavender

Herbs to harvest seasonally

Late spring
Angelica leaves and stems, borage leaves, chervil leaves, fennel leaves, Good King Henry leaves, sorrel leaves, sweet cicely leaves.

Early summer
Basil leaves, calendula flowers, dill leaves, elderflowers, lemon balm leaves, lovage leaves, nasturtium leaves, parsley leaves, sage leaves, tarragon leaves, thyme flowers and leaves.

Midsummer
Angelica seeds, camomile flowers, fenugreek leaves, lavender flowers, sweet marjoram flowers and leaves, mint leaves, St.-John's-wort flowers and leaves, summer savory leaves, sweet cicely seeds, horehound flowers and leaves, yarrow flowers and leaves.

Late summer
Bay leaves, chervil leaves, coriander seeds, dill seeds, elderberries, fennel seeds, garlic bulbs, horseradish root, lovage seeds.

Early Fall
Angelica root, dandelion root, sweet cicely root.

Dried herbs
Lavender stems retain their aroma better if hung upside down to dry in a warm space such as an airing cupboard.

Dried rosemary

Preserving herbs

Choosing the best leaves, flowers, and roots and preparing them for keeping is very much a part of managing your herb garden, and the more you do it, the more pleasure you will get from it. These methods make your herbs available as a constant source of flavoring and medicine.

Drying

This requires a quick and efficient way of drying herbs in which warm air circulates around them. Tie herbs like rosemary, sage, or thyme into small bunches and hang them upside down in a warm airing cupboard; they should dry in a week or so. Soft-stemmed or leaved herbs like lady's-mantle or flowers like calendula or camomile can be laid individually on cheesecloth on top of a cake-cooling tray so that air circulates freely. If you do not have an airing cupboard, you can place a tray or bunches of herbs tied together directly into a very cool oven at 90°F/33°C and leave the oven door ajar. This is a very good, quick way to dry herbs in a few hours or overnight and works well for juicier leaves like basil or lemon balm. Seeds should be dried in brown paper bags at room temperature for two to three weeks, completely away from moisture. Finally, roots need to be thoroughly washed and wiped, then either tied together in bunches to hang up or chopped into manageable pieces and dried on a tray.

Leaves are ready when they become brittle, flowers when they are like tissue paper, and roots when they snap easily when you bend them. Once your herbs are properly dried, store them in clean, glass screwtop jars clearly labeled with the contents. It is best to keep them out of direct sunlight in a cool, dark place. They will last for a year.

Preserving in sugar

This is wonderful for preserving the aroma of lavender flowers; simply strip a handful of blooms from several stems just as they are at their best and stir into 1¼ cups fine sugar (superfine sugar is best) in a screwtop jar. Store until needed—then sift away the flowers before use. The flavored sugar gives a lovely taste to cakes, biscuits, cookies, and jellies.

Preserving in salt

To make your own seasoning salt, pick a small bunch of mixed herbs such as chives (cut into small pieces), basil, thyme, sage, and rosemary (strip the leaves off the stems), and spread on a baking sheet. Pour over 4 oz/125 g sea salt, mixing the herbs into the salt, and leave in a cool oven at 90°F/33°C until the herbs are dry. Next grind the leaves and salt together with a pestle and mortar, then pour into a screwtop jar and use this delicious mix to season meat, fish, soups, or omelets.

Freezing

This works well for delicate leaves like basil, dill, fennel, or chervil; simply select small, perfect sprigs of herb, then place them in plastic bags and freeze them. Alternatively, you can make aromatic ice cubes by placing chopped peppermint and lemon balm leaves in ice-cube trays with water for freezing—great for drinks in the summer (see pages 116–117).

(see pages 116–117)

top row: left Harvest the herb leaves and stems by cutting with sharp scissors or shears.

top row: center Strip the leaves from the main stem.

top row: right Place on a drying rack in a warm place until brittle.

middle row: left Unearth the plant gently and wash the root to remove all the soil. Use a nail brush if necessary.

middle row: center Cut up the root.

middle row: right Spread the sliced roots onto a drying rack and place in the sun or a warm place until brittle.

bottom row: left For everyday use in the kitchen, you can store dried herbs in small jars with tight fitting lids.

bottom row: center Place dried or prepared herbs in dark jars and store in a cool place.

bottom row: right Place fresh herbs in small plastic bags and freeze.

Herbs in the wild

All herbs have wild origins, and in the past many people simply went out and gathered herbs from particular locations to take home and use. When Culpeper wrote his famous *Herbal* in 1649, he highlighted many plants that grew locally, preferring to use herbs and flowers that were native to Britain instead of exotic, imported species. His treatment involved explaining to his patients where they could collect the right herb for their condition so that they could medicate themselves! Since it was originally published, there have been more than 40 editions of Culpeper's *Herbal*, showing the popularity of this approach.

below There are many similar-looking species in the *Umbelliferae* family—some, like parsley, are edible but others can be toxic.

Nowadays there are important things you need to consider about gathering herbs from the wild. We do not live in the same environment as Culpeper did—there have been many changes. Farming methods are often intensive, meaning the development of huge fields of single crops with no hedgerows, and of course the extensive use of chemical sprays and fertilizers. Where you find herbs growing in fields, they are very likely to have been contaminated by pesticide or toxic residues; this will also be true for paths, roads, hedgerows, or waste land, especially if they are close to industrial areas, landfill sites for waste disposal, or heavy traffic.

Another issue is identification. There are many species of wild plants that look very similar, such as members of the *Umbelliferae* family. Fennel, parsley, and a whole host of other members of this family all have typical flat "umbels," umbrella-like spreads of tiny flowers. One of these is the giant hogweed, which can cause terrible burning skin reactions if you touch it. If you are interested in having a better understanding of wild plants, look out for guided walks or tours with experts—these are sometimes advertized in local newspapers—where you can be shown plants and learn their correct identification. There is great interest in herbs and foods that can be collected from wild sources; in France and other European countries, schoolchildren are taught how to identify and pick field mushroom species correctly. However, it is vital to know what you are doing.

Many wild species of herbs are also in danger of extinction and therefore protected by law. It is best to avoid gathering herbs from the wild and to concentrate either on growing your own herbs in your garden, or on purchasing herbs from garden and herb suppliers. This way you will know that what you are using is safe, organically sound and beneficial to your health.

Starting simply

There is no time like the present. However, after so much information in these pages, you may be feeling a little overwhelmed! Let's recap on some important aspects of herb growing and the reasons for doing it, and get a small project under way, to get you started. A thousand-mile journey starts with one step, and once you are on your way there is no stopping; however, the first step is sometimes the most challenging one!

Key things to remember

Your space

Spend time deciding what kind of herb garden you really want. Small herb plots (3–6 sq ft/ 1–2 sq m) are low-maintenance and can provide enough herbs to supply a family of four people for flavoring and simple medicines; you do not have to plan a huge herb garden, though if you have the space it can be a very satisfying task! Sketching the space and mapping out the sunny and shady areas, as well as knowing your soil, are crucial to selecting the kinds of plants that will grow well for you. If you don't want to do this, then simply potting herbs in compost and growing them is easy—just put them in the right place!

Your time

If you lead a busy life and do not have much time for gardening, then growing herbs is good to do because as plants, they are fairly easy-going and do not need a lot of attention. They provide a good yield as long as they have the right growing conditions. One of the big advantages of an aromatic space, particularly on a summer's evening, is that it encourages you to slow down, perhaps even stop and relax after a hard day at work. A herb plot can make a wonderful setting in which to eat al fresco, surrounded by colors and fragrances.

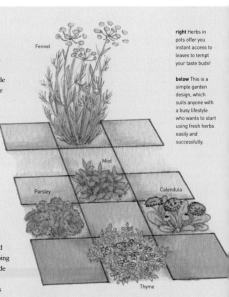

right Herbs in pots offer you instant access to leaves to tempt your taste buds!

below This is a simple garden design, which suits anyone with a busy lifestyle who wants to start using fresh herbs easily and successfully.

Fennel

Mint

Parsley

Calendula

Thyme

A checkerboard design like the one above lets you step on the pavers to reach your herbs easily and helps to ensure they don't spread too widely. This is a very easy herb plot to create and use, and requires little maintenance.

A simple herb project

Take four medium-size plant pots, and fill the
bases with stones or broken bits of pot. Add good-
quality soil-based compost mixed with a little
coarse sand for drainage. Plant the following four
useful herbs, then choose a window ledge that
gets warm sun for at least a few hours a day, and
put your pots in a long tray. Keep the compost
moist, but don't overwater.

Basil (Ocimum basilicum)

This is a wonderful green herb, vital for Italian
cooking, for pesto sauce and any tomato dishes.
The large, fresh green leaves give a piquant taste
to green salads and are also a key ingredient in
the Italian "Insalata tricolore." This is made with
ripe tomatoes, slices of mozzarella cheese, and
fresh basil leaves, drizzled with olive oil.

Dill (Anethum graveolens)

If you keep dill cropped, you will have an endless
supply of tasty leaves with a sharp, refreshing
flavor. Dill is extremely good with cucumber in
salads, as well as with fish like salmon or trout.
It is extremely beneficial to the digestion.

Parsley (Petroselinum sativum)

It's worth looking in garden centers for the
broad-leaved French variety of parsley, which has
a lovely pungent flavor. Rich in vitamins A, B, and
C and minerals, it tones the digestion as well as
bringing vital flavor to soups, stews, salads, and
mashed potato.

Spearmint (Mentha spicata)

This mild member of the mint family is wonderful
eaten freshly chopped over new potatoes or
fresh peas, or made into a soothing tea for the
digestion. Mixed with natural yogurt, it becomes
"raita," an Indian relish to cool the mouth when
eating curries.

herbs in the
kitchen

Why cook with herbs?

In this section, you will find ideas to inspire your cooking using herbs and spices. The recipes are easy and involve simple but very tasty combinations of flavors. People have been seasoning food throughout history, with every culture evolving its own dishes thanks to the diversity of plants available worldwide. In the 17th century, John Parkinson, the famous English herbalist at the Court of King James I, wrote that dried summer savory leaves ground up with bread crumbs "used to breade meate, be it fish or flesh, give it a quicker relish," meaning that it gives it a more exciting taste. So, the origin of meat or fish with a coating of herby bread crumbs is nothing new! There are very good reasons for using herbs in your cooking, linking to health as well as flavor.

Herbs are tasty

This is a fact—from fresh and pungent Mediterranean leaves to mild salads, from sweet spices to fiery peppers, the range of flavors is extremely wide. Culinary plants and spices work on the taste buds sitting on your tongue, helping to increase the amount of saliva in your mouth; this in turn improves the way you start digesting your food immediately. Another very important aspect of taste is linked to the sense of smell; well-flavored foods smell good even before you get to the table and this literally makes your mouth water—again, preparing for digestion. Research has shown that what you think you are tasting is, in fact, 80 percent of what you are smelling and 20 percent of what is registered by your tongue, which is why food is so bland when you have a cold and a blocked nose.

Herbs are healthy

Eating and drinking herbs in your diet has many benefits. The active ingredients in herbs pass into the digestive tract and through the system, helping various aspects of food absorption. Bitter leaves like dandelion (*Taraxacum officinale*) in salads,

for example, help increase the action of the liver to digest fatty foods. Aromatic leaves like peppermint (*Mentha x piperita*) are full of essential oil; the action of peppermint in the gut releases wind and improves the rhythmical movement of the intestines. Flowers like German camomile (*Chamomilla recutita*) have a soothing effect on the walls of the digestive tract and settle indigestion. Bulbs like garlic (*Allium sativum*) are well known for their antiseptic and immune-boosting properties.

Herbs give you variety

There is no doubt that using herbs and spices encourages you to experiment with flavors and tastes. This opens up new horizons in your cooking; you may find you become particularly interested in certain types of recipes from different cultures, such as Indian or Chinese, or in particular styles of cooking that demand specific herbs or flavorings. Searching out ingredients or growing and using them yourself becomes a fascinating journey.

left Using herbs and spices and experimenting with flavors can open up new horizons of taste and aroma.

Fresh and dried herbs

When you start using herbs in your cooking, you need to understand the difference between using them fresh or dried. There is a variation in taste and intensity, and this can make a big difference to the success of your dish. There is a trend toward using more fresh herbs in cooking with small pots of growing herbs available from many supermarkets, but sometimes the flavor of dried herbs or spices is needed because drying concentrates the essential oils in the plant, giving a powerful flavor.

Fresh herbs

These are at their best when taken straight from the garden, balcony, or windowsill. Although you can buy fresh herbs from the supermarket, they are often forced and may have been given artificial fertilizers to stimulate growth. Using organically grown herbs is tasty and healthy. Fresh leaves or flowers make the most delicious herbal teas, salads, and hot dishes. Fresh herbs like basil should be torn into small pieces with your fingers; this releases more flavor than slicing them with a knife. If you are adding fresh herbs to a hot dish, it is best to do this in the last 5–10 minutes of cooking because it enables the flavor to be more developed; prolonged heat destroys the aromatic essential oils in the plant, reducing the taste.

Dried herbs and spices

Dried herbs come into their own in the wintertime when fresh leaves are generally unavailable; leaves like thyme have a very strong taste because of the concentrated essential oil. Again, adding the herbs toward the end of cooking will give you a stronger flavor. You will notice that in recipes the amount of dried herb is always half the fresh herb, because dried herbs are more intense than fresh herbs, and this also applies when you are making herbal teas. Spices—fragrant seeds like cardamom, black pepper, and nutmeg, or bark like cinnamon—are always dried because this increases the pungent flavor. In Indian recipes, spices are often toasted in oil at the start of cooking to release the flavor and develop the taste even more.

above Bouquet garni means "gathered bunch"—an aromatic combination of thyme, parsley, and bay leaves.

right Fresh basil is a vital herb in Mediterranean dishes, especially with tomatoes.

below Dried herbs are particularly useful in winter—try creating your own combinations with your own herbs!

Pesto Sauce

Here is a recipe for a famous Italian sauce based around fresh basil, which is delicious stirred into cooked pasta.

SERVES 3–4
scant ¾ cup fresh basil leaves, bruised
3 garlic cloves, crushed
6 tbsp extra virgin olive oil
¼ cup grated fresh Parmesan cheese
1 tbsp pine nuts
12 oz/350 g cooked pasta, to serve

Place all ingredients except the pasta in a blender and whizz up to a fine purée. If you do not have a blender, slowly grind the ingredients together with a large pestle and mortar.

Combine the pesto with the pasta.

top Nutmegs need to be kept thoroughly dry to preserve their aromatic taste, and grated fresh when needed.

Nutmeg Sleeping Posset

In medieval times, a posset was a milk drink taken at night to help relaxation. This simple recipe goes back to the time of Chaucer in the 14th century. It is a lovely drink for cold winter nights; it calms the digestion and eases the mind.

SERVES 1
generous ¾ cup milk
grated nutmeg or 1 tsp of nutmeg spice

Heat the milk in a pan. As it boils, pour it carefully into a mug.

Grate a quarter of a nutmeg or sprinkle the nutmeg spice over the milk; it will smell warm and sweet. After a moment, stir the nutmeg into the milk and sip slowly.

Note Do not exceed the stated amount of herbs used in recipes.

73

A simple kitchen herb collection

Here is a chart of 25 common herbs and spices for all kinds of recipes.
Use it as a guide when you plan menus or as a reference to remind you
how to use these flavours.

Kitchen herbs and spices

Herb	Use
Basil	Fresh leaves for pesto; with raw or cooked tomatoes.
Bay	Dried leaves in soups, stock, Bolognese sauce, lentil dishes, or casseroles.
Black pepper	Dried, freshly ground peppercorns as a flavor enhancer for all savory dishes.
Cardamom	Dried seeds in cakes, cookies, coffee, or Indian dishes.
Chervil	Fresh leaves with egg dishes like omelets, or in soups and vegetable stews.
Chili	Small amounts of whole or ground spice in Indian, South American, or Thai dishes.
Chives	Fresh leaves chopped in egg and cheese dishes, savory butters; salads and soups as a garnish.
Cinnamon	Ground spice with apples (stewed or baked); also hot milk drinks and mulled wine.
Cloves	Whole cloves in roast ham or pork dishes, with baked apples or in mulled wine.
Coriander	Fresh leaves to garnish Indian dishes or soups, also in green salads; seeds as a pickling spice.
Dill	Fresh leaves in fish dishes and cheese dishes, also in pickles or vinegars; seeds in apple pies, cakes.
Fennel	Fresh leaves with chicken, pork, or fish dishes; seeds with oily fish or as herbal tea.
Garlic	Fresh crushed cloves in salad dressings, soups, butters, bread, Mediterranean or Indian dishes.
Ginger	Freshly chopped root in Indian, Thai, or Chinese dishes, and dried ground root in cakes, cookies, and baked apples.
Lovage	Fresh leaves in soups, stews, chicken, ham, or fish dishes.

Marjoram	Fresh or dried leaves in savory meat and vegetarian dishes, with cheese dishes or in herb butters.
Nutmeg	Ground spice in meat dishes, nut roasts, with baked or stewed apples, in milk drinks or egg desserts.
Oregano	In savory meat and vegetable dishes, in tomato-based pasta sauces.
Paprika	Ground sweet pepper in meat stews, with cheese or egg dishes, salad dressings, pasta sauces.
Rosemary	Fresh or dried leaves in lamb, pork, or chicken dishes, herb butters.
Sage	Fresh or dried leaves with pork, venison, or rich meat dishes; in apple sauce, cheese dishes.
Spearmint	Fresh leaves with new potatoes, fresh peas, or sprinkled in summer punches.
Summer savory	Fresh or dried leaves in fish or meat coatings; also with beans, cabbage, or cauliflower dishes.
Tarragon	Fresh or dried leaves in chicken, fish, or lamb dishes; with omelets and herb butters.
Thyme	Fresh or dried leaves in Italian pasta sauces; with fish, lamb, pork, or beef; also feta cheese.

Herb equipment

To process your herbs, the following equipment is useful:

• Kitchen scissors to snip fresh herbs and chop up leaves
• Sharp knives for chopping leaves and stems
• A good-quality press to crush fresh garlic
• A pestle and mortar to grind up whole spices

Food as medicine:
a Western approach

Traditional Western natural medicine respects food as a medicinal tool that is very able to affect and maintain health. These days, the effects of overconsumption of salt and sugar as well as of saturated fat and artificial flavorings are well known as major contributors to heart disease, diabetes, and obesity. Understanding the benefits of particular ingredients and ways of eating can help you change the way you see food, not just as something tasty and filling, but also as a source of strength and well-being.

Hippocrates

As far back as Ancient Greece, Hippocrates (c.460–370 BC), the father of Western medicine, said in his writing: "Let food be your medicine and medicine be your food." He was a naturopath, a healer who worked with aspects of diet and fasting to improve his patients' health, as well as using bathing and massage. Other recommendations included watercress (*Nasturtium officinale*) in the diet as a respiratory tonic, expectorant, and digestive tonic—particularly chewing the leaves raw to help strengthen the gums.

Hildegard of Bingen

One of the most influential and famous healers of the Middle Ages was the abbess Hildegard of Bingen (1098–1181), whose amazing life included a vast literary output, much of which concerned medicine and food. To this day, her principles of medicinal eating are followed in the Rhineland area in southern Germany, where she lived. Hildegard saw food as spiritual energy as well as physical nourishment; she also believed in the qualities of different foods to cleanse away negativity, or dark "humors," from the body and mind. She regarded imbalances of the four humors—blood, phlegm, and yellow and black bile—as being responsible for all disease.

Many of her healing recipes are simple and extremely tasty. She used a whole range of herbs and spices in her practice for specific reasons: here are some examples.

Watercress

Lavender

Lavender wine was Hildegard's remedy for detoxifying and supporting the liver, which she believed was crucial to health. Empty a bottle of red table wine into a steel pan. Add 5 tbsp of fresh lavender flowers stripped off the stems. Bring the liquid to a boil, then reduce the heat and simmer for 35–40 minutes to evaporate the alcohol. Let cool, then strain and rebottle. Take 2 tsp of the mixture 3–4 times daily for up to 10 days. (Instead of wine, Hildegard suggests that you can use scant 3 cups water and add 3 tbsp honey, then simmer the lavender flowers as above.)

Hot porridge made with flakes of oats or spelt (*Triticum vulgare*—a variety of wheat) and eaten in the mornings is Hildegard's remedy for stress or nervous tension. Oats are still used in modern herbal medicine as a nerve tonic.

Sweet chestnuts (*Castanea sativa*) boiled in water and mashed are seen by Hildegard as strengthening to the body and the brain. They make an excellent nut roast, and modern practitioners recommend them for convalescence after infectious illness because they are an excellent source of vitamins A, B, and C.

Fennel seeds (*Foeniculum vulgare*) chewed after a meal will neutralize stomach acid, sweeten the breath, and help digest fatty foods. Hildegard believed fennel to be one of the best all-round herbs.

far left Hildegard of Bingen believed that food and health were absolutely linked.

above Oats are excellent for breakfast—they release energy slowly throughout the morning and keep food cravings at bay.

left Lavender flowers make an unusual health tonic from Hildegard's time.

Food as medicine: an Eastern approach

The Ayurvedic tradition in India, some 4,000 years old, is an astonishing heritage where the boundaries between body and mind, spirit and matter, food and medicine dissolve, and what is eaten is seen as potentially balancing to all aspects of life. The tradition teaches that from primal energy comes Akasha, or "ether," the element beyond physical form. Out of that come four more elements of air, fire, water, and earth. The human body is seen as being made up of all these five elements, which settle into what are called three "doshas," or typical physical types. While we are made up of all three, one will tend to dominate. This will influence the types of foods and medicinal help that suit us individually.

The three doshas are:

Vatta

These are said to be wind-dominated individuals prone to insomnia, who dislike cold and find it painful; they tend to have dry skin and sparse hair. They often suffer from constipation and their mouths are frequently dry. They have a tall, thin physical frame. Hot and moist foods suit them, such as dishes made with eggs, fish, kidney beans, sweet potatoes, and wheat; they also need sour tastes like lemon or yogurt.

Pitta

These are bile-dominated individuals—they tend to sweat a lot and be angry. They are lovers of flowers and aromas. Their faces tend to have a flushed look; they are quick-tempered and easily excited. They are hungry and thirsty a lot of the time, eat a lot, and can become overweight. Cool, heavy, and dry foods balance this temperament, such as unripe bananas, pumpkin, and zucchini.

Kapha

These are mucus-dominated individuals—they are well-built, handsome, and symmetrical with broad foreheads and thick hair. They sleep soundly and have good digestion, eating moderately. They can be susceptible to coughs, colds, and immune problems. Hot, light, dry foods suit this temperament, such as dates, honey, lentils, onions, and peas, particularly flavored with black pepper, ginger, or chili.

Doshas and health

This distinction between types does not mean that you should eat only the foods relating to your main dosha, but if you feel unwell or lacking in energy it can help to concentrate on foods more suited to your temperament.

Zucchini

Lentils

Yogurt

Common foods and flavorings

Here is how the Ayurvedic tradition uses some common foods and flavorings:

Food	Use
Carrots	These help stimulate the kidneys to eliminate toxins, helping digestion and cleaning the stomach and intestines, and are also a good source of vitamin A.
Cucumbers	These are light and cooling, helping any burning in the stomach and protecting the system against over-acidity. They are best eaten mixed with plain yogurt.
Bay leaves	These help skin problems like rashes or irritations and can be drunk as a tea. Eaten in food, they ease the pain of hemorrhoids/piles and diarrhea, and help improve liver function.

Black peppercorns	These are seen as vital to good digestion and extremely beneficial for asthma, coughs, colds, and flu. They also help the digestion of fatty foods.

right Black peppercorns are vital in Ayurvedic healing to tone and energize the respiratory, digestive, and immune systems.

Herb **butters** and **dips**

Mixing simple combinations of herbs with butter, mayonnaise, yogurt, or oil brings out the flavor and is an easy way of incorporating them into quick dishes that make very tasty light suppers. Any of the ideas below would work with a baked potato and salad, or broiled meat or fish, or with vegetarian burgers. Dips are also delicious at parties or grills as appetizers, eaten with sticks of fresh raw carrots, celery, sweet peppers, cucumber, and quartered tomatoes.

right Guacamole is a smooth textured yet spicy dip, excellent with raw vegetables.

below Aïoli is a really powerful garlic relish, which is extremely pungent!

Herb Butter

Herb butter or its variations work as an accompaniment or are delicious with warmed bread.

SERVES 4
1 stick good quality unsalted butter at room temperature
scant ½ cup chopped fresh parsley
¼ cup chopped fresh chives
Pepper
A squeeze of lemon juice

Cut the butter into pieces in a small bowl and beat it with a fork.

Add the parsley, chives, pepper, and lemon juice and continue beating to a smooth paste.

Cover the bowl and put it in the refrigerator for at least an hour.

VARIATIONS

Substitute scant ½ cup fresh dill leaves and 1 tbsp lemon juice for a butter to accompany fish like salmon or trout; or in addition to parsley and chives add 2 crushed garlic cloves. Spread in a baguette, then wrap in foil and place in the oven for 20 minutes at 400°F/200°C.

Aïoli

This is a famous French garlic mayonnaise from Provence—definitely for garlic lovers! The French eat it with fish, but it is also delicious with grilled meats or good-quality sausages.

SERVES 4
3 large garlic cloves, finely chopped
2 egg yolks
1 cup extra virgin olive oil
1 tbsp lemon juice
1 tbsp lime juice
1 tbsp Dijon mustard
1 tbsp chopped fresh tarragon
salt and pepper
sprig of tarragon, to decorate

For best results, all the ingredients should be at room temperature. Put the garlic and the egg yolks into a food processor and process until well blended.

With the motor running, pour in the oil teaspoon-by-teaspoon until it starts to thicken, then pour in the remaining oil in a thin stream until a thick mayonnaise forms.

Add the lemon and lime juices, along with the mustard and tarragon, and season to taste with salt and pepper. Blend until smooth, then transfer to a nonmetallic bowl. Decorate with a sprig of tarragon.

Cover with plastic wrap and refrigerate until needed.

Note This recipe contains raw eggs so is not suitable for all.

Guacamole

It is fortunate that this spicy Mexican dip is so speedy to prepare because you cannot make it too far in advance. If you do, the avocados will discolor.

SERVES 6

4 avocados
2 garlic cloves
4 scallions
3 fresh red chilies, deseeded
2 red bell peppers, deseeded
5 tbsp olive oil (1 tbsp for drizzling)
juice of 1½ limes
salt
chopped fresh parsley leaves, to garnish
tortilla chips, to serve

Cut the avocados in half lengthwise and twist the halves to separate. Remove and discard the pits and scoop the flesh into a large bowl with a spoon. Mash coarsely with a fork.

Finely chop the garlic, scallions, chilies, and bell peppers, then stir them into the mashed avocado. Add 4 tablespoons of the oil and the lime juice. Season to taste with salt and stir well to mix. If you prefer a smoother dip, process all the ingredients together in a food processor.

Transfer the guacamole to a serving bowl. Drizzle the remaining oil over the top and sprinkle with the parsley, then serve with tortilla chips.

Herb and Yogurt Dip

This is a creamy dip made with strained plain yogurt, which has a thicker consistency. If you want a lighter version, use lowfat yogurt.

SERVES 4

1 cup strained plain yogurt
1tbsp lemon juice
a pinch of salt
freshly ground black pepper
3 tbsp fresh sage leaves
3 tbsp fresh marjoram leaves, finely chopped
1½ tbsp fresh thyme leaves

Simply mix all the ingredients together and refrigerate.

Garlic, Herb, and Tomato Dip

This is a Mediterranean-style dip with a lovely color and flavor—especially wonderful if you grow your own tomatoes.

SERVES 4

3–4 medium-size tomatoes, skinned
4 tbsp chopped fresh chives
1 clove garlic, crushed
5 fresh basil leaves
a pinch of salt
freshly ground black pepper

Skin the tomatoes by dropping them into a bowl of boiling water for a second or two. The skin can then be removed easily.

Chop the tomatoes into very small pieces. Add the chopped chives and basil torn into small pieces, followed by the seasoning. Alternatively, put all the ingredients into a blender and blend to an even consistency.

VARIATION

Instead of the basil, add 1 tsp finely chopped onion and ½ tsp dried chili powder for a spicy version.

Herb **vinegars**

Vinegar is one of the most ancient preserving mediums, and is made by souring wine, cider, or beer. The name comes from the French *vin aigre*, meaning sour wine. The sour taste arises because the alcohol content turns into acetic acid, which is then usually present at around 6% by volume. Making your own herb and spice vinegars is easy and adds a wonderful range of flavors to salad dressings, to stock for poaching meat or fish, or to sauces and soups. If you choose attractive bottles, these can also make lovely gifts.

below Make your aromatic vinegars in unusual bottles—they look interesting and make individual, homemade gifts.

Choosing the best vinegars:

Wine vinegar from grapes can be red or white, and the best quality comes from Orléans in France, where it is matured slowly in oak casks. It works well with mild herbs because it has a subtle rounded flavor and does not mask their taste.

Cider vinegar from apples is extremely helpful in the diet because it neutralizes excess stomach acid, improves digestive function, and cleanses the whole system. It has a very strong taste and works only with pungent herb or spice combinations. Look out for cider vinegar matured in wooden casks to obtain the full health benefits.

Note Malt vinegar is made from beer and, although it works well for pickling, it has too strong a flavor to use with herbs.

Making herb vinegars

Tarragon and Lemon Wine Vinegar

18 fl oz/500 ml bottle of white wine vinegar
3–4 long sprigs of fresh tarragon, washed and any damaged leaves removed
3–4 strips of fresh unwaxed lemon peel

Pour off a little vinegar from the top of the bottle and push in the herbs and the lemon peel. Re-seal the bottle and let stand on a sunny windowsill for 2–3 weeks.

You can remove the old herbs and replace the sprigs with fresh ones, which will intensify the flavor. As long as the bottle stays well sealed, the vinegar can last up to 2 years.

RECIPE SUGGESTION
For a salad dressing for cold chicken and a selection of fresh green leaves.

2 tbsp tarragon and lemon wine vinegar
2 tbsp olive oil
salt and pepper

Mix the vinegar with the olive oil. Add a pinch of salt and freshly ground black pepper.

Garlic and Rosemary Vinegar

This robustly flavored vinegar will complement winter salads made with beans or lentils.

18 fl oz/500 ml bottle of cider vinegar
3–4 garlic cloves, each sliced in half
3 sprigs of fresh rosemary (tender young tips, each sprig around 4 inches/10 cm long)

Pour off a little vinegar, then push the sprigs of rosemary and the garlic cloves into the bottle.

Re-seal and let stand in a sunny place for 2–3 weeks.

Four-spice Vinegar

A little of this spicy vinegar adds a powerful flavor to chili dishes, either meat or vegetarian versions.

18 fl oz/500 ml bottle of red wine vinegar
1 tsp dried coriander seeds
1 tsp black peppercorns
2 tsp dill seeds
1 tsp dried chili

Lightly grind the coriander, peppercorn, and dill seeds using a pestle and mortar. Add the dried chili.

Carefully add them to the vinegar, then seal the bottle and let stand for 2–3 weeks.

Strain the liquid and re-bottle it before using.

Herb oils for cooking

Aromatic herbs contain essential oils, which are responsible for their flavors. These can be absorbed from the plant fibers using a vegetable oil, which preserves their active properties. Well-flavored herb oils are excellent bases for a whole range of recipes; they can be used to sweat onions at the start of making soups, in meat, fish, or vegetarian hot dishes, and also in salads as dressings. Experiment with your own combinations!

below Herb oils have subtle flavors, which delicately enhance your recipes.

Oils to choose

Olive oil (*Olea europea*) is full of nutrients, especially if it is of cold-pressed, extra-virgin quality. It does have its own distinctive taste and aroma, so it is best used with pungent herbs, pepper, and garlic.

Grape seed oil (*Vitis vinifera*) is a light, dark-green vegetable oil with no taste, so it can be used as a base for many herb combinations.

Sunflower seed oil (*Helianthus annuus*) is golden colored and a good source of linoleic acid, which helps the digestion as well as the skin and nails. It has no taste and can also be used for a whole variety of herb or spice combinations.

Buying vegetable oils

You are strongly advised to obtain vegetable oils from health food stores or good supermarkets—look for cold-pressed oils where possible, and of organic quality. Many cheap vegetable oils have been heat-treated and bleached and have no nutrient value.

Garlic, Peppercorn, and Marjoram Oil

This oil makes a lovely base for meat pasta sauces or for sprinkling over steaks on the grill.

18 fl oz/500 ml bottle of extra virgin olive oil
3–4 garlic cloves, chopped in half
1 tsp black peppercorns, slightly crushed
4 sprigs of fresh marjoram, each around 6 inches/
   15 cm long, washed with damaged leaves removed

Pour a little oil out of the bottle and push in the garlic cloves, peppercorns, and marjoram.

Make sure the oil comes up to the very top of the bottle.
Re-seal and let stand on a sunny windowsill for 2 weeks.
Every so often, give the bottle a little shake to mix it.

After 2 weeks strain the oil and re-bottle, then it is ready to use; it will last up to 3 months.

Fennel and Dill Oil

18 fl oz/500 ml bottle of sunflower seed oil
4 sprigs of fresh fennel leaves, washed
4 sprigs of fresh dill leaves, washed

Pour a little oil out of the bottle and push in the fennel and dill leaves.

Make sure the oil comes up to the very top of the bottle.
Re-seal and let stand it on a sunny windowsill for 2 weeks.
Every so often, give the bottle a little shake to mix it.

After 2 weeks strain the oil and re-bottle, then it is ready to use; it will last up to 3 months.

RECIPE SUGGESTION
This combination makes an excellent summer salad dressing.

2 tbsp of Fennel and Dill Oil
1 tbsp lemon juice
salt and pepper

Combine the oil, lemon juice, and salt and pepper and pour over green leaves.

Spice Oil

18 fl oz/500 ml bottle of grape seed oil
1 tbsp coriander seeds
1 tbsp cumin seeds
1 tsp black peppercorns
1 tsp dried chili

Grind the coriander, cumin, and peppercorns in a pestle and mortar. Add the chili. Pour a little oil out of the bottle and add the ground seeds.

Make sure the oil comes up to the very top of the bottle.
Re-seal and let stand on a sunny windowsill for 2 weeks.
Every so often, give the bottle a little shake to mix it.

After 2 weeks strain the oil and re-bottle, then it is ready to use; it will last up to 3 months.

This is an excellent base for curry recipes, for frying meat, or a salad dressing for chickpeas or lentils.

RECIPE SUGGESTION
2 tbsp of Spice Oil
2 tbsp lemon juice
a pinch of salt

Mix the oil, lemon juice, and salt together and use as a winter salad dressing for chickpeas or lentils, garnished with cilantro leaves or in a salad.

Green herb salads

Salads need never be boring, and there are some wonderful variations on the endless bags of tasteless leaves available in supermarkets. Many herbs like fennel, dill, lemon balm, or borage are excellent additions to a green salad. They add flavor and texture to the mixture of leaves. Also, remember the more old-fashioned salad herbs mentioned on pages 48–49, like Good King Henry and salad burnet, or watercress, or mint leaves. Assembling a salad can be so exciting when you have different-shaped and -tasting leaves to use, and of course, they are even better when you grow them yourself.

Here are some ideas:
Dandelion, Watercress, and Lettuce Mix

This is a lovely spring mix with the pungent taste of the dandelion and watercress, both rich in vitamin C.

1 small flat lettuce
3 oz/85 g young dandelion leaves
3 oz/85 g watercress
scant ½ cup chopped chives

Combine the dandelion leaves, watercress, and chives.

Good King Henry, Chervil, and Corn Salad Mix

This is an interesting combination of pungent and mild leaves.

4½ oz/125 g Good King Henry leaves
4½ oz/125 g corn salad
1¼ oz/55 g chervil leaves
1 lettuce

Combine to make a salad mix.

Nasturtium, Spinach, Watercress, and Arugula Mix

This is a very tasty summer combination and you can eat the flowers!

6 oz/175 g spinach leaves
1 large bunch of watercress
4 oz/115 g arugula leaves
6–8 nasturtium flowers

Mix together the spinach leaves, watercress, and arugula leaves. Scatter the nasturtium flowers over the top to add a glorious splash of color.

below A mixed salad with colorful ingredients and a yogurt dressing makes a delicious summer lunch.

Salad dressings

Commercial salad sauces are packed with artificial flavors and preservatives. Once you know how easy it is to make your own and how good they taste, you will never need to buy them again. The Italians dress a salad simply and superbly with lemon juice, olive oil, and a little salt and pepper. You can also use your flavored vinegars or oils.

French Dressing

This dressing is very tasty over any green salad combinations. If you wish, you can add a crushed garlic clove to the blend.

¾ cup extra virgin olive oil
4 tbsp white wine vinegar
1 tsp French mustard (preferably Dijon)
2 tsp chopped chives or parsley
a pinch of sugar
salt and pepper

Put all the ingredients in a clean, screwtop jar. Put on the lid and shake the jar.

Keep the dressing in the refrigerator and use within 1 week.

Salad with Yogurt Dressing

This is a very quick and refreshing salad, using a whole range of colorful ingredients, which make it look as good as it tastes. Put the dressing on the salad just prior to serving.

SERVES 4
2¾ oz/75 g cucumber, cut into sticks
6 scallions, halved
2 tomatoes, deseeded and cut into eight
1 yellow bell pepper, cut into strips
2 celery stalks, cut into strips
4 radishes, cut into fourths
2¾ oz/75 g arugula
1 tbsp chopped mint, to serve

DRESSING
2 tbsp lemon juice
1 garlic clove, crushed
⅔ cup plain yogurt
2 tbsp olive oil
salt and pepper

Mix the cucumber, scallions, tomatoes, bell pepper, celery, radishes, and arugula together in a large serving bowl.

To make the dressing, stir the lemon juice, garlic, yogurt, and olive oil together. Season well with salt and pepper.

Spoon the dressing over the salad and toss to mix. Sprinkle the salad with chopped mint and serve.

Herb soups

Herb soups are very easy to make, and there are so many combinations of vegetables, greens and herbs that can be used that the possibilities are endless. They really come into their own in the wintertime—on a cold winter's night, there is nothing more warming and satisfying than a tasty bowl of soup with fresh bread and perhaps some well-flavored Cheddar cheese. To give soup a robust taste, you can use yeast extract or good-quality soy sauce, or there are additive-free dried vegetable stocks you can buy as powder or cubes. Herbs also give soups pungent flavors.

Sorrel Soup

This is a wonderful green soup, which makes an early spring tonic, especially good when sorrel leaves are young and tender. They are rich in vitamin C and have a slightly lemony taste. It is best enjoyed as an occasional seasonal treat.

SERVES 4
1 small onion, finely chopped
1 tbsp sunflower seed oil
1–2 garlic cloves, crushed
generous handful of fresh young sorrel stems
    and leaves, washed and roughly chopped
3½ cups water
2 tsp dried vegetable stock powder or 1 cube
salt and pepper
⅔ cup light cream
ground nutmeg, to garnish

Gently cook the onion in the sunflower seed oil until it is soft, then add the sorrel leaves and garlic and continue cooking for 1 minute.

Pour over the water and stir in the dried stock. Bring to a boil, then reduce the heat and simmer for 15 minutes.

Add salt and pepper to taste. If you wish, you can pour the soup into a blender and blend until smooth.

Pour a swirl of light cream into the bottom of 4 soup bowls, then gently pour over the soup. Garnish with a sprinkling of grated nutmeg.

below Cilantro leaves have a fresh, slightly lemony tang to complement all the flavors in this soup.

Cold Cilantro Soup

This soup brings together Thai flavors for a cool, refreshing appetizer.

SERVES 4

2 tsp olive oil
1 large onion, finely chopped
1 leek, thinly sliced
1 garlic clove, thinly sliced
4 cups water
1 zucchini, peeled and chopped
scant ⅓ cup white rice
2-inch/5-cm piece lemongrass
2 lime leaves
1 cup cilantro leaves and soft stems
chili paste (optional)
salt and pepper
finely chopped red bell pepper and/or red chilies, to garnish

Heat the oil in a large pan over medium heat. Add the onion, leek, and garlic, then cover and cook for 4–5 minutes, or until the onion is softened, stirring frequently.

Add the water, zucchini, and rice with a large pinch of salt and some pepper. Stir in the lemongrass and lime leaves. Bring just to a boil and reduce the heat to low. Cover and simmer for about 15–20 minutes, or until the rice is soft and tender.

Add the cilantro leaves, pushing them down into the liquid. Continue cooking for 2–3 minutes, or until they are wilted. Remove the lemongrass and lime leaves.

Let the soup cool slightly, then transfer to a blender or food processor and purée until smooth, working in batches if necessary. Scrape the soup into a large container. Season to taste with salt and pepper. Cover and refrigerate until cold.

Taste and adjust the seasoning. For a more spicy soup, stir in a little chili paste to taste. For a thinner soup, add a small amount of iced water. Ladle into chilled bowls and garnish with finely chopped red bell pepper and/or chilies.

Herb soups

Turkey Soup with Rice, Mushrooms, and Sage

A rich, hearty soup, which can work well using the remains of the Thanksgiving turkey and its stock.

SERVES 4

generous ⅓ stick butter

1 onion, chopped finely

1 celery stalk, chopped finely

25 large fresh sage leaves, finely chopped

4 tbsp all-purpose flour

4 cups turkey or chicken stock

½ cup brown rice

9 oz/250 g mushrooms, sliced

7 oz/200 g cooked turkey, chopped

generous ¾ cup heavy cream

freshly grated Parmesan cheese, to serve

Melt half the butter in a large pan over medium-low heat. Add the onion, celery, and sage, and cook for 3–4 minutes, or until the onion is softened, stirring frequently. Stir in the flour and continue cooking for 2 minutes.

Add about a quarter of the stock a little at a time, and stir well, scraping the bottom of the pan to mix in the flour. Pour in the remaining stock, stirring to combine completely, and bring just to a boil.

Stir in the rice and season to taste. Reduce the heat and simmer gently, partially covered, for about 30 minutes, or until the rice is just tender, stirring occasionally.

Meanwhile, melt the remaining butter in a large skillet over medium heat. Add the mushrooms and season with salt and pepper. Cook for about 8 minutes, or until they are golden brown, stirring occasionally at first, then more often after they start to color. Add the mushrooms to the soup.

Add the turkey to the soup and stir in the cream. Continue simmering for about 10 minutes, or until heated through. Taste and adjust the seasoning, if necessary. Ladle into warm bowls and serve with Parmesan cheese.

below Turkey and mushroom soup is a really delicious winter warmer!

Bacon, Lentil, and Sage Soup

This hearty soup is a nourishing meal in itself on a cold night.

SERVES 4

1 tbsp sunflower seed oil
3 strips of lean bacon, chopped into
  small pieces
1 onion, finely chopped
generous 1 cup split red lentils, rinsed and any grit
  picked out
5 cups water
3 tsp dried vegetable stock or 1½ stock cubes
4 fresh sage leaves, finely chopped
1 bay leaf
salt and pepper

Heat the oil in a large pan and gently cook the bacon pieces until they are lightly browned. Add the chopped onion and cook until soft. Add the lentils and turn them in the onions and bacon until they are coated with oil.

Add the water and the dried stock, chopped sage leaves, and bay leaf. Bring the soup to a boil, stirring all the time.

Reduce to a very low heat and put the lid on the pan. Simmer slowly for 45 minutes, or until the lentils are very soft and creamy. Stir occasionally; a little more water may need to be added toward the end.

Before serving, add salt and freshly ground pepper to taste. Lift out the bay leaf and pour into 4 large bowls.

VARIATION

For a vegetarian version of this delicious soup, leave out the bacon.

Chicken and Thyme Broth

This is a delicious, light, and economical soup you can make with chicken drumsticks. The French way of making tasty soup with wonderful concentrated flavors is to simmer it slowly on very low heat. Slow simmering draws flavor out of the bones as well as the meat, giving a wonderful aroma. You can add herbs early on if you are using this method, as the low heat will draw out their aroma without destroying the taste.

SERVES 4

6 chicken drumsticks, washed under cold water,
  skins removed
1 onion, finely chopped
2 garlic cloves, chopped into several pieces
3 sprigs of fresh thyme, washed
1 bay leaf
3½ cups water
2 tsp dried vegetable stock or 1 cube
salt and pepper

Place the drumsticks in the bottom of a large pan. Scatter the onion, garlic, thyme, and bay leaf over the top. Pour over the water, then add the stock and slowly bring to a boil.

Turn down to a very low heat and simmer slowly for 1 hour with the lid on the pan.

Lift out the drumsticks and remove the meat from the bones. Cut up the meat finely, removing any gristle, and return it to the pan to warm through again. Add salt and pepper to taste. Lift out the bay leaf and thyme, then serve.

VARIATION

For a richer soup, stir in ⅔ cup light cream just before serving.

Herbs with meat

Cooking meat with herbs adds flavor as well as easing the digestive process; herbs stimulate the digestive juices through taste and smell even before the food has entered the mouth, and this helps absorption. There are many traditional combinations of particular herb tastes with particular meats.

Pork Chops with Fennel and Juniper

The addition of juniper and fennel to the pork chops gives an unusual and delicate flavor to this dish.

SERVES 4
½ fennel bulb
1 tbsp juniper berries, lightly crushed
about 2 tbsp olive oil
finely grated rind and juice of
** 1 orange**
4 pork chops, about 5½ oz/150 g each
fresh bread and a crisp salad, to serve

Using a sharp knife, finely chop the fennel bulb, discarding the green parts.

Grind the juniper berries using a pestle and mortar. Mix the crushed juniper berries with the fennel flesh, olive oil, and orange rind.

Using a sharp knife, score a few cuts all over each chop. Place the pork chops in a roasting pan or an ovenproof dish. Spoon the fennel and juniper mixture over the pork chops. Carefully pour the orange juice over the pork chops, cover and then let marinate in the refrigerator for about 2 hours.

Cook the pork chops under a preheated broiler for 10–15 minutes, depending on the thickness of the meat, until the meat is tender and cooked through, turning occasionally.

Transfer the pork chops to serving plates and serve with a crisp, fresh salad and plenty of fresh bread to mop up the cooking juices.

below The sweet anise taste of fennel complements the flavor of the pork.

Pan-fried Lamb Chop with Fresh Rosemary and Garlic

Sometimes you may be at home on your own and feel like eating something special. Here is a lamb dish created for one person; simply multiply the proportions if you are cooking for more people.

SERVES 1

1 lamb chop

2 tbsp extra virgin olive oil

2 cloves garlic, crushed

scant ¼ cup fresh rosemary leaves or 2 tsp
  dried rosemary

⅓ cup red wine

salt and pepper

2 tbsp light cream

TO SERVE

mashed potato and steamed broccoli

Rinse the chop under cold water, then dry with paper towels. Rub a little salt and fresh pepper on both sides.

Heat the oil in a skillet and add the chop, cooking it on medium heat for 5–10 minutes each side, depending on the thickness. Sprinkle over the fresh rosemary leaves and garlic and continue cooking for 1 minute, turning the chop over once or twice.

Pour over the red wine and bring it to a boil, then turn down the heat and simmer for 10 minutes. Add salt and freshly ground black pepper to taste.

Remove from the heat and add the cream to the sauce, stirring gently.

Serve with some mashed potato and steamed broccoli.

Chicken-breast Slices in Tarragon and Cream Sauce

Tarragon is a strong-tasting herb with a distinctive, almost minty flavor. It adds zest and interest to chicken, which can be so bland. If you can, buy organic free-range meat as it does taste better.

SERVES 2

2 organic free-range chicken breasts

2 tbsp sunflower seed oil

1 shallot, finely chopped

1 garlic clove, crushed

scant ¼ cup fresh tarragon leaves

1 tsp lemon juice

salt and pepper

⅔ cup light cream

TO SERVE

new potatoes, steamed carrots, and snow peas

Wash, dry, and slice the chicken pieces.

Heat the oil in a skillet over medium heat, and add the chicken slices, turning them until lightly browned. Add the garlic, shallot, and a pinch of salt and pepper and continue turning for 5 minutes.

Sprinkle over the tarragon leaves and add the lemon juice; then put a lid on the skillet and cook over low heat for another 10 minutes. Just before serving, check the seasoning, then remove from the heat and stir in the cream.

This is delicious served with baby new potatoes, steamed carrots, and snow peas.

Herbs with **meat**

Pork, Sage, and Cider Casserole

Stronger-tasting meats like pork (or beef) can be cooked with pungent herbs like sage, which adds an almost spicy flavor. Fresh sage leaves are best if you have them; they have a peppery taste, as compared to dried leaves, which are sweeter and milder. Bay leaves also work well because they are full of zesty aromatic oil, which brings out the taste of the meat. Pork with apple and cider is a traditional combination with a sweet yet aromatic flavor. Sage just lifts these two and adds a warm, fresh, spicy taste.

below Lemon and tarragon are fresh, light flavors which work well with all poultry—here with squab chickens.

SERVES 4
4 pork steaks
3 tbsp sunflower seed oil
1 large cooking apple, peeled, cored, and chopped
1 large onion, finely chopped
scant ¼ cup fresh chopped sage leaves or
    2 tsp dried sage
3 tbsp all-purpose flour
generous 1¾ cups hard cider
salt and pepper

TO SERVE
mashed potatoes with mustard and green beans

Remove the fat from the pork and cut into small pieces. Heat the oil in a skillet and brown the pork cubes, lifting them out into the casserole as they are cooked. Sprinkle the apple pieces over the meat.

Cook the onion and once it is soft add the sage leaves and flour, stirring together. Pour over the cider and stir until the mixture thickens. Add a generous pinch of salt and freshly ground pepper, then pour into a flameproof casserole over the meat. Stir it all together, and put a lid on the casserole.

Cook the dish in the middle of the oven at 350°F/180°C for 45 minutes. Serve with mashed potatoes with a little Dijon mustard added in, and green beans.

Lemon and Tarragon Squab Chickens

Broiled spatchcocked squab chickens, or poussins, are complemented by the delicate fragrance of lemon and tarragon.

SERVES 2

2 poussins
4 sprigs fresh tarragon
1 tsp oil
2 tbsp butter
rind of ½ lemon
1 tbsp lemon juice
1 garlic clove, crushed
salt and pepper
tarragon and orange slices, to garnish

Prepare the poussins by turning them breast-side down on a cutting board and cutting them through the backbone using kitchen scissors. Crush each bird gently to break the bones so that they lie flat while cooking. Season each with salt.

Turn them over and insert a sprig of tarragon under the skin over each side of the breast. Brush the chickens with oil, using a pastry brush, and place under a preheated hot broiler about 5 inches/13 cm from the heat. Grill the chickens for about 15 minutes, turning half way, until they are lightly browned.

To make the glaze for the chicken, melt the butter in a pan, then add the lemon rind and juice and the garlic, and season to taste.

Brush the chickens with the glaze and cook for an additional 15 minutes, turning them once and brushing regularly so that they stay moist. Garnish the chickens with tarragon and orange slices and serve with new potatoes.

Bolognese Sauce

This sauce is an Italian classic, which is also called "ragu." The addition of strong aromatic herbs like basil, oregano, and bay really improves the flavor of the beef that is the basis of the sauce, and they also complement the tomatoes and garlic. This is another recipe that benefits from longer simmering at low temperature—perfect if your guests are late!

SERVES 4

3 tbsp extra virgin olive oil
1 large onion, finely chopped
1 celery stalk, finely chopped
6 oz/175 g lean unsmoked bacon, diced
1–2 garlic cloves, crushed
1 lb/450 g lean ground beef
2 tbsp tomato paste
14 oz/400 g canned tomatoes
⅔ cup red wine
salt and pepper
1 tsp dried basil or 4 fresh basil leaves
1 tsp dried oregano or 3 sprigs fresh oregano
1 bay leaf

TO SERVE

cooked spaghetti
Parmesan cheese, for sprinkling

Cook the onion, celery, and bacon together in the oil over medium heat for 3–5 minutes, stirring occasionally.

Add the garlic and the ground beef and cook until the meat is browned. Add the tomato paste and stir in, then add the tomatoes and wine, stirring into a thick sauce. Add a pinch of salt and pepper, then add the herbs and bring to a boil; turn the heat down low and simmer for at least 45 minutes.

Serve with spaghetti for the classic Italian dish; or you can use this recipe for making a meat lasagna. Don't forget a sprinkling of fresh Parmesan cheese for an authentic flavor!

Herbs with fish

Cooking fish can provide a protein-rich meal in very little time. Frying or broiling are simple methods that bring out the flavor. It is very easy to obtain filleted fresh fish from supermarkets, already cleaned and ready to cook. When buying fish, look out for shiny bright scales or, in the case of salmon, plump peach-colored flesh. If you are using frozen fish, let it thaw completely before cooking.

Lime and Basil-Cured Salmon

The combination of herbs with citrus fruit creates light and tangy flavors that are simply delicious with fish. It is very important to use fresh salmon for this dish. The salt and sugar draw the moisture from the fish, leaving it raw but cured and full of flavor.

SERVES 6
2 lb/900 g very fresh salmon fillet, from the head
    end, skinned
¼ cup sugar
1¾ oz/50 g sea salt
5 tbsp chopped fresh basil
finely grated rind of 2 limes
1 tsp white peppercorns, lightly crushed

DRESSING
generous ¾ cup rice vinegar
5 tbsp sugar
finely grated rind of 1 lime
½ tsp English mustard
3 tbsp chopped fresh basil
1 tbsp Japanese pickled ginger, finely shredded
5½ oz/150 g mixed salad greens, to serve

TO GARNISH
lime wedges
basil leaves

Remove any small bones that remain in the salmon fillet. Wash and dry the fish. Place the salmon in a large nonmetallic dish and sprinkle evenly with the sugar, sea salt, basil, lime rind, and peppercorns. Cover and chill for 24–48 hours, turning the fish occasionally.

For the dressing, put the rice vinegar and sugar in a small pan and stir gently over low heat until the sugar has dissolved. Then, bring to a boil and simmer for 5–6 minutes, or until the liquid is reduced by about one-third. Remove the pan from the heat and stir in the lime rind and mustard. Put the pan to one side.

Remove the salmon fillet from the marinade, wiping off any excess with paper towels. Slice very thinly.

To serve, stir the chopped basil and ginger into the dressing. Toss the salad greens with a little of the dressing and arrange on 6 serving plates. Divide the salmon slices between the plates and drizzle a little dressing over. Garnish with lime wedges and basil leaves.

below Lime is a green and zesty aroma, which lifts the delicate taste of salmon fillet.

Herb-crusted Haddock with Tomato Salsa

We recommend you buy a good quality salsa, which contains onions, tomatoes, bell peppers, and spices.

SERVES 4

2 cups fresh white bread crumbs
3 tbsp lemon juice
1 tbsp Pesto Sauce (see page 73)
2 tbsp chopped fresh parsley
salt and pepper
vegetable oil spray
4 haddock fillets
1 tub tomato salsa, to serve

Put the bread crumbs, 2 tablespoons of the lemon juice, the Pesto Sauce, parsley, and salt and pepper in a bowl and mix together well.

Line a broiler pan with aluminum foil and spray with vegetable oil. Place the haddock fillets on the foil and sprinkle with the remaining lemon juice and more salt and pepper, then cook under a preheated broiler for 5 minutes.

Turn the haddock fillets over and spread the herb and bread crumb mixture over the top of each.

Cook for an additional 5–10 minutes, or until the haddock is tender and the crust is golden brown.

Serve with the tomato salsa spooned over the top of each fish.

Trout with Almonds, Lemon, and Parsley

Trout is a sweet and mild fish with a lovely flavor, well-complemented by lemon and the flat-leaf parsley, if you can get it; otherwise the curly-leaved version will be fine.

SERVES 2

2 fresh trout
½ stick salted butter
2 oz/55 g slivered almonds
2 tbsp fresh flat-leaf parsley, washed and chopped
3 tbsp fresh lemon juice
salt and pepper
selection of steamed vegetables, to serve

Season the fish with salt and pepper on both sides before cooking. Melt the butter in a large skillet and cook the trout on each side for 6–8 minutes, or until golden brown and cooked through.

Remove the fish to a heated serving dish and place in a warm oven.

Add the slivered almonds to the skillet, turning until they are golden brown. Add the parsley and the lemon juice, which will all combine into a lovely herby, lemony sauce.

To serve, put the trout on plates and spoon over the sauce. The fish is delicious with a selection of steamed vegetables such as baby carrots and corn, broccoli, and some new potatoes.

below Tasty herby bread crumbs make a delicious crunchy topping for the haddock.

Herbs with fish

Mediterranean Cod Steaks with Thyme and Marjoram

If you have packages of cod steaks in the freezer, here is an easy dish to be baked in the oven. It has a robust tomato flavor, complemented by aromatic thyme and marjoram, which makes a simple supper. This makes a great supper dish, and once it is cooking you will notice a mouth-watering aroma, helped by strong herbs like thyme.

SERVES 4

4 cod steaks, defrosted if frozen
2 tsp fresh lemon juice
2 tbsp extra virgin olive oil
1 onion, finely chopped
2 garlic cloves, crushed
1 tbsp tomato paste
14 oz/400 g canned tomatoes
scant ¼ cup fresh thyme leaves or 2 tsp dried thyme
2 tsp fresh marjoram leaves or 1 tsp dried marjoram
2 tbsp green olives stuffed with pimento, halved
salt and pepper

TO SERVE
boiled plain rice and a leafy salad

Place the cod steaks in a flameproof casserole and sprinkle them with lemon juice.

In a large pan, heat the oil and cook the onion until soft, then add the garlic and tomato paste. Add the tomatoes, herbs, and olives. Season to taste with salt and pepper.

Cook on medium heat for about 10 minutes, then pour the sauce over the fish. Put a lid on the casserole and bake on a high shelf in the oven for 25–30 minutes at 190°C/375°F.

Serve the dish with freshly boiled plain rice and a leafy green salad.

Herrings with Orange Tarragon Stuffing

The fish are filled with an orange-flavored stuffing and are wrapped in kitchen foil before being baked on the grill.

SERVES 4

1 orange
4 scallions
scant 1 cup fresh whole-wheat bread crumbs
1 tbsp fresh tarragon, chopped
4 herrings, cleaned and gutted
salt and pepper
green salad, to serve

TO GARNISH

2 oranges
1 tbsp light brown sugar
1 tbsp olive oil
sprigs of fresh tarragon

To make the stuffing, grate the rind from half of the orange, using a zester. Peel and chop all of the orange flesh on a plate in order to catch all of the juice.

Mix together the orange flesh, juice, rind, scallions, bread crumbs, and tarragon in a bowl. Season with salt and pepper to taste.

Divide the stuffing into 4 equal portions and use it to fill the body cavities of the fish. Place each fish on to a square of lightly greased kitchen foil and wrap the foil around the fish so that it is completely enclosed. Grill over hot coals for 20–30 minutes, or until the fish are cooked through—the flesh should be white and firm to the touch.

Meanwhile, make the garnish. Peel and thickly slice the 2 oranges and sprinkle over the sugar. Just before the fish is cooked, drizzle a little oil over the orange slices and place them on the grill for about 5 minutes to heat through.

Transfer the fish to serving plates and garnish with the grilled orange slices and sprigs of fresh tarragon. Serve with a green salad.

left Sweet, citrusy orange and fresh, aromatic tarragon enhance the flavor of the herrings.

Herbs in vegetarian dishes

Herbs and spices really combine well with protein-rich pulses to make delicious and economical entrées. They taste wonderful and also help the digestion of pulses. Indian recipes combine tasty spices and garlic to add flavor, and Western dishes use powerful herbs like savory leaves to add a pungent aroma.

below Pungent and slightly peppery, arugula adds a contrasting taste to this dish.

Wild Arugula and Tomato Risotto with Mozzarella

Never let the rice dry out when cooking.

SERVES 4

2 tbsp olive oil
¼ stick unsalted butter
1 large onion, chopped finely
2 garlic cloves, chopped finely
generous 1½ cups risotto rice
½ cup dry white vermouth (optional)
6¼ cups vegetable stock, simmering
6 vine-ripened or Italian plum tomatoes, deseeded and chopped
4½ oz/125 g wild rocket
handful of fresh basil leaves
1 cup freshly grated Parmesan cheese
8 oz/225 g fresh Italian buffalo mozzarella, grated coarsely, or diced
salt and pepper

Heat the oil and half the butter in a large skillet. Add the onion and cook for about 2 minutes, or until the onion just begins to soften. Stir in the garlic and rice, and cook, stirring frequently, until the rice is translucent and well coated with the butter and garlic.

Pour in the white vermouth, if using; it will bubble and steam rapidly and evaporate almost immediately. Add a ladleful (about 1 cup) of the simmering stock and cook, stirring constantly, until it is absorbed.

Continue adding the stock, about half a ladleful at a time, letting each addition be absorbed before adding the next.

Just before the rice is tender, stir in the chopped tomatoes and arugula. Shred the basil leaves and stir them into the risotto immediately. Continue to cook, adding more stock, until the risotto is creamy and the rice is tender but firm to the bite.

Remove from the heat and stir in the remaining butter, and the Parmesan and mozzarella. Season to taste with salt and pepper. Cover, and let stand for about 1 minute. Serve immediately, before the mozzarella melts completely.

Red Lentil and Spinach Curry

This is a very easy and lightly spiced curry with a mild nutty flavor from the lentils, combined with nutritious spinach.

SERVES 4

2 lb/900 g fresh spinach
generous 1 cup red lentils, washed and any grit picked out
2 tbsp sunflower seed oil
1 large onion, finely chopped
2 garlic cloves, crushed
1-inch/2.5-cm piece fresh gingerroot, peeled and very finely chopped
1/4 tsp dried chili powder
1 tsp dried cumin
1 tsp dried coriander
1 tbsp fresh lemon juice
salt and pepper

TO SERVE

basmati rice, a salad of cucumber slices mixed with plain yogurt

Wash the spinach leaves and put them in a large pan with a very small amount of water and a pinch of salt. On medium heat they will cook in just 5–7 minutes, reducing dramatically. Drain the cooked leaves very thoroughly. Chop them finely and put to one side.

Put the washed lentils and a pinch of salt into another pan. Pour over generous 1¾ cups water and simmer slowly for about 15 minutes until the lentils go creamy.

In a large skillet heat the oil and cook the onion, garlic, ginger, and chili for 5 minutes. Then add the cumin and coriander and continue cooking for 3 minutes, followed by the spinach and lemon juice, stirring in well. Turn down the heat and keep stirring occasionally.

Check the lentils are soft, then pour the cooked spices and spinach into the lentils, mixing thoroughly. Add salt and freshly ground pepper to taste. Serve immediately with boiled Indian basmati rice, and a salad of cucumber slices mixed with plain yogurt.

Wax Bean, Mushroom, and Summer Savory Salad

This lovely bean salad makes a delicious summer lunch.

SERVES 2

8 oz/225 g mushrooms
4 tbsp extra virgin olive oil
1 clove garlic, crushed
8 oz/225 g canned wax beans, drained and rinsed
2 tbsp fresh lemon juice
scant 1/2 cup fresh summer savory leaves, slightly bruised
salt and freshly ground pepper

TO SERVE

green salad, fresh whole-wheat rolls

Wash or wipe the mushrooms and slice them.

Heat half of the olive oil in a skillet. Cook the mushrooms with the garlic and a pinch of salt and pepper for 5 minutes.

Pour the mushrooms and their juice into a bowl. Add the wax beans, the rest of the olive oil, the lemon juice, and savory leaves. Stir together lightly. Add salt and pepper to taste.

Serve with a green salad and fresh whole-wheat rolls.

Herbs in *vegetarian dishes*

Basil and Tomato Pasta

Roasting the tomatoes gives a sweeter and smoother flavor to this sauce. Try to buy Italian tomatoes, such as plum or flavia, as these have a better flavor and color.

below A classic basil and tomato combination—bursting with flavor.

SERVES 4

1 tbsp olive oil

2 sprigs rosemary

2 garlic cloves, unpeeled

1 lb/450 g tomatoes, halved

1 tbsp sun-dried tomato paste

12 fresh basil leaves

salt and pepper

1lb 8 oz/675 g fresh farfalle or
    12 oz/350 g dried farfalle

basil leaves, to garnish

salt and pepper

Place the oil, rosemary, garlic, and tomatoes, skin-side up, in a shallow roasting pan. Drizzle with a little oil and cook under a preheated broiler for 20 minutes, or until the tomato skins are slightly charred.

Peel the skin from the tomatoes. Coarsely chop the tomato flesh and place in a pan. Squeeze the pulp from the garlic cloves and mix with the tomato flesh and sun-dried tomato paste. Coarsely tear the fresh basil leaves into smaller pieces and then stir them into the sauce. Season with a little salt and pepper to taste.

Cook the farfalle in a pan of boiling water according to the directions on the package or until it is cooked through, but still has "bite." Drain.

Gently heat the tomato and basil sauce. Transfer the farfalle to serving plates and serve with the basil and tomato sauce.

Special Nut Roast

This vegetarian dish is ideal for a special occasion. It is flavored with garlic and fresh rosemary for a delicious taste. As it does not contain any egg, it will also suit people who do not eat dairy products.

SERVES 4

2 tbsp sunflower seed oil

1 large onion, finely chopped

scant 1¼ cups water

2 tsp yeast extract

4 oz/115 g cooked sweet chestnuts, peeled and finely chopped

2 oz/55 g hazelnuts, finely ground or very finely chopped

½ cup walnut pieces

2 cups whole-wheat bread crumbs

scant ¼ cup fresh rosemary leaves

2 garlic cloves, crushed

salt and pepper

steamed snow peas or green beans, to serve

In a pan, heat the oil and cook the onion gently until soft. Add the water and yeast extract and gently bring to a boil.

In a bowl, put the nuts, bread crumbs, rosemary, and garlic and stir together; then add the liquid and stir with a fork until the consistency is thick and slack. Add a pinch of salt and pepper.

Pour into a greased shallow baking dish, preferably nonstick, and bake in the middle of the oven for 30 minutes at 350°F/180°C, or until golden brown. If you let it cool for 10 minutes, it is easier to slice.

Potato, Cheese, and Oregano Bake with White Wine

Here is an aromatic potato dish.

SERVES 4

1 lb/450 g potatoes, peeled and very finely sliced

1½ cups finely grated sharp Cheddar or Gruyère cheese

scant ½ cup fresh oregano leaves or 1 tbsp dried oregano

2½ cups hot water

2 tsp dried vegetable stock or 1 cube

1 glass dry white wine

salt and pepper

steamed snow peas or green beans, to serve

Pour a little cold water into the bottom of a large pan. Add the potato slices and simmer gently for about 10 minutes to soften them.

Grease a large shallow heatproof dish with a little oil, then put a layer of potato in the bottom. Sprinkle it with grated cheese, a tiny pinch of pepper, and a few oregano leaves, then repeat the layers of potato and cheese until the dish is full.

Add the dried stock to the hot water and stir in, followed by the wine. Pour this carefully over the potatoes and make sure the top layer has a generous amount of cheese and oregano with a pinch of salt and pepper.

Put the dish on a high shelf and cook for 30–45 minutes at 350°F/180°C, until the potatoes are tender. Serve with green beans or snow peas.

Herbs in desserts

Herbs such as mint can be used to make
lovely fresh-flavored summer desserts,
which are great for summer parties
or barbecues.

Minted Pears

These sweet pears are straightforward to make and
taste delicious. They can be made in advance and left
to chill, making them an ideal, easy dessert after a
more complex entrée.

SERVES 4
4 large pears
4 tbsp superfine sugar
4 tbsp clear honey
2 tbsp green crème de menthe
fresh mint sprigs, to decorate

Peel the pears and stand them upright in a heavy-
bottom pan. Add enough water to cover. Bring to a boil,
then reduce the heat and simmer, covered, for 25–30
minutes, or until the pears are tender. Pour away half
the cooking water, then add the superfine sugar to the
pan and simmer for an additional 10 minutes.

Transfer the pears to a bowl with a slotted spoon. Pour
²/₃ cup of the cooking water into a measuring cup and
stir in the honey and crème de menthe. Pour the syrup
over the pears.

Set the pears aside to cool, then cover with plastic wrap
and chill in the refrigerator for 1–2 hours. Transfer the
pears to individual serving bowls and spoon the mint
syrup over them, then serve decorated with fresh mint.

below A delicate
minty flavor
complements the
sweetness of
poached pears.

Spearmint, Apple, and Lemon Fool

SERVES 4

1 lb/450 g cooking apples, peeled and sliced

scant ¼ cup soft brown sugar

2 tbsp water

rind of 1 unwaxed lemon, washed

scant ½ cup fresh spearmint leaves, washed

⅔ cup whipping cream

fresh mint leaves, to serve

EGG CUSTARD

3 egg yolks

scant 1¼ cups light cream

1 tbsp superfine sugar

1 tbsp corn starch

2 drops vanilla extract

Put the apple slices, sugar, water, lemon rind, and mint leaves in a pan and simmer until the apples turn very soft.

Take out the mint leaves and purée the apple, either in a blender or food processor, or with a fork. Let stand in the pan to cool.

To make the custard, whisk together the egg yolks, superfine sugar, cornstarch, and vanilla extract. Heat the light cream in a pan until it boils, then turn down the heat and pour in the egg mixture, stirring all the time until it thickens. Let cool.

Whip the cream until it forms soft peaks, and carefully fold in the apple mixture, followed by the custard. Don't mix it too much—the swirling effect of the layers is attractive.

Spoon into individual glass dishes and chill before serving; decorate with fresh mint leaves.

Chilled Rose Cheesecake

In the Middle East, rose is seen as a digestive and liver tonic, which is why rosewater, Turkish Delight, or candied rose petals are so popular as desserts after rich main dishes. This is a light and delicious floral dessert flavored with rose water distilled from rose petals. You can buy this in health food stores or from herbal/essential oil suppliers.

SERVES 6–8

FOR THE BASE:

8 oz/225 g graham crackers, crushed with a rolling pin

¾ stick butter, melted

FOR THE FILLING:

1½ cups cream cheese

4 tbsp clear honey

⅔ cup lowfat plain yogurt

grated rind of 1 unwaxed lemon (wash fruit first)

2 tbsp rosewater

½ oz/15 g gelatin soaked in 3 tbsp water

3 egg whites

rose and candied petals, to decorate

Mix the graham-cracker crumbs with the melted butter and press into the base of a 8-inch/20-cm loose-bottom cake pan and refrigerate until solid.

In a bowl mix together the cream cheese, honey, yogurt, lemon rind, and rosewater.

Put the soaked gelatin in a bowl over a pan of simmering water until it dissolves, then stir into the mixture. Whisk the egg whites until they form stiff peaks, then fold into the filling. Pour over the cracker base and refrigerate for at least 2 hours until set.

To decorate before serving, choose a perfect budding rose from the garden as a centerpiece and surround it with candied rose petals.

Note This recipe contains raw eggs, so it is not suitable for all.

Herbs in desserts

Banana and Allspice Crêpes with Orange

Allspice is usually a blend of nutmeg, cloves, ginger, and cinnamon; combined with citrus fruit, it is an immediately uplifting fragrance. The crêpes can be made to any size—smaller ones around 6 inches/15 cm diameter, or larger ones the size of the pan. A skillet is essential, and you can easily turn crêpes with a spatula.

SERVES 8–10
scant ⅔ cup whole-wheat flour
1 large free-range egg, lightly beaten
1¼ cups milk
sunflower seed oil
1 small banana, mashed to a pulp
1 tsp allspice
grated rind of 1 unwaxed orange, washed

TO SERVE
whipped cream
juice of 1 orange

Pour the flour into a bowl. Make a well in the center and pour in the beaten egg. Using a balloon whisk, start beating in the milk slowly, bringing in more of the flour as you go, until you have a smooth batter. Beat in 1 tsp sunflower seed oil, banana, allspice, and orange rind.

Heat 2 tsp sunflower seed oil in a skillet until very hot. Pour in 3–4 tbsp batter, tilting the skillet so the bottom is coated. Cook for 2 minutes, then flip over and cook the other side.

Transfer to a warm plate while you carry on cooking the rest of the crêpes.

Serve with cream, sprinkled with freshly squeezed orange juice.

Dried Fruit, Cinnamon, and Almond Crumble

Mouth-watering spices like cinnamon, cardamom, or ginger are very good with sweet fruit, adding a warm, zesty aroma. This hearty winter dessert is both warming and satisfying. The combination of soaked dried fruit with the spicy topping is delicious and very aromatic. You can serve it with hot fresh custard or light cream.

SERVES 4
1 cup dried apricots
⅓ cup dried figs
⅓ cup dried golden raisins
1¼ cups pure apple juice
2 tsp ground cinnamon

FOR THE TOPPING
generous 1½ cups whole-wheat flour
¾ stick butter or generous ⅓ cup margarine at
   room temperature
½ cup soft brown sugar
1 oz/25 g slivered almonds

Put the dried fruit in a bowl and cover with the apple juice, then let stand overnight. Chop the soaked fruit into small pieces and transfer it with its juice into a heatproof dish, then sprinkle it with cinnamon.

To make the topping, sift the flour into a bowl. Cut the fat into small pieces and rub it into the flour until it is light and crumbly. Stir in the sugar and then pour the topping over the fruit. Scatter slivered almonds over the dish to finish.

Bake in the top of the oven at 350°F/180°C, or until it has nicely browned.

right A heavenly summer combination— strawberries, rose petals, and meringue.

Strawberry Rose Meringues

Rose water gives an exotic fragrance
to the delicious whipped cream filling
in these attractive strawberry meringues.

SERVES 4–6
2 egg whites
generous ½ cup superfine sugar

FILLING
⅓ cup strawberries
2 tsp confectioners' sugar
3 tbsp rose water
⅔ cup heavy cream

TO DECORATE
12 fresh strawberries
rose petals

Line 2 large baking sheets with nonstick parchment
paper. Place the egg whites in a large, spotlessly clean,
greasefree bowl and whisk until it forms stiff peaks.
Whisk in half the sugar, then carefully fold in the
remainder.

Spoon the meringue into a pastry bag fitted with a large
star tip. Pipe 24 x 3-inch/7.5-cm lengths onto the baking
sheets. Bake in the oven at 225°F/110°C for 1 hour,
or until the meringues are dry and crisp. Let cool on
wire racks.

To make the filling, place the strawberries in a blender
or food processor and process to a purée. Strain the
purée into a bowl and stir in the confectioners' sugar
and rose water. Place the cream in a separate bowl and
whip until thick. Stir into the strawberry mixture and
mix well together.

Sandwich the meringues together with the strawberry
cream. Cut 6 of the strawberries in half and use to
decorate the meringues. Scatter rose petals over
the top and serve immediately with the remaining
whole strawberries.

Herbs in biscuits

Biscuits are very easy to make and best eaten on the day of cooking. Biscuit dough should be soft but not sticky, and it should not be over-handled, or it will become tough. Aromatic flowers and leaves add unusual tastes.

Lavender Biscuits

These are surprisingly good, especially in the summertime with some fresh raspberry or strawberry jelly, and maybe a little whipped cream for a real treat. They are best made in late June to early July, when lavender flowers are at their best; their special taste comes from the flower's essential oil.

SERVES 4

generous 1⅓ cups white self-rising flour

a pinch of salt

⅓ stick soft butter or 3 tbsp margarine

1 tsp superfine sugar

1 tbsp fresh lavender flowers

⅔ cup milk

Sift the flour and salt into a bowl and rub in the fat until the mixture is like fine bread crumbs.

Stir in the lavender flowers and the sugar, and then add enough milk to make a soft but not sticky dough. Turn onto a floured counter and roll out until ½ in/1 cm thick. Cut out 8 biscuits with a pastry cutter.

Place on a greased and floured baking sheet and bake in the oven at 425°F/220°C for 10–15 minutes, until risen and golden.

Cheese and Herb Biscuits with Yogurt

This is a whole-wheat version with a savory, slightly spicy taste, excellent with a leafy green salad or tomato and red onion salad for a light summer lunch. This recipe uses Red Leicester cheese which gives it a mild flavor, but you can use any local hard cheese. The marjoram adds a light herbal flavor and the biscuits can be made with either fresh or dried leaves. The plain yogurt makes them extremely moist.

SERVES 4

generous 1⅓ cups whole-wheat flour

1½ tsp baking powder

pinch of salt

1 tbsp margarine

¾ cup finely grated Red Leicester cheese

1 tsp paprika

scant ¼ cup fresh marjoram leaves, or

1½ tsp dried marjoram

⅔ cup lowfat yogurt at room temperature

Sift together the flour, baking powder, and salt. Rub in the margarine until the mixture is fine and crumbly. Stir in the cheese, paprika, and marjoram.

Add the yogurt, mixing to a soft dough, adding a little milk if needed. Knead lightly on a counter and roll out to approximately ½ in/1 cm thickness.

Cut out 8 biscuits with a pastry cutter. Place on a greased and floured baking sheet and bake in the oven at 400°F/200°C for 15–20 minutes, or until golden brown.

Savory Chive Biscuits

Savory scones make a delicious alternative to
sandwiches at tea-time and they are ideal for serving
with soup.

SERVES 4

generous ⅔ cup white self-rising flour,
   plus extra for dusting

generous ⅔ cup whole-wheat self-rising flour

1 tsp baking powder

pinch of salt

⅓ stick butter, plus extra for greasing

¾ cup finely grated Cheddar cheese

2 tbsp snipped fresh chives

3 tbsp milk

fresh chives, to garnish

Preheat the oven to 425°F/220°C, then grease a baking
sheet. Sift the 2 flours, baking powder, and salt into a
bowl. Rub in the butter until the mixture resembles fine
bread crumbs, then stir in ½ cup of the grated cheese
and chives. Stir in up to 1 tablespoon of milk to make a
fairly soft, light dough.

On a floured counter, roll out the dough to ¾ inch/
2 cm thick and stamp into circles with a 2½-inch/
6-cm plain cutter. Gather the trimmings, then re-roll
and stamp out more biscuits until the dough is used up.

Place the biscuits on the prepared baking sheet, then
brush the tops with the remaining milk and sprinkle with
the remaining grated cheese. Bake in the preheated
oven for 10 minutes, or until well risen and golden.
Garnish with fresh chives and serve warm or cold.

below Cheese
and chive biscuits
make a tasty
and unusual
tea-time treat.

Herbs in **cakes** and **cookies**

Baking your own cakes and cookies is surprisingly easy and takes very little time. As well as making your home smell wonderful, home-baking tastes fresh and is satisfying to do. Including herbs and spices adds particular succulent aromas to simple recipes. You only need simple equipment; a good nonstick baking sheet is very useful.

Lavender Cupcakes

Lavender gives a special fragrance and flavor to these little cakes.

SERVES 4–6
generous ½ cup golden superfine sugar
1 stick butter, softened
2 eggs, beaten
1 tbsp milk
1 tsp finely chopped lavender flowers
½ tsp vanilla extract
generous 1 cup self-rising flour, sifted
1¼ cups confectioners' sugar

TO DECORATE
lavender flowers
silver dragées

Place 12 paper cake cases in a muffin pan. Place the superfine sugar and butter in a bowl and cream together until pale and fluffy. Gradually beat in the eggs. Stir in the milk, lavender, and vanilla extract, then carefully fold in the flour.

Divide the mixture between the paper cases and bake in the oven for 12–15 minutes at 400°F/200°C, or until well risen and golden. The sponge should bounce back when pressed. A few minutes before the cakes are ready, sift the confectioners' sugar into a bowl and stir in enough water to make a thick frosting.

When the cakes are baked, transfer to a wire rack and place a blob of frosting in the center of each one, letting it run across the cake. Decorate with lavender flowers and silver dragées and serve as soon as the cakes are cool.

below Lavender's soft and sweet aroma adds a magical twist to these cupcakes.

Apple and Nutmeg Cakes

These are so homely and yet so simple, with a delicious spicy taste. Be warned—they tend to disappear very quickly!

SERVES 6

1½ cups white self-rising flour
pinch of salt
1 tsp grated lemon rind
1 tsp ground nutmeg
1½ sticks butter or ¾ cup margarine cut into
   small pieces
¼ cup superfine sugar
1 large, free-range egg, beaten
2 cooking apples, peeled, cored, and grated

Sift the flour and salt into a bowl. Add the lemon rind and nutmeg, then the butter and rub in until the mixture is like fine bread crumbs.

Stir in the sugar, then add the egg and beat the mixture well to a thick consistency. Add the apple.

Place 12 heaped spoonfuls of the mixture on a greased baking sheet and bake in middle of the oven at 375°F/190°C for 20–25 minutes, or until risen and golden brown.

Let the cakes cool for 5 minutes before transferring them to a wire rack.

Oat Cookies with Oregano

This recipe makes lovely nutty cookies, which are delicious at the end of a meal with a selection of cheeses. They are extremely easy to make and best eaten on the day of baking; however, they will keep for a few days in an airtight container. Dried oregano is a softly aromatic herb and here it lifts the taste.

SERVES 10

generous 1 cup whole-wheat flour, plus extra
   for sprinkling
generous ½ cup oat flakes
1 tsp baking powder
pinch of salt
1 tsp dried oregano
¾ stick butter or scant ⅓ cup margarine
3 tbsp milk

In a bowl, mix together the flour, oats, baking powder, salt, and oregano.

Rub in the butter until the mixture is like fine bread crumbs, then slowly stir in the milk using a fork until the ingredients are well worked together. Sprinkle flour on a clean counter and roll out the dough until it is ¼ inch/5 mm thick.

Use a pastry cutter to stamp out 18 cookie shapes. Place on a greased baking sheet and bake on a mid-to-high shelf at 350°F/180°C for 20–25 minutes, or until golden brown. Lift the cookies carefully onto a wire tray to cool, then store in an airtight container.

VARIATIONS

Instead of the oats, try 1½ oz/40 g sunflower seeds for a crunchy texture or 1½ oz/40 g sesame seeds for a milder, sweeter taste.

Herb rolls and tea bread

Making your own bread always sounds somewhat daunting, so it is a relief to know there are very simple ways of making rolls that do not require yeast or long rising times.

Rosemary Soda Rolls

Soda bread is a traditional Irish loaf, best eaten on the day of making, and it requires only baking soda to make it rise. Whole-wheat flour gives it a nutty taste, and the addition of herbs like fresh rosemary adds an unusual twist. These lovely rolls are excellent for a packed lunch, split and filled with grated cheese and sliced fresh tomato, or sliced ham and lettuce leaves. You can vary the herbs as you wish. They are also a very quick standby if you run out of bread!

SERVES 4

2¾ cup whole-wheat flour
1 tsp salt
2 tsp baking soda
2 tbsp butter
2 tsp chopped fresh rosemary leaves
1¼ cups milk

Sift the flour, salt, and baking soda into a bowl. Add the butter and rub in until the mixture is like fine bread crumbs. Stir in the rosemary.

Make a well in the middle and, using a fork, beat in the milk, then gradually knead with your hands to make a dough.

Turn it out on to a floured counter and split into 4 segments, shaping each one lightly into a circle. Place them on a greased baking sheet. Bake in the middle of the oven at 425°F/220°C for 30–35 minutes, or until risen and golden, then cool on a wire rack.

Cheese, Onion, and Marjoram Tea Bread

Tea breads are also very easy, needing only baking powder and eggs as raising agents, and here is an onion bread with fragrant marjoram to add aroma. This tea bread is lovely served sliced and buttered with a bowl of homemade soup, or as an accompaniment to a vegetable bake or stew, as a light supper.

SERVES 4

2 cups white self-rising flour
1 tsp salt
¼ cup margarine
1 small onion, peeled and finely chopped
1 cup finely grated well-flavored Cheddar cheese
1 tsp dried marjoram
1 large egg, beaten
⅔ cup milk

Sieve the flour and salt into a bowl. Rub in the margarine until the mixture is like fine bread crumbs, then add the onion, cheese, and marjoram and mix well. Add the beaten egg and milk and mix to a soft dough, then place it into a 1-lb/450-g greased loaf pan.

Bake in the middle of the oven at 375°F/190°C for 1 hour, until risen and golden brown. Let cool for 5 minutes, then turn onto a wire rack. This bread is delicious eaten warm.

VARIATIONS

Instead of the onion and marjoram, try adding ½ cup finely chopped walnuts and 1 tsp dried rosemary; or 2 celery stalks very finely chopped and 2 tsp fresh chopped parsley.

Cheese, Herb, and Onion Rolls

Great texture and flavor are achieved by mixing white and granary flours together with minced onion, grated cheese, and fresh herbs.

SERVES 4

1½ cups white bread flour

1½ tsp salt

1 tsp mustard powder

good pinch of pepper

generous 1⅓ cups granary or malted wheat flour

2 tbsp chopped fresh mixed herbs

2 tbsp finely chopped scallions

1¼–1¾ cups grated lowfat Cheddar cheese

½ oz/15 g compressed fresh yeast; or

   1½ tsp instant dry yeast plus

   1 tsp superfine sugar; or

   1 envelope active dry yeast plus 1 tbsp oil

1¼ cup warm water

Sift the white flour with the salt, mustard, and pepper into a bowl. Mix in the granary flour, herbs, scallions, and most of the cheese.

Blend the fresh yeast with the warm water or, if using dry yeast, dissolve the sugar in the water, then sprinkle the yeast on top and let stand in a warm place for about 10 minutes, or until frothy. Add the yeast mixture of your choice to the dry ingredients and mix to form a firm dough, adding more flour if necessary.

Knead until smooth and elastic. Cover with oiled plastic wrap and let stand in a warm place to rise for 1 hour, or until doubled in size. Knock back and knead the dough until smooth. Divide into 10–12 pieces and shape into round or long rolls, coils, or knots.

Alternatively, make one large braided loaf. Divide the dough into 3 even pieces and roll each into a long thin sausage and join at one end. Beginning at the joined end, braid to the end and secure. Place on greased baking sheets, then cover with an oiled sheet of plastic and let rise until doubled in size. Remove the plastic.

Sprinkle with the rest of the cheese. Bake in a preheated oven at 400°F/200°C for 15–20 minutes for the rolls, or 30–40 minutes for the loaf.

below Mixed herbs and spring onions give these rolls a strongly savoury aroma.

Herb breads

Here are some herbed breads to make, including some that use Italian-style dough.

Mixed-herb Pizza Dough

Making your own pizza is great fun; there are literally hundreds of toppings to try.

FOR ONE PIZZA BASE [SERVES 4]
⅓–½ cup hand-hot water
¼ tsp sugar
1½ tsp instant dry yeast
1½ cups all-purpose flour
1 tsp salt
½ tsp dried thyme
½ tsp dried basil
½ tsp dried oregano
1 egg, beaten
1 tsp extra virgin olive oil
various toppings, to serve

Pour ⅓ cup of the water into a bowl, then stir in the sugar and dried yeast and let stand in a warm place for 10–15 minutes, or until frothy.

Sift the flour and salt into a bowl and stir in the dried herbs, then add the yeast mixture and beaten egg and work into a dough, adding a little more water if necessary.

Turn the dough onto a floured counter and knead for 5–10 minutes; then wrap it in a piece of plastic wrap moistened with the olive oil. Put it in a warm place until it has doubled in size. Unwrap it, then knead again for about 5 minutes, and it's ready; roll it out to about ¼ inch/5 mm thick and lay on a greased baking sheet.

To make pizza, brush the base with olive oil. Cover with a thin layer of tomato paste, then add layers of sliced vegetables, or olives, capers, or anchovies, or combinations of chopped ham, sliced salami, or fish like tuna. Finish with slices of mozzarella cheese or grated Cheddar and bake at the top of a hot oven [500°F/250°C] for 15 minutes.

Garlic and Sage Bread

This freshly made herb bread is an ideal accompaniment to salads and soups and is dairy-free. You could also use rosemary, marjoram, or thyme.

SERVES 6
oil, for greasing
1½ cups strong whole-wheat bread flour
1 envelope active dry yeast
3 tbsp chopped fresh sage
2 tsp sea salt
3 garlic cloves, finely chopped
1 tsp clear honey
⅔ cup hand-hot water

Grease a baking sheet. Sift the flour into a large mixing bowl and stir in the bran remaining in the strainer.

Stir in the active dry yeast, chopped fresh sage and half of the sea salt. Reserve 1 teaspoon of the chopped garlic for sprinkling and stir the remainder into the bowl. Add the honey and hand-hot water and mix together to form a dough.

Turn the dough out onto a lightly floured counter and knead it for about 5 minutes, or until smooth and elastic [alternatively, use an electric mixer with a dough hook].

Place the dough in a bowl greased with oil, then cover with lightly oiled plastic wrap and let rise in a warm place until doubled in size.

Knead the dough again for a few minutes. Roll it into a long sausage and then shape it into a ring. Place on the prepared baking sheet. Cover and let rise for 30 minutes, until springy to the touch. Sprinkle with the remaining sea salt and garlic.

Bake the loaf in a preheated oven, 400°F/200°C for 25–30 minutes. Transfer the bread to a wire rack to cool before serving.

below A strongly flavored bread with garlic—try your own combinations of herbs!

Herb Focaccia

Rich with olive oil, this bread is so delicious it would turn a simple salad or bowl of soup into a positive feast.

SERVES 6

2⅔ cups unbleached white bread flour, plus extra
   for dusting
1 envelope active dry yeast
1½ tsp salt
½ tsp sugar
1¼ cups hand-hot water
3 tbsp extra virgin olive oil, plus extra for greasing
4 tbsp finely chopped fresh herbs
sea salt, for sprinkling

Combine the flour, yeast, salt, and sugar in a bowl and make a well in the center. Gradually stir in most of the water and 2 tablespoons of the olive oil to make a dough. Gradually add the remaining water, if necessary, drawing in all the flour.

Turn out onto a lightly floured counter and knead. Transfer to a bowl and lightly knead in the herbs for 10 minutes until soft but not sticky. Wash the bowl and lightly coat with olive oil.

Shape the dough into a ball, then put it in the bowl and turn the dough over. Cover tightly with a dish towel or tightly greased plastic wrap and set aside in a warm place to rise until the dough has doubled in volume. Meanwhile, sprinkle polenta over a baking sheet.

Turn the dough out onto a lightly floured counter and knead lightly. Cover with the upturned bowl and let stand for 10 minutes. Roll out and pat the dough into a 10 inch/25 cm circle, about ½ inch/1 cm thick, and carefully transfer it to the prepared baking sheet. Cover the dough with a dish towel and let rise again for 15 minutes.

Using a lightly oiled finger, poke indentations all over the surface of the loaf. Drizzle the remaining olive oil over and sprinkle lightly with sea salt. Bake in a preheated oven, 450°F/230°C, for 15 minutes, or until golden and the loaf sounds hollow when tapped on the bottom. Transfer the loaf to a wire rack to cool completely.

below Herb focaccia is delicious with any summer salad combination—take it on a picnic!

Herbal **drinks**

Herbs are very much part of traditional
drink recipes, whether alcoholic or not.
Mulled wine in the winter is a classic
heady spicy treat. In medieval times the
tradition was to plunge a red-hot poker
into the drink to heat it; nowadays, using
a pan is simpler but less dramatic.
Summer drinks with combinations of herbs
are also delicious—cooling to the mouth
and soothing to the digestion.

Lime and Lemon Grass Cooler

A refreshing drink for a hot summer's day.
The lemon grass complements the lime perfectly.

SERVES 4
- egg white and superfine sugar, to frost
- 2 limes, peeled and each cut into 8 pieces
- 1 small lemongrass stem, coarsely chopped
- 3 tbsp superfine sugar
- 4 crushed ice cubes
- ½ cup water
- 4 slices of lime
- soda water, to top up

To frost the rim of the glasses, pour a little egg white
into a saucer. Dip the rim of each glass briefly into
the egg white and then into a saucer of the sugar.

Place the lime pieces and lemongrass in a food
processor with the sugar and crushed ice cubes.

Add the water and process for a few seconds, but not
until completely smooth. Strain the mixture into the
frosted glasses. Add a slice of lime to each glass and
top up to taste with soda water. Serve at once.

Summer Borage Punch

In the 16th century, the herbalist Gerard was a great
fan of borage in drinks, saying "it maketh a man
merrie and joyfull." Flowers add decoration as well
as a mild taste, and leaves add flavor.

SERVES 4–6
- 4 cups dry white wine
- 1¼ cups good-quality lemonade
- grated rind of 1 unwaxed lemon (wash fruit first)
- 1 unwaxed lemon cut into thin slices
- several borage flowers and leaves, rinsed, to decorate

Pour the wine and the lemonade into a bowl, and stir in
the lemon rind. Add the slices of lemon, then sprinkle
over the borage flowers and leaves and chill until needed.

above Lime and
lemon grass are
two perfectly
complementary
flavors full of
summer zest.

right Aromatic spices mixed with ice cream—an unusual summer treat!

Christmas in Summer

A blend of traditional winter spices makes this a cool drink to be enjoyed in summer.

SERVES 2
scant ⅓ cup cranberry cordial
2 allspice berries, crushed
2 slices of orange
2 cinnamon sticks
1 cup boiling water
2 scoops of luxury vanilla ice cream

Ensure that you use glasses which are suitable for holding boiling water.

Divide the cranberry cordial between the glasses, then add a crushed allspice berry, an orange slice, and a cinnamon stick to each glass.

Pour the boiling water into the glasses. Let cool, then chill.

When you are ready to serve, float a scoop of ice cream on the top of each glass.

Mulled Wine

A traditional winter favorite.

SERVES 4–6
1 bottle red table wine
3 tbsp brandy
4 cups fresh orange juice
2 sticks cinnamon
8 cloves
1 tsp dried nutmeg
3 tbsp runny honey
1 unwaxed orange, washed and sliced

Pour the wine into a large steel pan and start to gently warm it over medium heat. Add the brandy, orange juice, spices, and honey, and keep stirring until the mixture gets hot and the honey melts.

Add the orange slices and turn down the heat, simmering slowly for 10–15 minutes; then you can add more honey to taste. Serve immediately.

VARIATION

For hot mulled cider, use 2½ cups hard cider, 1¼ cups apple juice, 3 tbsp honey, 8 cloves, 2 cinnamon sticks.

Herbal teas

Herbal teas or infusions are one of the easiest ways to enjoy
herbs, as well as to get the benefits of their active ingredients.

The proportion is always twice as much volume
of fresh herb to dried herb:

FOR 1 LARGE CUP OR MUG
1 tsp dried herb (or 2 tsp fresh herb)
1 cup boiling water

Use a special tea infuser, which you simply hang
in the cup, or use a small teapot. Alternatively,
add the herbs to the cup, then pour over the
boiling water and put a saucer on top for 15
minutes to infuse the tea. The heat in the water
draws out the active ingredients. You can strain
the tea if you like before drinking. Add a slice of
lemon for vitamin C and flavor, and a spoonful of
honey to sweeten if needed.

There are so many examples of herbs for tea—
here is a chart showing some of the most
common, and a few unusual ones.

Types of Teas and their Uses

Tea	Use
Peppermint (also apple mint or spearmint)	The leaves settle the digestion and calm the stomach, as well as refreshing the mouth. The tea is excellent drunk after a meal.
Camomile	Soothing and calming, the flowers of either Roman or German camomile can be infused to help with tension, headaches, stress, or anxiety.
Lemon balm	The lemony sweet leaves help calm the digestion and soothe the mind—a very calming drink at the end of the day. Lemon balm can also be combined with any of the mints.

Fennel
The seeds make the most potent tea with a peppery and anise-like flavor. It is very good as a digestive aid after rich foods in particular.

Elderflower
Delicate pale elderflowers give a lovely flowery and slightly lemony taste. This tea is calming and soothing. In equal parts with mint and yarrow leaves, it supports the immune system in the early stages of influenza.

Lavender
Lavender flowers, either fresh or dried, make a soft, slightly pungent tea, which is very good for headaches and insomnia. It will usually need a teaspoon of honey to sweeten it.

Rosemary
Fresh and zesty leaves makes a warm and aromatic tea, helpful for headaches and supportive to digestion.

Sage
This is a peppery and almost spicy tea, warming in the winter when you feel chilled or tired, or perhaps have a cold.

Thyme
The leaves have a powerful aroma and are a very good antiseptic if you have a sore throat or a cough.

Ginger
Fresh root in particular (a ½-in/1-cm piece, finely chopped) is a very powerful immune support for coughs, colds, and influenza, good with honey and lemon.

Cardamom
3–4 pods crushed will make a lovely sweet, aromatic tea, very good for sore throats or a runny nose.

Dandelion
Fresh young leaves make a wonderful bitter cleansing tea— it stimulates the kidneys. Drink it in small amounts.

Feverfew
This is a herb reputed to be very helpful for migraine sufferers, and it also calms stress.

herbs for
health

Herbs for a **healthy lifestyle**

This section will show you ways to use herbs to support your health and well-being. In today's busy world, it is becoming increasingly important to rebuild vitality and strength. Emotional, work, or environmental stresses are undermining general health patterns, and conventional medicine does not always have the answer. Using herbs for their healing properties can help to prevent problems from occurring by working gradually to increase general energy levels—so your body can fight potential problems itself.

below Using herbs to support your health helps you make gradual changes to your lifestyle, bringing balance and new levels of focus.

What does the idea of "health" mean to you? Perhaps it might seem like the absence of illness—just simply not being sick. Is there more? Could "health" mean something much wider and deeper than this? If you consider that "being healthy" may mean maintaining a state of harmony where all systems in the body and mind are functioning as they should, then this begins to change the picture. Your body is an incredible organism capable of immense feats of self-repair and renewal, yet it needs help to keep doing all this. You know you need some support when you are tired, when you are stressed or lack the energy to do what you want to do, or maybe you are having some symptoms that are bothering you. You need help, but where do you look? Some people may reach for the quick highs of sugar or caffeine, or artificially flavored food, or alcohol, or chemical drugs for pain relief. Yet none of these things solve the problems—they just mask them for a while, and in the end they may make the underlying situation worse.

Herbs are not the answer to everything and it would be a mistake to see them as yet another crutch. They are plants that offer a level of support which is gentle; after years of experiencing the effects of synthetic chemicals in your system, you may find it hard to feel what they are actually doing—at first. If you start using herbs for health as part of a gradual change in your lifestyle toward more natural food, simpler eating patterns, and a closer relationship to nature, then you really start to feel the benefits. Your digestion functions better, your mind is calmer, you have improved levels of energy—these are some of the noticeable effects you begin to experience.

This section guides you through making simple herbal preparations to use, like ointments and balms, and also gives you a brief introduction to aromatherapy—the use of essential oils extracted from aromatic plants. You will then be guided through sections relating to the main body systems with information on how they function and how herbs can be used to support them. The emphasis is on self-help, with clear suggestions to follow.

It is very important to be aware of your own body and its symptoms. If you feel unwell or have pain, are pregnant or have any serious condition, you should always consult your physician, who will provide you with conventional treatment for your condition. If you want to use herbs to support you in any of these circumstances, you should consult a qualified herbal practitioner who is trained to give you expert advice and help.

below Herbs can be used to promote health and a sense of well-being for all members of the family.

What is **herbal medicine?**

Every culture on the planet has its own traditional remedies made from local plants. Humankind has evolved this very close relationship with the plant kingdom since the beginning of our evolution, selecting particular leaves, roots, or flowers for the effects they give.

Even today, there are still areas of the planet where instinctive and sensitive ways of connecting with plants are being used. In the Amazon basin, Kayapo Indian medicine men continue to seek out new plants to use according to their own tradition, in which they "dream" the remedy for the person and then go out into the forest and find it. Even though the rainforest is being destroyed in many areas, there are still botanical treasures to be found.

Herbal medicine follows different traditions in different parts of the world.

The Western approach

Western herbal tradition goes back to Ancient Greece, to practitioners like Hippocrates and Dioscorides, who cataloged plants and wrote down their remedies, forming a body of knowledge that was used for centuries after their deaths. Hippocrates in particular followed a very "holistic" model, by which remedies were part of a whole plan for the patient, which included fasting, massage, and special baths; he believed very much in the notion of "a healthy mind in a healthy body." Today, in modern herbal practice, the same thing applies—changes in diet will be advised as the result of extensive questioning and examination of lifestyle habits and stress levels. Support using herbs as supplements, or as teas or infusions, will be advised, and a program designed for the client to follow. This is designed to help the body to detoxify itself from the effects of years of imbalance. Sometimes the effects can be dramatic, and although the strict regime may be challenging to follow, the end results are long-lasting. Modern Western herbal practitioners train for at least five years and have detailed understanding of the pharmacological effects of the herbs they use as remedies.

Eastern approaches

Eastern herbal medical practices are also thousands of years old and are unbroken traditions that exist alongside conventional drug therapy. In China, Traditional Chinese Medicine employs literally thousands of ingredients, many from plants but some also derived from animal sources. These are made up into powders, which the client has to drink over a period of time. Chinese herbal practitioners see the body as energetic as well as physical; they assess energy imbalances and see these as contributing to physical problems. Their map of the body includes the "meridians," or lines of energy that cover the entire three dimensions of the body, passing through all surfaces and organs. They will assess energy levels before prescribing remedies. In India, the ancient tradition of Ayurveda (see pages 78–79) maintains health in the body through massage, fasting, and particular foods, as well as remedies made from herbs and spices. Both of these traditions demand at least five years of training before practitioners are qualified.

Herbal medicine has an enormous body of knowledge behind it. It is from the Western tradition that the following self-help guide is drawn.

top left Herbal teas or infusions have many different effects, including calming the mind and soothing the digestion.

top right Indian spices have pungent aromas and powerful effects on the immune system, building vitality and strength.

bottom left Chinese herbs are combined in thousands of ways to rebalance the whole system and cleanse the internal organs.

bottom right Camomile flowers are a gentle remedy—they can be made into a skin wash to soothe irritated or problem areas.

Active herbal ingredients

All plants contain hundreds of ingredients and are extremely complex organisms. Herbs contain particular active substances that can help the human body cope with different problems. These ingredients are now known by chemical names as the result of more scientific analysis, whereas in the past the plants were selected because their effects had been observed through use.

Herbal medicine differs from synthetic drug therapy because the whole herb is used, even if only one ingredient in the plant is actively required to treat the problem. Plants contain hundreds of natural chemicals or phytochemicals, which all work together with the active constituents, helping to prevent any side-effects. In synthetic drug therapy, a single concentrated active ingredient is often used and this may require other drugs to counteract it.

Many common synthetic drugs are actually derived from plant remedies. One example is white willow (*Salix alba*), where the bark is a traditional remedy for pain relief because it contains salicylic acid, known chemically as aspirin. Foxglove (*Digitalis purpurea*) was used as a heart tonic in traditional herbal practice; the modern heart drug digoxin is derived from this plant.

right Foxgloves were traditionally used as a heart tonic and are the source of some common drugs for heart conditions.

Active ingredients in herbs

- **Mucilages** are gel-like substances that cool, soothe, and protect the skin as well as the delicate membranes of the digestive, respiratory, and urinary systems. Comfrey leaves are rich in mucilage, as are aloe vera leaves.

- **Saponins** are ingredients that can produce a lather when mixed with water. In the past, saponin-rich herbs were used as skin washes, hair rinses, or antiseptic skin cleansers. Good examples are oats, calendula, or yarrow.

- **Tannins** are substances that have a protective effect on the skin, shielding it against infection and helping inflammation. Examples of tannin-rich herbs are horsetail, elderflower, and raspberry leaf.

- **Alkaloids** are the most powerful of all plant constituents, which affect the nervous system. Many alkaloid-rich herbs are not suitable for home use; milder examples are herbs like borage or comfrey.

- **Flavonoids** are ingredients mainly found in plant tissues with yellow or white pigments; they help the circulation, protect blood-vessel walls, and help reduce inflammation. Examples are St.-John's-wort, yarrow, and elderflower.

- **Essential oils** are found in microscopic specialized cells inside leaves, flowers, roots, woods, fruit peel, or berries; they have a powerful aroma and give the plant its unique fragrance. They are usually extracted by distillation and are used in aromatherapy (see pages 138–141). Lavender, rosemary, or rose are examples.

- **Bitter principles** taste bitter and they increase the flow of digestive juices, improving all aspects of absorption and elimination. They are found in herbs like dandelion, calendula, or camomile.

- **Vitamins and trace elements** assist in building vitality and are essential to overall health. All herbs are rich in these.

Herbal **safety**

In order to obtain the maximum benefit from using herbs, it is very important to use them safely and correctly. In this way you will be able to experience the benefits herbs can bring as well as know you are using them effectively. Although the dosage amounts may seem small, they are therapeutically active and you will feel the improvements they can bring. These can include a calmer mind, better digestion, and improved sleep.

below left Herbal teas are a simple, refreshing, and effective way to enjoy the active properties of leaves and flowers.

right Syrups [see page 135] are pleasant-tasting blends of herbs or berries, which make effective winter remedies for colds or coughs.

General safety advice

Safety advice is particularly relevant when it comes to taking herbs internally, which you will do when you drink infusions—herbal teas, for example—or swallow tinctures, decoctions, or syrups (see pages 135–137 for directions on making these). The active ingredients in the herbs are much more easily absorbed through the moist lining of the digestive tract. It is important not to exceed the suggested dosages, as shown opposite. Certain herbs in the Directory in Part 4 (see pages 178–251) have particular individual safety guidelines you should follow.

As a general guideline, if you have acute physiological symptoms and have used any oral herbal method without success for 3 or 4 days, discontinue and seek professional advice from a physician or herbal practitioner. If your symptoms are milder and more chronic, you can use low doses of herbs over a longer period, but you should still seek professional guidance after 4 weeks.

Simple methods of use, like facial steams, baths, balms, compresses, and ointments, are very mild; but you must follow the given directions (see pages 130–135).

A full guide to safety using essential oils is found on page 141.

Herbs in pregnancy

If you are pregnant, you are strongly advised to consult a professional herbal practitioner for advice on what is best for you to use. This is so that you can have confidence in your plan to support yourself and your baby through the process of pregnancy. In the past, herbs were used by women while carrying the baby and also during the birth itself. They can be an excellent support; however, every woman should have her needs assessed individually.

The following common herbs are best avoided medicinally during pregnancy, because they may cause the uterus to contract or can stimulate menstrual bleeding (see the Directory, pages 178–251 for individual profiles).

Agnus castus, aloe vera *(orally)*, angelica, basil, calendula *(orally)*, clary sage, fennel, fenugreek, horehound, hyssop, juniper, lady's-mantle, lavender, lovage, oregano, parsley seeds, raspberry leaf *(can be used in labor)*, rosemary, sage (common), savory (summer), sorrel, tarragon, thyme.

Note Herbs in this list are not dangerous just used as flavorings in cooking in their correct amounts.

Dosages for oral use

Adult Infusion (teal): 1 cup (9 fl oz/250 ml), 3 times daily.
Decoction ¼ cup (2 fl oz/50 ml), 3 times daily.
Tincture 20 drops in water, 3 times daily.
Syrup 2 tsp, 3 times daily.

Person over 70 Half the adult dosages.
Child aged 9–14 Half the adult dosages.
Child aged 5–9 One quarter the adult dosages.
Babies and infants aged 1–5 Infusion only—1 tsp, 3 times daily.

Oil-based herbal preparations

In oil-based herbal preparations, vegetable oil is a very good fatty medium that dissolves or absorbs the active ingredients out of plant fibers. The results are strongly aromatic ointments or balms with skin-smoothing properties, helping to ease dryness and cracking.

The oily base also helps some of the active ingredients to pass through the upper layers of the skin, improving their effects. In older herbals, Vaseline or petroleum jelly may be used as bases; these make a barrier across the skin but do not penetrate it in the same way as vegetable-oil bases. It is much better to use good-quality vegetable oils, which are rich in their own nutrients and which also enable herbal ingredients to be absorbed.

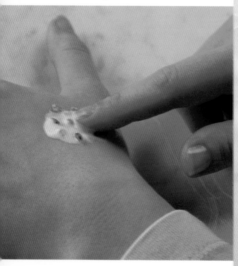

Ointments

Making nourishing herbal ointments is a bit like making mayonnaise the old-fashioned way—you just need to be patient while beating in the oil!

TO MAKE ONE 4 oz/115 g POT OF OINTMENT,
YOU WILL NEED:

A clean, dark brown glass jar with a screwtop lid
    (4 oz/115 g size)
A small, heavy-bottom pan
A heatproof glass dish you can sit over the pan so it
    does not touch the bottom
A small metal whisk to stir the ingredients

2 tbsp grated beeswax OR 2 tbsp cocoa butter
4 tbsp herbal infusion, e.g. comfrey or elderflower
    or camomile
4 tbsp sunflower seed oil

Pour cold water to cover the bottom of the pan up to 1 inch/2.5 cm, and gently heat until simmering. In the heatproof dish, place the infusion and the grated beeswax or cocoa butter; place the dish in the pan over the simmering water and whisk until the wax has dissolved. Then start whisking in the oil, just a few drops at a time; keep stirring vigorously. When you have used all the oil, take the dish off the heat and continue beating until the ointment begins to cool down, becoming thicker; pour into the jar, then seal and refrigerate to set it. It will keep for 4 weeks. After this time, you must discard the mixture.

Rosemary

Herbal balms

These are vegetable oils heated with herbs to make very aromatic skin balms, excellent for aching muscles as well as dry skin. They require very similar equipment.

YOU WILL NEED:
A medium, heavy-bottom pan and lid
A heatproof glass dish that sits over the pan without touching the bottom
A clean, dark glass bottle, at least 8 oz/225 ml capacity

scant 1 cup sunflower seed oil
A generous handful of fresh herbs and flowers, e.g. a mixture of lavender stems and rosemary sprigs, lightly rinsed and shaken dry

Pour water into the pan to a depth of 1 inch/2.5 cm and heat until simmering; keep the heat low. Pour the oil into the heatproof dish and add the herbs, pressing them in well. Place the dish in the pan over the simmering water, then cover with the pan lid and let simmer over low heat for 1 hour. Check the pan does not boil dry. Lift out the heatproof dish and let cool, then strain the oil into a glass pitcher, and carefully pour into the bottle. It will keep in a dark place for 4–6 weeks. After this time, you must discard the mixture.

Some good combinations of fresh herbs

Lavender flowers and rosemary leaves for aching muscles

Marjoram and myrtle leaves for calming the mind

Peppermint leaves and camomile flowers for stomach tension

Marjoram

Water-based herbal preparations

Water absorbs active ingredients very effectively out of plant fibers, especially when it is heated. Our bodies are made up of approximately 80% water, which is vital to all our bodily functions, especially elimination. We can easily absorb the healing properties of herbs by using methods that are water-based and very easy to try.

Infusions

Standard infusions (1 tsp dried herbs or 2 tsp fresh leaves/flowers in 1 cup boiling water, infused for 10–15 minutes)

These are herbal teas that can be drunk as refreshing caffeine-free drinks, as on pages 118–119, or as simple soothing remedies (for example, fresh sage-leaf tea with 1 tsp honey is very helpful for sore throats).

Strong infusions (2 tsp dried herbs or 4 tsp fresh leaves/flowers in 1 cup hot water, infused for 20–30 minutes)

These are useful as cleansing or soothing skin lotions, for wound-cleaning, or as rinses for shiny, healthy hair (for example, a strong infusion of 2 tsp fresh rosemary leaves and 2 tsp fresh nettle leaves in 1 cup water makes a revitalizing rinse for dark hair).

Facial steams or inhalations

Fresh leaves or flowers can help to deep-cleanse the skin or ease chesty congestion if you have a cold or flu. Pour 5 cups boiling water into a heatproof dish and set on a table. Scatter your choice of herbs into the water. Sit down and lean over the fragrant steam with a towel over your head like a tent, and steam for 10–15 minutes. If you have a cold, steam in the morning and evening.

To deep-cleanse the skin
generous ⅔ cup fresh camomile flowers
OR generous ⅔ cup fresh lavender flowers
OR generous ⅔ cup fresh myrtle flowers

To clear the sinuses, head, and chest
generous ⅔ cup fresh eucalyptus leaves, broken into pieces
OR generous ⅔ cup fresh rosemary leaves, chopped
OR generous ⅔ cup fresh peppermint leaves, chopped

Baths

Herbal baths cleanse and soothe the skin. There are two ways to try—either just scatter your chosen leaves and flowers into the water or, if you prefer, put the herbs in a small cheesecloth bag and hang it over the hot-water faucet so that the water runs through as the bath fills. Baths are very therapeutic and also a chance to relax after the stresses of the day; soak for at least 20 minutes.

Some choices to try:

Relaxing

generous ⅔ cup fresh lemon balm leaves
OR generous ⅔ cup fresh myrtle leaves
OR generous ⅔ cup fresh sweet marjoram leaves

Invigorating

generous ⅔ cup fresh rosemary leaves
OR generous ⅔ cup fresh yarrow leaves
OR generous ⅔ cup fresh sage leaves

You can vary the bath by mixing two favorite herbs to make up the amount. If you want to soften the water, add 2 tbsp oats to a cheesecloth bag and hang over the faucet; the bath water will look slightly milky and oats soothe your skin.

Water-based herbal preparations

Using herbs soaked in water is an effective way to treat many skin problems or minor injuries like bruises. The water soothes and moistens the skin so that the active ingredients in the plants are absorbed more easily. Boiling herbs or berries in sugar and water helps to preserve the active ingredients and makes a syrup that is very pleasant and easy to take, particularly in the wintertime as a tonic or to help coughs.

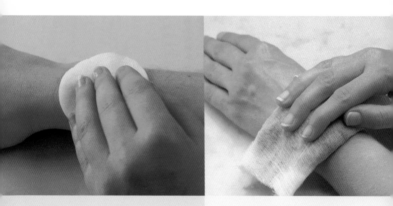

Compresses

Here you soak a pad of lint or absorbent cotton in a strong infusion and apply it directly to the problem area. For cold application, let the infusion cool completely. *Cold* compresses are particularly good for sprains or muscular injuries; herbs like camomile or comfrey help to relieve pain and reduce swelling. *Hot* compresses are used to draw infected matter out of wounds; a strong horsetail infusion applied to the area will help expel the poison and speed up healing. Apply hot or cold compresses for 15–20 minutes; in acute cases, repeat application immediately.

Poultices

These are pastes made of herb combinations that improve circulation, draw out infection, reduce inflammation, and speed up healing. Hot poultices need to be at a bearable heat so that they do not burn the skin. Simply make up a strong infusion, then strain out the plant material and mash it into a paste. Take a piece of gauze and fold it in half; sandwich the paste inside the folded material and apply directly to the area. Hold it in place with a towel or a bandage and leave it there until it cools. An example would be a combination of calendula flowers and borage leaves and flowers to treat an inflamed, infected cut.

Syrups

Make your own syrup to take as a natural remedy in the cold months of the year. Elderberries are an excellent source of vitamin C and are also antiviral—very effective in wintertime against colds and, more importantly, influenza. They soothe the chest, ease coughing, and will induce sweating, which helps move the infection through the body.

Elderberry syrup

2 lb/900 g ripe elderberries
1 cup soft brown sugar

In a large, heavy-bottom pan put the ripe elderberries, washed and picked off the stems.
Crush them with a potato masher.

Add the soft brown sugar, then stir in and simmer until the juice is thick.

Let it cool, then pour into dark glass bottles and seal them.

Keep in a cold, dark, dry place.

Note if you cannot tolerate cane sugar, you can add honey instead, or apple juice concentrate, which is sold in health food stores.

Other herbs used to make syrups include **white horehound, ginger,** or **thyme,** all of which are excellent as respiratory and immune tonics.

The proportions are 2 tbsp dried or 1 cup fresh herb to 2½ cups water; simmer for 20–30 minutes, then strain out the herb. Add generous ½ cup honey or 1 cup sugar to the liquid and simmer gently until thick. Cool and bottle as before, and take your dose as directed above.

Elderberry

left Use a funnel to pour the syrup safely into a dark glass bottle; then seal it well and store in a cool, dark place to preserve the active ingredients.

Dosage

Adults Can take 2 tsp mixed in scant ¼ cup (3½ fl oz/100 ml) hot water, 3 times a day.
Children or elderly people Take half the adult dose.

To make a tincture

Take scant ½ cup fresh herb or generous ¾ cup dried herb, then bruise it slightly in a pestle and mortar and place in a large dark glass jar or bottle, at least 10 fl oz/300 ml capacity. Pour over 1 cup brandy or vodka, making sure all the herb is covered. Close the jar or bottle tightly and let stand in a cool, dark place. Shake the bottle daily, and after 3 weeks strain the liquid to obtain the tincture. Store it in dark glass bottles in a cool, dry cupboard.

Alcohol-based herbal preparations

Alcohol is a very efficient medium to use for drawing out active ingredients in herbs and preserving these over time. Once alcohol-based remedies are made, they will remain potent for several years if stored tightly closed in a cool, dark place. They are used in small quantities; if you are traveling, a small 1 fl oz/30 ml bottle of remedy will serve your needs for several weeks because you need to take only a small number of drops diluted in water.

Tinctures are the most commonly used alcohol-based remedy. They have been in use for hundreds of years; the name comes from the Latin word "tingere," to dye, which links to the fact that the alcohol draws the pigments out of the plant, giving the remedy a dark color. There are many tinctures available commercially in health food stores and drug stores; however, you can make your own with good-quality brandy or vodka as a base and a preservative.

It is best to take tinctures on an empty stomach, just before meals. The adult dose is 20 drops or 1 ml of tincture in a small glass of water 2–3 times daily; children aged 9–14, half this dose; and age 5–9, quarter this dose. To measure the drops or 1 ml, you can buy graduated glass droppers from your local drug store.

Flower remedies are another example of plant remedies preserved in alcohol. They were originally invented by Dr Edward Bach in the early 20th century, as a way of using native wild plants and trees in nearly homeopathic potencies to treat emotional and psychological problems that lead to personality issues like extreme stubbornness, mental weariness, or deep melancholy. The imbalances at a physical and spiritual level are healed. The 38 original Bach Flower remedies also include a "Rescue Remedy" made up of 5 plants; this is used for acute emotional shock and distress. These remedies are now sold throughout the world, and new flower remedies are being made from local plants in countries such as Australia and the USA. One way to take flower remedies is to put 4–6 drops in a glass of water and drink (twice daily).

below A glass dropper helps you count the exact number of drops of tincture you need.

Essential oils: herb fragrances

Aromatic flowers and herbs, such as rose, lavender, sweet marjoram, or myrtle, contain special sacs within the cellular structure of their leaves and flowers. As the plants mature during the summer season, these sacs gradually fill up with globules of highly fragrant essential oil, which give the plants a very strong perfume.

Rose petals

These wonderful natural aromas have been prized as fragrances for hundreds of years. The first documented attempt at extracting them was the work of the Arab physician, astrologer, and scholar Abu Ibn Sina, also known as Avicenna (AD 980–1037). He used a very simple still to extract rose water from rose petals. By the 13th century, the "perfumes of Arabia" were celebrated all over the known world.

In Europe, in the 16th century, equipment for distillation became more refined, and larger quantities of what were called "chymical oils" were produced from plants like lavender, rosemary, and thyme, which were used as fragrances and natural antiseptics. The perfume industry centered around Grasse in Southern France is still world-renowned for the production of what we now call essential oils. These are used in perfumery, in the making of soaps and toiletries, in pharmaceutical preparations like liniments for sports massage, and even in the food industry as natural flavorings. Essential oils are also used in Aromatherapy (see pages 140–141), where the natural fragrances of these aromatic plants are used in massage and other ways to enhance body and mind.

Essential oils are highly concentrated; it takes approximately half a ton of lavender flowers and stems to produce about 4 cups of essential oil; with rose, it takes approximately 100 blooms of *Rosa damascena* to create ONE DROP of rose essential oil! Modern distillation techniques pump steam through the plant material, which lifts the aromatic molecules out of the fibers; the scented steam passes through a cooling chamber, where it turns back to water with essential oil floating on top. Distillation is used to extract most oils; citrus oils from fruits like lemon or orange are simply pressed out of the peel; and highly expensive flowers like jasmine are chemically processed to obtain absolutes, very concentrated and complex floral aromas.

Essential oils are now widely available from good drug stores and health food stores. They should be sold in dark glass bottles with a drop dispenser in the neck; this way you can accurately count the number of drops you need. Very small quantities are used on the skin because of the concentration; in aromatherapy the essential oil is always mixed with a vegetable carrier oil to dilute it before applying to the skin.

Essential oils come from all around the globe and are traded worldwide as powerful natural fragrances and therapeutic remedies.

right: top left
The peel of fresh lemons releases a zesty bright citrus aroma.

right: bottom right
A field of lavender produces large quantities of flowers for distillation.

below Rose essential oil is very costly to produce—but has an exquisite fragrance.

Where essential oils are found in plants:

Flowers   Lavender, rose, neroli
(orange blossom), jasmine,
ylang-ylang, camomile.

Leaves   Rosemary, tea tree, eucalyptus,
peppermint, lemon balm, pine.

Roots   Ginger, turmeric, vetiver.

Berries/seeds Cardamom, coriander,
black pepper, juniper.

Fruits   Lemon, orange, mandarin,
grapefruit, bergamot, lime.

Woods   Sandalwood, cedarwood,
rosewood.

Resins   Frankincense, myrrh.

Simple aromatherapy

The term "aromatherapy" was created by a French perfume chemist called Gattefosse, in the early 20th century. He had a laboratory accident in which he burned himself, and when he poured pure lavender oil over the injury (after mistaking it for water) he found it healed incredibly quickly, leaving no scar. He began to investigate the healing powers of essential oils, which had been known in the past but had largely been forgotten.

Now there is a worldwide expansion of aromatherapy as a healing art, with qualified aromatherapists offering treatments using essential oils and massage to help ease tension and anxiety. Many modern ailments are stress-related, and using aromatherapy can help ease symptoms as well as improve mental energy. Self-help with essential oils is a very good way of learning to manage your own stress levels.

There are three simple ways of using essential oils on yourself:

Baths Run the bathwater and add 4 drops of your chosen essential oil, then swish the water and soak for 20 minutes.

Vaporizing There are many essential-oil vaporizers and diffusers available, some flame-driven and others electrical. Use 6 drops of essential oil in the diffuser according to the manufacturer's guidelines; this will vaporize a room for up to 1 hour.

Massage To massage a whole body, measure 2 tbsp vegetable oil such as sweet almond or grapeseed into a bottle, and add 6 drops of your chosen essential oil. Shake the bottle and the oil is ready for application.

Essential oil safety guidelines

Like herbs, essential oils need to be used with care. Here are some key points:

• Never swallow essential oils, because they are so concentrated. They are safe if used as directed above, but note—for external use only.

• Keep all essential oils in a cool, dark place. Citrus oils (orange, lemon, etc.) will last for up to 6 months after opening; all other oils up to 1 year.

• Keep all essential oils out of the reach of small children.

• The massage dosage above (6 drops in 2 tbsp vegetable oil) is very mild and is fine to use on most skin types and also on children aged 5 upward. In cases of very sensitive skin, use only 3 drops in the same amount of vegetable oil. For babies; ONE DROP only of lavender in 1 tbsp carrier oil.

• If you are pregnant, use only the relaxing or refreshing oils for self-help. You are advised to consult a professional aromatherapist for more detailed guidance.

Aromatherapy is a gentle healing art with calming and subtle effects on body and mind. It is well worth taking a short class on self-help techniques to expand your use of essential oils on yourself and your family or friends.

Nine simple essential oils for a starter kit

Relaxing oils to de-stress and help you sleep:
• **Lavender**   (Lavandula angustifolia)
• **Sweet orange**   (Citrus sinensis)
• **Sandalwood**   (Santalum album)

Reviving oils to boost your immunity and wake up your mind:
• **Rosemary**   (Rosmarinus officinalis)
• **Eucalyptus**   (Eucalyptus globulus)
• **Tea tree**   (Melaleuca alternifolia)

Refreshing oils to uplift depression and ease anxiety:
• **Ylang-ylang**   (Cananga odorata)
• **Grapefruit**   (Citrus paradisi)
• **Mandarin**   (Citrus reticulata)

The **musculoskeletal** system

Our musculoskeletal system is made up of our bone structure—the skeleton itself—and the muscular tissue that attaches to it. This defines our physical shape and influences how we move through everyday life.

Nettles

A healthy musculoskeletal system depends not just on good posture and exercise, but also on diet and metabolism—how efficiently our body transforms the foods and drinks we take in to repair, rebuild, and protect our physical frame.

The skeleton is our main support. It is made up of bone, cartilage, and bone marrow, where our red blood cells are formed. Bone stores minerals like sodium, calcium, and phosphorus. The more weight-bearing exercise we do, the more our bone-forming cells, called osteoblasts, are encouraged to create more tissue; our bones are therefore strong if we move and exercise, and have a tendency to waste if we do not. Within the skeleton our vital organs are protected; the skull supports the brain, the rib cage shields our heart and lungs, and the spinal column protects the delicate spinal cord, which connects to the brain. There are approximately 206 bones in the skeleton in total. Joints—where two or more bones meet—are held together by pads of cartilage and ligaments; some of them are almost fixed, such as the joints between the bones in the skull, and others move very freely, such as the shoulder or the knee.

Muscles attach to bones and help us to move. The body contains around 640 muscles that maintain our posture, and like bones, they maintain their strength as long as they are kept working. If you lead a very lazy, sedentary life, your muscles will start to waste! In most people, the muscles account for about half the body weight. We have two kinds of muscles in the body—*voluntary* muscles, such as those we use for walking, running, sitting, or chewing, and which we are aware of, and *involuntary* muscles, such as the bands around the large intestine, which are not under our conscious control. Our muscles are stimulated by nerve impulses from the brain, which cause the fibers in them to contract, making us move. Muscle movement generates heat in the body, circulating blood around the system to warm us up.

Herbs help the musculoskeletal system in different ways:

• **Cleansing herbs** like nettle help eliminate toxins that can build up in muscle tissue.

• **Relaxing herbs** like valerian help release muscle tension, particularly if this links to stress.

• **Anti-inflammatory herbs** like comfrey help reduce swelling, particularly in joints.

• **Antirheumatics** like yarrow help ease the pain and discomfort of rheumatism.

• **Diuretics** like dandelion help the kidneys to eliminate waste products.

• **Circulatory stimulants** like rosemary help improve blood supply to the muscles.

• **Bone tonics** like horsetail are rich in silica, which helps support bone formation.

Helping **musculoskeletal** problems

Conditions that affect this system tend to be associated with tension and stress; for example, emotional upsets, poor posture, and bad sitting habits are often the cause of muscular spasm and aches in the shoulders or back. Over a longer period, poor diet and buildup of toxins in the system can cause more painful problems like arthritis. When helping musculoskeletal issues, simple lifestyle changes can make a big difference.

below Massage needs to be given gently and carefully, especially around any painful areas.

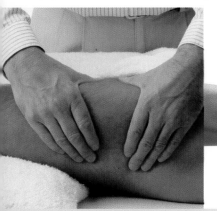

Muscular aches and pains

Chronic aches and pains, which are there most of the time in a milder way and do not stop normal activity, can be treated with self-help methods. However, it is also useful to see a structural specialist such as an osteopath, chiropractor, or physiotherapist to correct any skeletal misalignment that may cause muscular tension. For herbal treatment, the herbal balms on pages 130–131 are very useful, applied using gentle massage to the affected area. Stand a bottle of herbal balm in a bowl of hot water first so that the oil goes onto the skin warm, which is very soothing. Good combinations of herbs to put in a muscle balm are: rosemary and ginger (both circulatory stimulants,

helping stiffness); camomile and lavender (soothing and pain relieving, useful for night application); and St.-John's-wort and comfrey (these soothe pain in muscles and nerves). Lifestyle adjustments include checking posture, particularly at work; addressing emotional issues; and exercising or stretching regularly to ease out affected areas.

Acute aches or pains—often due to injury, accidents, or trauma—need assessment first. Your action here from a self-help perspective links to first aid. Cold compresses applied directly to injury sites are very helpful: use anti-inflammatory herbs like camomile, comfrey, or common daisy to reduce swelling and relieve pain.

Arthritis

To select suitable herbs, it is important to know which type of arthritis you are addressing. Please discuss any use of herbs with your physician if you are receiving medical treatment.

Osteoarthritis is caused by injury, or by general wear and tear of the joints as the body ages, leading to stiffness, immobility, and muscular pain. It can be helped by massaging in herbal balms containing circulatory stimulant herbs like ginger and peppermint, or rosemary and eucalyptus. Drinking infusions of ginger can also improve the circulation. A useful lifestyle change is to exclude specific foods from the diet, such as members of the nightshade family—eggplants, tomatoes, potatoes, and bell peppers, which are known to increase symptoms.

Rheumatoid arthritis is an inflammation response in the body linked to the immune system.The body is attacking its own tissues, particularly the lining of the joints, making them swollen and misshapen. Sufferers often feel very low and depleted, and joints "flare up" at different times. Women are three times more likely to experience it than men. It is important to use anti-inflammatory herbs like camomile, either in balms for gentle application externally, or as an infusion drunk three times daily to ease painful symptoms. Infusions of cleansing herbs like dandelion or yarrow will help to gently improve elimination of toxins. Lifestyle adjustment involves removing citrus fruit, other acidic fruit like gooseberries, and also vinegar from the diet, as these can aggravate symptoms.

right These are all herbs that improve the circulation and help relieve muscular pain.

Ginger

Yarrow

Mint

St.-John's-wort

The **digestive** system

The digestive tract is a long tube that runs all the way through the body; it is around 36 ft/11 m long. The tract is lined with a moist membrane that secretes digestive juices to help the absorption of food. Our total health and vitality depends on good digestive function; the foods we eat are full of the nutrients we need to absorb to help our body repair and renew itself, as well as energy, which we need to live our lives.

When we eat food, the teeth and saliva in the mouth help to reduce it to a smooth paste, which we swallow down into the stomach. There it begins to be broken down and digested; in the small intestine, more nutrients are absorbed and mixed with even more digestive juices. Bile, produced in the liver, and insulin from the pancreas help this process so the nutrients can begin to be absorbed into the bloodstream. Through the large intestine, the remains of the food are excreted by the body as waste products.

The digestive tract has a muscular coating that works involuntarily, so the contractions that move the food through the tract are not generally felt. However, these muscles are under the control of the autonomic nervous system, which is also very influenced by stress levels. When we are under emotional pressure, this is usually felt through changes in bowel movement, either in regularity or ease. To help digestive issues from a more holistic point of view, the underlying stress needs to be helped as well as the more obvious physical symptoms, such as constipation or diarrhea.

Effective digestion is also a matter of rhythm. Our eating habits are constantly under pressure from busy lifestyles, which lead to us skipping meals, eating while on the move, and eating too quickly or when emotionally upset. Poor chewing can cause the digestive system to be overloaded with nutrients it finds difficult to assimilate. High intake of stimulants like tea and coffee, sugar, and refined foods also add strain. It is important to allow time for meals, to try and adapt to a slower pace, for long-term digestive health. Also the old saying "breakfast like a king, lunch like a prince, and dine like a pauper" is the best way to spread the digestive load throughout the day.

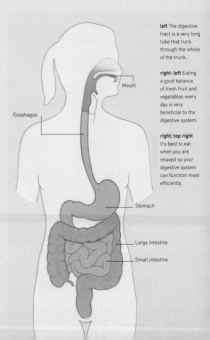

left The digestive tract is a very long tube that runs through the whole of the trunk.

right: left Eating a good balance of fresh fruit and vegetables every day is very beneficial to the digestive system.

right: top right It's best to eat when you are relaxed so your digestive system can function most efficiently.

Mouth

Esophagus

Stomach

Large intestine

Small intestine

Types of herbs that help the digestive system are:

• **Demulcents**, such as comfrey, which soothe and protect the delicate membrane.

• **Astringents/anti-inflammatories**, such as raspberry leaf, which calm inflammation.

• **Bitters**, like dandelion or camomile, which stimulate the flow of bile from the liver.

• **Carminatives**, like cinnamon or peppermint, which help ease wind in the gut.

• **Antispasmodics**, such as lemon balm, which ease pain or spasm in the gut.

• **Tonics**, like angelica, which help to increase digestive juices.

• **Relaxants**, like lavender, which help to counter emotional stress linked to digestive problems.

Helping **digestive** problems

It is very important to distinguish between acute and chronic problems. Acute situations like sudden diarrhea or vomiting mean the body is trying to get rid of something that is irritating or attacking it, and these symptoms need to be supported with frequent water intake to stop dehydration. If acute symptoms persist, you should always seek medical help. Chronic problems like constipation over a longer period may benefit from a look at lifestyle to see if there are any stress factors that may be contributing to the condition.

Camomile

Indigestion

This is a combination of feelings of bloating, heaviness, or dull pain after eating. Infusions of peppermint, fennel, or dill all contain essential oils, which help to counteract over-acidity and settle the digestion. If indigestion is due to emotional stress, drink an infusion of lavender flowers. Frequent episodes of the problem could benefit from looking at lifestyle factors like hurrying or eating too quickly.

Diarrhea

This is often due to irritation or invasion of the intestinal tract by unfriendly microorganisms. It can be accompanied by nausea and vomiting. In an acute situation like this, it is vital to keep giving fluid to the body to stop dehydration; a cup of warm water with 1tsp honey helps to restore energy. Infusion of gingerroot and cinnamon powder helps to reduce cramps and nausea. As you recover, eat small amounts of live yogurt to re-introduce friendly bacteria into the gut. If the condition lasts for more than 6 hours, seek medical help.

Constipation

Here, the normal rhythm of the gut is interrupted due to an over-sedentary lifestyle, emotional upset, or simply a lack of water. The bowel should normally empty itself at least once a day, but the above factors can interfere with this pattern so the abdomen becomes bloated and movements, when they occur, cause straining, pain, and sometimes rectal bleeding. Constipation benefits from infusions of herbs like fennel or raspberry leaf; if the condition is stress-related, try camomile or lemon balm. A varied diet with fresh vegetables and salads, plenty of water, and moderate exercise are recommended. (Note: any signs of bleeding need medical attention.)

left Honey and ginger are traditional remedies that help to ease spasm in the gut.

right These herbs are very useful aids for easing digestive cramps and wind.

Irritable bowel syndrome

This is a condition in which there are alternating bouts of constipation and diarrhea, sometimes with mucus in the feces and varying levels of pain in the abdomen. These symptoms can be accompanied by nausea, headaches, or depression. Herbs can help to reestablish normal bowel rhythm and reduce spasm in the gut. One of the most useful is peppermint in an infusion; it is also available as an essential oil in special capsules, which can be taken internally. Peppermint is antispasmodic, and it also soothes the intestinal wall. Other useful herbs for infusions are camomile or ginger. Flax seed (2 tsp) taken daily sprinkled over breakfast cereal helps soothe the bowel and absorb excess gastric juices.

Liver support

The liver is vital to our health, as a chemical factory and storehouse of nutrients. It is the major detoxifying organ of the whole body. Traditional herbal medicine recognizes this role by supporting the liver with herbs like nettle or dandelion—in springtime, young leaves drunk as infusions will help cleanse and regulate liver function.

Cinnamon

Comfrey

Dandelion

Angelica

Raspberry leaf

The **respiratory** system

Our respiratory system extracts oxygen from the air we breathe and keeps us alive. Breathing correctly is vital to the smooth function of the body and also plays a big part in balancing our emotions. Many imbalances of the respiratory system can be improved by concentrating on the quality of the breath, making it slower and more regular. The practice of meditation is very helpful in achieving this.

right: top The practice of yoga or meditation helps to steady the breath and ease stress.

right: bottom Regular exercise and deep breathing will keep the lungs healthy.

Every cell in our bodies relies on oxygen as the fuel for energy. We can survive for long periods without food, for a few days without water, but only for a few minutes without oxygen. When we breathe in, the muscles between the ribs lift the rib cage and flatten the diaphragm, which is a large muscle below the lungs. Air comes into the lungs via the nose and mouth. As we breathe out, the chest and diaphragm relax, the lungs deflate, and we release carbon dioxide into the air. The lungs are made up of many folds of tiny sacs called alveoli, which are enveloped in an extensive network of blood vessels; oxygen and carbon dioxide molecules can pass across the vessel walls to and from the bloodstream.

The upper respiratory tract is made up of the nose, mouth, throat, larynx (voicebox), and sinuses in the head. The lower respiratory tract is made up of the windpipe, bronchi, lungs, and diaphragm. The whole of the respiratory tract is lined with a mucus membrane, which keeps the surfaces moist.

If we are at rest, we breathe about 15 times per minute; this rate increases as we become active and our muscles demand more oxygen. Regular exercise, deep breathing, and disciplines such as yoga or t'ai chi all help to establish a nourishing respiratory rhythm, which is vital to overall health. They are particularly helpful if you suffer from stress. Research has shown that asthmatics who take up singing, improve their lung capacity and suffer fewer asthma attacks.

Many problems that occur in the respiratory tract are linked to the immune system, such as colds or influenza, which are caused by airborne microorganisms that we breathe into the body.

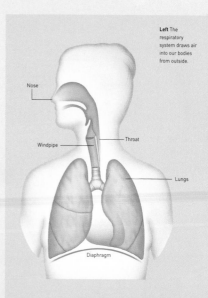

Left The respiratory system draws air into our bodies from outside.

Nose

Windpipe

Throat

Lungs

Diaphragm

Types of herbs that help the respiratory system include:

- **Anticatarrhals** such as sage and yarrow, which help reduce excess mucus in the tract.

- **Antimicrobials** such as echinacea and garlic, which help the body fight bacteria and viruses that cause colds and influenza.

- **Antiseptics** such as eucalyptus and rosemary, which are aromatic herbs containing powerful essential oils that fight infection.

- **Antispasmodics** such as camomile and red clover, which help reduce unproductive coughing.

- **Diaphoretics** such as elder and peppermint, which induce sweating, helping the body eliminate toxins and fight viral infections.

- **Expectorants** such as garlic and thyme, which help the body expel excess mucus.

Helping **respiratory** problems

The respiratory system is one of the most common areas to experience problems, especially in the colder months of the year. Different herbs and methods can be used to help either the upper or lower part of the respiratory tract. As a respiratory infection progresses, it is important to support changes in symptoms using varied remedies.

A major lifestyle consideration, particularly if you suffer regularly from colds, coughs, or excess mucus, is to try excluding mucus-forming foods from your diet. Two groups of foods to target are dairy products—particularly milk and cheese—and wheat, oats, or barley. Very persistent catarrh may benefit from excluding other mucus-forming foods like bananas or potatoes. Replace these with varied fruits and vegetables, rice and beans, and goat's or soy milk.

Upper respiratory tract conditions
Colds

These are caused by a range of viruses that lead to sneezing, stuffy heads, sore throats, and running noses. Elderberry syrup helps soothe sore throats and support the immune system; a hot infusion of dried cinnamon and fresh ginger with lemon and honey will do the same. A famous herbal combination for a cold is an infusion of equal parts of yarrow, peppermint, and elderflower, which can be drunk 4–6 times daily.

Catarrh

The respiratory tract is lined with mucus, which is needed to keep the area moist. Overproduction can lead to congestion and discomfort. Infusions of camomile, peppermint, or elderflower help to tone the mucus membrane and the body to detoxify itself. A steam inhalation with 3 drops eucalyptus and 3 drops rosemary essential oil will loosen stubborn mucus.

Sinusitis

This is an infection of the cavities inside the head, causing extreme pain in the cheeks and face. Tincture of echinacea and infusion of thyme and peppermint help to support the immune system as well as helping to ease inflammation. A steam inhalation with 4 drops lavender essential oil soothes the inflamed areas. Eat 2 raw garlic cloves in your diet each day as an immune booster.

Lower respiratory tract conditions
Dry coughs

Infection spreading from the nose, ears, and sinuses can irritate the throat. Honey is an antiseptic and soothing remedy in its own right; an infusion of fresh comfrey leaf with 2 tsp honey and a slice of fresh lemon soothes irritation.

Productive coughs

These are a response from the body to rid itself of excess mucus and might also be a sign of infection, especially if the cough is painful deep in the chest. Drink infusion of thyme and sage to fight infection; regular steam inhalations of tea tree essential oil clear phlegm and support the immune system (4 drops in generous 2 cups boiling water; inhale steam for 15 minutes). If your symptoms persist, consult your physician.

right These herbs help to enhance the function of the respiratory and immune systems.

Dried sage

Garlic

Sage

Thyme

Elderberry
flowers

Red clover

Lavender

Echinacea

The **immune** system

The immune system protects the body from invading microorganisms like bacteria, viruses, parasites, and fungi. We are surrounded by these, breathing them into the body as well as touching them in our daily life.

We take our general resistance to these organisms for granted most of the time because we are not affected by them; we are unaware of the vital role played by our immune defenses. We take notice when signs of illness show themselves—the message is that the immune system needs extra support and help.

The bone marrow is the factory that makes key cells for the immune system, called lymphocytes. These cells migrate to particular areas in the body, such as the thymus gland in the chest, the spleen, and the tonsils, and also circulate in the blood. They operate by destroying toxins and microbes. In the event of an invasion by a microorganism, the body also produces extra white blood cells, which can neutralize invaders.

Immunity also relies on another response, where antibodies are produced to neutralize the same invading organism when it reappears. This is called acquired immunity and is the result of experiencing childhood illnesses like measles, for example; once the body has produced antibodies, the condition should not recur.

Allergies are an exaggerated version of this response. Lining the mucus membranes are special cells called mast cells; these produce special antibodies called immunoglobulins. Sometimes, on repeated exposure to the same substance, the immunoglobulins overreact, triggering the release of histamine, which causes an inflammation at the contact site, accompanied by reactions like itching, sneezing, watering eyes, swelling, or headaches. Once the body is hypersensitive, the reaction will recur, and the only real solution is to avoid the

trigger. In some cases, the immune system can become confused and can start attacking its own tissues. This is called an autoimmune condition; an example is rheumatoid arthritis, when the body produces inflammation in the linings of the joints.

The immune system is affected by our moods and our energy levels; high levels of stress, emotional upset, and physical tiredness will reduce the production of defensive cells, making us more likely to pick up an infection. Holistic treatment with herbs works to build the strength of the immune system.

right: top A high temperature and shivering are signs of immune system infection.

right: bottom Keeping mind, body, and emotions in balance helps to promote a healthy immune system.

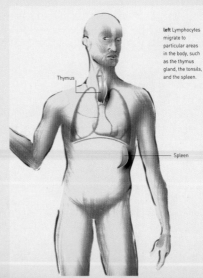

left Lymphocytes migrate to particular areas in the body, such as the thymus gland, the tonsils, and the spleen.

Thymus

Spleen

Types of herbs for immune system support include:

- **Alteratives** such as echinacea and red clover, to detoxify the blood and renew tissue.

- **Antimicrobials** such as garlic and thyme, to destroy microorganisms.

- **Anti-inflammatories** such as calendula and aloe vera, to soothe skin irritation.

- **Diuretics** such as dandelion and nettle, to improve elimination.

- **Adrenal tonics** such as ginger and rosemary, to boost the body during long periods of ill-health.

- **Sedatives** such as lemon balm and lavender, to reduce nervous anxiety.

Helping **immune** conditions

When the immune system is severely depleted, the body needs rest. Its reactions
to infection usually make the body feel weak, and this is a clear sign to slow down.
Unfortunately, this sign is often ignored in the modern world and the system is put under
enormous pressure, especially through over-the-counter chemical remedies containing
caffeine, which gives the illusion of energy but actually depletes the system even more.
Taking time out will, in the end, shorten the period of the illness and help you recover
more quickly.

Fever

This is a response to an infection, either bacterial
or viral; it raises body temperature so that the
microorganism cannot survive. Fever is actually a
defensive reaction. Appetite will decrease, but lots
of fluids are vital. Herbs can be used to support
the body through a fever; the classic mixture of
infusion of equal parts of yarrow, peppermint, and
elderflower is again crucial here. Elderflowers are
diaphoretic and help to encourage sweating and
toxin elimination. Antimicrobials like echinacea
tincture can also be taken, and immune-boosting
garlic can be eaten in the diet once appetite
returns. Sponging the body with a cool infusion
of camomile eases discomfort. Most fevers will
pass in about 48 hours; medical help must be
sought if fever lasts longer than this or is
consistently over 102°F/39°C in children, or
104°F/40°C in adults, or if the temperature drops
suddenly to below 95°F/35°C and the skin
becomes very clammy.

Influenza

This is a viral infection where the body
experiences stabbing pains, shivers, and total loss
of energy. A bout of flu will last about 7–10 days,
and total bed rest is advised. Appetite will be low,
but again lots of fluids are needed; add honey and
fresh lemon to infusions to help boost energy
levels. Fresh ginger tea warms the body and

supports the immune system, as do other spices
like cardamom and nutmeg; a spicy infusion of
these three is very refreshing. Again, echinacea
tincture is advised 3 times daily, and once appetite
returns eat 2 raw garlic cloves in food for a
powerful cleansing effect.

Chronic immune conditions

If the immune system is depleted over a long
period, this can lead to severe exhaustion,
sometimes known as post-viral fatigue or
ME. This is a condition best supported by a
professional herbalist; however, the body can be
supported by using infusions of sedative herbs
like sweet marjoram, lavender, or lemon balm.
Taking echinacea tincture helps boost immune
function and oat tincture eases chronic stress
levels. Infusions of alterative herbs like calendula,
nettle, or red clover can help to cleanse and
detoxify the blood and lymphatic system.

For recovery after periods of immune depletion,
lifestyle help includes plenty of fresh fruit,
vegetables, and fresh herbs in the diet, at least
6 large glasses of spring water per day, and also
using methods like yoga or meditation to balance
stress. Walking in the fresh air is a gentle way to
begin exercising to rebuild physical strength.
Essential oils like lemon and sweet orange have an
uplifting effect on mood; try 3 drops each of these
oils in a vaporizer.

right These herbs
are effective at
relieving stress as
well as helping
the immune
system.

Lemon verbena

Rosemary

Calendula

Aloe vera

Ginger

Nettles

The skin

The skin envelops us completely, a supple surface well-supplied with blood and nerve endings; it enables us to touch, sense, and feel our world. It regulates our temperature via the sweat glands; a day's average activity will see us lose about 2½ cups of sweat, far more if we exercise or do physical work. This is why it is so important to drink at least 10 cups of water a day. The skin is sometimes called the "third kidney" because it is such an important organ of detoxification for the body.

The three main layers of the skin

The **epidermis**, or outer surface, is made up of layers of cells containing keratin, also found in our hair and nails. Wearing clothes and rubbing the skin constantly removes dead cells, which are replaced from the lower epidermal layers.

Beneath it, the **dermis** is a layer that contains a network of fine blood vessels, sensory nerve receptors, sweat glands, hair follicles, and the important sebaceous glands, which secrete lubrication onto the surface of the skin to keep the epidermis supple. Muscle fibers also pass through this area. In our armpits and groin areas are special exocrine glands, which secrete hormonal male and female odors.

The lowest layer is the **subcutaneous fat**, which conserves body heat.

The health of the skin relies far more on what is put into the body than what is applied externally. Just drinking plenty of spring water each day keeps the skin cells plump and supple. Eating moderate amounts of good-quality vegetable oils like extra virgin olive, sunflower seed, or evening primrose provides strength and suppleness to the skin, avoiding dryness. Fresh fruit and vegetables in the diet provide vitamins and nutrients to promote healthy cell growth and renewal.

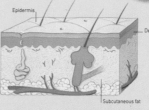

Epidermis

Dermis

Subcutaneous fat

Smoking severely depletes the skin of collagen fibers, which maintain elasticity. Poor elimination and lack of sleep, fresh air, and exercise can also give it a pale and lackluster appearance. Our skin flushes when we are agitated and pales when we are afraid; it is also a mirror of our emotional state. This is because when we are in the womb, the skin and nervous system actually develop together. Simply working on the external appearance will not bring long-term relief from skin problems; assessing lifestyle issues like diet and stress levels as well as symptoms is a combined approach that is more likely to succeed. You do need to be patient because improvements may not be immediate.

left The skin has three important layers which interact with each other to protect the body.

above Drinking water is a simple way to keep a supple and youthful complexion.

right Eating fresh fruits and vegetables provides skin-enhancing vitamins and minerals.

top right Lovely skin requires a good diet, good sleep, and careful skincare.

Types of herbs to help skin problems include:

- **Alteratives** such as red clover and nettle, to cleanse and detoxify generally.

- **Anti-allergics** like yarrow, Roman or German camomile, or marigold to reduce itching, redness, and heat resulting from nettlerash, prickly heat, or minor skin allergies.

- **Anti-inflammatories** such as camomile and comfrey, to soothe soreness.

- **Antimicrobials** such as thyme and echinacea, to fight infection.

- **Cytophylactics** such as lavender and myrtle, for healthy skin growth.

- **Diuretics** such as yarrow and nettle, to help elimination of waste products via the kidneys.

- **Hormone balancers** such as fennel, agnus castus, or clary sage to balance hormonal fluctuations leading to skin blemishes.

- **Sedatives** such as lemon balm and sweet marjoram, to ease stress.

- **Vulneraries** such as horsetail and oat, to promote wound healing.

159

Helping **skin** problems

After cleaning and soothing damaged skin with strong infusions (see pages 132–133), ointments (see pages 130–131) are excellent for helping to promote skin regeneration. These combined methods help treat the appearance of the skin; remember, there may also be other lifestyle patterns that need addressing.

above Herbal oils can help to soothe and ease damaged skin.

right Effective skin herbs repair skin damage and heal infections.

Cuts and wounds

Cleansing the area with a strong infusion of horsetail and yarrow has an antiseptic effect and helps to stop excessive bleeding. Always ensure the wound is as clean as possible before applying any ointment. If infection sets in, hot compresses of antimicrobials like thyme or garlic will help draw out pus. Healing ointment made from herbs like calendula, comfrey, or St.-John's-wort will help the wound heal cleanly. If there is shock from the injury, a soothing tea made with lavender will help steady the nerves.

Acne

A series of red pustules with yellow heads can appear over the face, neck, shoulders, or back. The sebaceous glands become blocked and inflamed, often as a result of hormonal changes, but also due to poor diet and elimination. The skin needs gentle but thorough cleansing with herbs like dandelion and camomile, and toning with herbs such as witch hazel to help fight infection. Ointment with red clover and calendula, or with essential oils like lavender and tea tree, can help reduce infection and heal the lesions.

Boils

These are localized infected areas swollen with a bacterial infection. Hot compresses with herbs like thyme help to draw out infection, and camomile will also soothe inflammation. Again, ointment with calendula and comfrey will speed up healing, and the same dietary changes as for acne should be adopted.

Eczema

This is a condition with a very strong link to the emotions, always worse during periods of stress. Small lesions break open into reddish, weeping areas, particularly between fingers or in creases or folds of skin. After a while, the skin may become hard and scaly as the epidermis thickens to try and protect itself. A strong camomile infusion can be used as a cool compress to calm inflammation. Soothing and skin-repairing combinations, such as lavender and borage or red clover and calendula, can be combined in ointments to ease the chapping. Any treatment is best applied at night to give time for it to work. Many people with eczema are allergic to dairy products, so excluding these from the diet is advised, at least temporarily; other trigger foods that make it worse are citrus fruit, tomatoes, sugar, and food additives.

Psoriasis

Although there are several forms of psoriasis, the most common type is where large patches of the lower epidermal layer are replaced more quickly than necessary, shedding silvery skin cells and exposing red inflamed areas. These are often found on the elbows or knees. Sometimes psoriasis can lead to localized arthritis. Skin oil balm with lavender flowers and comfrey is extremely soothing applied externally; other calming herbs like calendula and red clover can also be used. Infusions of sedative herbs like lemon balm or lemon verbena help to calm the system and ease underlying stress.

Marjoram

Nettle

Calendula

Comfrey

Red clover

Camomile

Witch hazel

Skin care using herbs

Using herbs to take care of your skin is very satisfying because you are using totally natural ingredients, avoiding any harsh chemicals. Most commercial skin products are full of artificial colorings or preservatives. Simple, natural skincare is a wonderful treat using time-honored ingredients, traditionally valued for their cleansing and nourishing properties. These preparations must be used fresh to maximize their effectiveness.

Dandelion and Comfrey Cleanser

This is a wonderful rejuvenating milk with young leaves of dandelion to deep-cleanse the pores and comfrey to soothe the skin. Make a strong infusion with 3 tbsp chopped fresh dandelion and 3 tbsp chopped fresh comfrey leaves in 1 cup boiling water. Let infuse for 2 hours, then strain the liquid. In a bowl whisk together generous ¾ cup infusion with generous ¾ cup whole milk, then pour into a large bottle and refrigerate. Shake before using. This milk will last for 1 week. After this time, you must discard the mixture.

Jojoba and Cocoa Butter Face Cream with Lavender and Myrtle

This light, nourishing face cream is suitable for all skin types. Make an infusion of 1½ tbsp fresh lavender flowers and 1½ tbsp fresh myrtle leaves in 1 cup boiling water; let infuse for 15 minutes, then strain the liquid. In a small, heavy-bottom pan, pour 1 inch/2.5 cm water and simmer gently. In a heatproof glass dish pour 4 tbsp infusion and add 1 oz/30 g solid cocoa butter. Place the dish in the pan over the simmering water and whisk until the cocoa butter melts. Measure 4 tbsp jojoba oil into a small pitcher and add to the mixture in the dish a few drops at a time, whisking until all the oil is used. Remove the dish from the heat and continue whisking until the mixture thickens, then pour into a dark glass jar (4 oz/115 g capacity). Refrigerate to set the cream. The shelf life is 3–4 weeks; keep it cool. After this time, you must discard the mixture.

Oatmeal and Honey Mask with Camomile

The oats in the mask help to gently exfoliate the skin, and the honey is a well-known skin soother. Camomile infusion is anti-inflammatory and calming. This mask suits all skin types. Make up a standard infusion of camomile—1 tsp dried or 3 tbsp fresh flowers in 1 cup boiling water—and infuse for 15 minutes. In a bowl, put 4 tbsp fine oatmeal and 3 tbsp of the infusion; stir this into a paste. Add 2 tsp runny honey, then stir and apply the mask to clean skin. Leave on for 20 minutes, then wash off with warm water. Pat the skin dry; it should feel very soft. Use this mask fresh, discarding any remaining paste.

Herbal toning waters

You can make very simple and effective facial toning waters just by using standard infusions of particular herbs (1 tsp dried herb or 3 tbsp fresh herb to 1 cup boiling water, infused for 15 minutes, then strained and cooled).

Keep the infusion in a glass bottle; refrigerate and use up in 3–4 days. After this time, you must discard the mixture.

Some examples:

Oily skin Rosemary and myrtle leaves

Dry skin Lavender and camomile flowers

Mature skin Calendula flowers and lemon balm leaves

Acne Red clover flowers and comfrey leaves

163

The **female reproductive** system

For centuries, women have used herbs to take care of their hormonal system. Generations of grandmothers and mothers passed on acquired knowledge of herbal combinations to regulate menstruation, ease pain, or help the process of childbirth. Science has now identified ingredients in certain herbs, called plant steroids, which support hormonal function because they are similar to our own hormones. Using balancing and toning herbs helps to support the female reproductive system through its cyclical swings and changes.

right: top For centuries, women have relied on herbs to balance hormones and support the reproductive organs.

right: bottom Certain herbs can be used in pregnancy to gently support the system.

The female reproductive organs are:

• The **ovaries**, which are two organs, each the size of a small nut, made up of a large number of small sacs called follicles, each one containing an egg (ovum). The ovaries release an egg approximately every 28 days during a woman's reproductive life, and produce the hormones estrogen and progesterone, which control changes during the menstrual cycle.

• The **Fallopian tubes**, which connect the ovaries to the womb.

• The **uterus** or womb, which is pear-shaped and fits inside the pelvis between the bladder and the rectum. The lower part of the womb, the cervix, fits inside the vagina. The wall of the uterus is about 1 in/2.5 cm thick and is lined with a special membrane called endometrium. This thickens each month, and is then discharged as menstruation, the monthly "period," if the released egg is unfertilized.

• The **breasts**, which consist of fatty fibrous tissue; they form and store milk to feed a baby. The menstrual cycle is linked to the moon; most women bleed approximately 13 times per year in line with lunar phases. The cycle starts on the first day of bleeding; by days 14–16, the lining of the womb has thickened and an egg has been released. If the egg is not fertilized, the lining of the womb will degenerate and be lost as the following menstrual flow. If the egg is fertilized, the lining will thicken even more as the embryo embeds itself and starts growing into a baby.

In later years, the frequency of menstruation slows and hormonal changes take place until it ceases. This change is called the menopause, and it can be accompanied by changing moods and symptoms like night sweats or hot flushes. Herbs can help to balance the hormones and ease menopausal discomfort.

below The female reproductive system is best helped by using baths and massage with herbs.

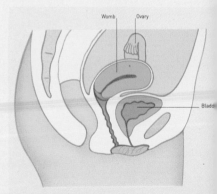

Womb   Ovary

Bladd

Types of herbs to help female reproduction are:

• **Astringents** such as yarrow and nettle, which help to tone excess menstrual bleeding.

• **Antispasmodics** such as lavender and camomile, which help ease menstrual cramps.

• **Emmenagogues** such as cinnamon and ginger, which initiate menstrual flow, particularly if it is scanty or absent. (Note: it must be established that the woman is not pregnant before using these herbs, as they should not be used in pregnancy.)

• **Hormone regulators** such as agnus castus and sage, which balance the female sex hormones estrogen and progesterone.

• **Nerve tonics** such as lemon balm and St.-John's-wort, which help to calm stressful mood swings.

• **Uterine tonics** such as lady's-mantle and raspberry leaf, which tone and strengthen the reproductive organs and their function.

Helping female reproductive problems

You can use a variety of herbal methods to help female reproduction. Massaging oil balms into the abdomen, drinking teas, and taking tinctures are all beneficial. A diet rich in fresh fruits, vegetables, beans and whole grains, along with drinking herbal infusions and plenty of water, ensures good nutrient supply to the pelvic area via the blood circulation, as well as healthy elimination. Regular supplements of vitamin E and evening primrose oil taken over time can help to balance the cycle and reduce menstrual discomfort.

Raspberry leaf

Pre-menstrual syndrome (PMS)

This is the name given to a wide range of symptoms experienced during the latter part of the menstrual cycle, such as mood swings, temporary weight increase, abdominal bloating, or headaches. Taking tincture of agnus castus (15 drops in water on waking for 4–6 months) can significantly improve symptoms—however, it is slow acting and takes up to 25 days to become effective. Drinking standard infusion of lady's-mantle and calendula helps, particularly during the last week of the cycle. Include cleansing salad herbs in your diet, such as dandelion or watercress leaves.

Irregular periods

These are erratic in rhythm and vary in amount of flow. They are a sign of hormone imbalance and may be due to thyroid dysfunction or lifestyle factors. Any sudden change in menstrual rhythm or flow must be discussed with your physician, particularly if the periods stop. Infusion of lady's-mantle and yarrow in equal parts is helpful drunk regularly over a 3–4 month period, as is taking agnus castus tincture as above; it is useful to consult a qualified herbalist for individual assessment and advice.

Painful periods

There are two types—the first, where intense cramping begins with the onset of the period and

lasts for about 48 hours, accompanied by heavy bright-red flow, and the second where dull pain starts 2–3 days before menstruation, and flow is dark and heavy with clotting. Pain is caused by poor circulation in the pelvic area as well as high levels of prostaglandins, hormone-like substances that cause contractions in muscle fibers. Evening primrose oil supplementation for at least 6 months is helpful for balancing prostaglandin formation, and a standard infusion of equal parts of yarrow, rosemary, and lady's-mantle is a useful soothing blend taken twice a day for at least 2–3 months. If you are tense and exhausted, use a lemon balm infusion. Make a skin balm with lavender flowers and sweet marjoram leaves (see pages 130–131) and massage into your abdomen every evening during the last week of the cycle and as your period begins.

Menopausal symptoms

These include headaches, hot flushes, heart palpitations, mood swings, insomnia, and low libido, which are all due to lowered hormone levels. Herbs with estrogen-like effects include agnus castus, taken as a tincture as above, as well as clary sage or fennel, which can be drunk as standard infusions. Yarrow infusion can help night sweats or hot flushes by helping control the circulation. Discuss the use of herbs with a medical doctor or medical herbalist.

right These herbs help to balance the hormones and support the nervous system.

Yarrow

St.-John's-wort

Agnus-castus

Lady's-mantle

Lemon balm

Watercress

167

The male reproductive system

Smooth function of the male reproductive system requires a balance between physical, emotional, and mental well-being. In today's goal-driven world, there is heavy emphasis on performance and achievement, which if taken to excess can severely deplete energy levels and also self-esteem. It is important to address the whole lifestyle pattern when addressing male issues, looking at areas of stress and ways to adapt different strategies to rebuild energy and vitality.

The organs of male reproduction are:

• The **testes**, which produce sperm and also secrete testosterone, the male sex hormone that is responsible for bone and muscle growth as well as sexual development.

• The **scrotum**, which is the sac that contains the testes. It allows sperm to develop at a lower temperature outside the body. Internally it is divided in two halves, each containing a testis. Each testis is suspended by a spermatic cord, inside which is the tube that transports sperm to the penis.

• The **penis**, which is the male sex organ through which semen (sperm swimming in fluid) and urine pass. It contains erectile tissue, which causes it to lengthen and stiffen during sexual arousal.

• The **prostate gland**, which is about the size of a walnut, situated under the bladder and in front of the rectum. It produces fluids that are mixed with sperm during ejaculation. It grows to full size during puberty due to increased male hormone levels; in many men it can enlarge further after the age of 50, causing urinary problems.

Addressing male reproductive problems requires lifestyle adjustments to help increase sperm formation, tone up the sexual organs, and also deal with underlying emotional stress and anxiety. A balance between work and leisure and a variety of activities that allow time for mental expansion and creativity as well as physical exercise are highly beneficial. It is not enough to wait for the yearly holiday to relax—if stress levels are high, you may be too exhausted to enjoy it.

Fertility issues can apply to males as well as females; high levels of stress, smoking, poor diet, and alcohol can all reduce male sperm count. As well as using tonic herbs, it is very important to review eating and drinking patterns, especially if a couple are trying to conceive, and include plenty of fresh fruit and vegetables as well as nuts and seeds, which are good sources of zinc, B vitamins, and vitamin E, to encourage healthy levels of male sex hormones.

right: top An over-busy schedule can affect male hormone production.

right: bottom Stress-relieving herbs give important support for emotional problems.

below The male reproductive system is very influenced by lifestyle factors such as stress.

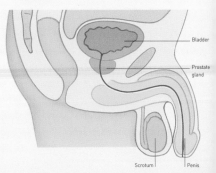

Bladder

Prostate gland

Scrotum

Penis

Types of herbs that can help support male reproduction are:

- **Adrenal tonics** such as borage or celery, to help with exhaustion and low energy.

- **Antiseptics** such as thyme and calendula, to help deal with any infection.

- **Demulcents** such as comfrey and aloe vera, to soothe inflamed membranes.

- **Diuretics** such as horsetail and yarrow, to improve elimination.

- **Tonics** such as ginseng and ginger, to tone the sexual organs.

Helping male reproductive issues

Herbs can be used in a number of ways to help male reproduction. Drinking herbal infusions or using baths and massage balms for relaxation are useful methods. You can also include supportive ingredients in the diet, like fresh ginger, black pepper, and garlic to tone the circulation or seafoods like oysters or crab, which are rich in minerals like zinc to support the production of male sex hormones.

above Crab is a seafood rich in zinc, which helps the production of male sex hormones.

right Effective herbs soothe, cleanse, and support the male reproductive system.

Impotence

The physical sign of this condition is a man's inability to achieve or sustain an erection; however, this is often a symptom of more complex underlying patterns linked to worry, stress, levels of physical energy, and lack of true relaxation. Dietary factors play a big part in rebuilding vitality (see page 168), which is the main route to improving the condition. Tonic herbs like ginger, ginseng, and nettle, taken either as supplements or infusions, help to renew energy levels; St-John's-wort as a supplement or a tincture is helpful for feelings of depression or depleting anxiety. Massage with relaxing essential oils like lavender or sandalwood helps to improve sleep quality and daytime energy levels (see pages 140–141).

Prostate enlargement

This is a common condition affecting one in three males over the age of 50. Due to hormonal fluctuations at this time, the prostate gland can enlarge, causing it to press on the bladder and creating a frequent need to pass urine. However, a reduction in flow of urine means the bladder does not feel completely empty. Infusions of tonic and astringent herbs like horsetail and nettle can be drunk 2–3 times daily to help restore flow; however, the condition should also be monitored by a physician. Include lots of seeds like pumpkin and sunflower in salads—these are rich in essential fatty acids, which help reduce discomfort.

Prostatitis

This is a bacterial infection in the prostate gland, which needs medical support because there will be fever and lower back pain and burning on urination. Infusions of antiseptic herbs like thyme, anti-inflammatory herbs like camomile, or diaphoretic herbs like elderflower or sage can help ease fever and pain, and can be drunk 2–3 times daily in an acute case; use of herbs can be tried alongside conventional medication. Echinacea tincture can be taken to support the immune system.

Note Seek medical help for any unusual swelling or pain in the lower abdomen.

A health drink

Any urinary difficulties can also be helped by drinking fresh carrot, celery, and cucumber juice. Making this drink requires an electric juice extractor—there are many models available on the market. You will need 2–3 large carrots, 3–4 celery stalks, and 1 large cucumber (all peeled and chopped, then juiced) to make approximately 1 cup of pure vegetable juice. Drink it diluted, half-filling a glass with juice and topping up with cold spring water. As well as delivering vital nutrients, carrot, celery, and cucumber juice helps reduce the acidity of the urine and therefore cools and soothes the urinary tract. Drink a large glass 3–4 times daily.

Ginseng

Calendula

Borage

Thyme

Horsetail

Aloe vera

Ginger

171

The **nervous** system

The nervous system is a complex communication network, which links the brain to the body so electrical messages can pass to and fro. The body then adjusts itself to changes in external environment as well as internal fluctuations. The nervous system also signals responses to stress, and these cause the brain to adjust the internal chemistry of the body.

Feverfew

The nervous system is made up of:

• The **brain**, which is housed inside the bony skull, and is the nerve center of the system. Protected by layers of membrane called the meninges, it is composed of three main parts:

The *cerebrum*, divided into two hemispheres on the left and right, is the gray matter of the brain. It controls voluntary movement, processes that we sense through touch, and is also the area where our faculties of intelligence, memory, and sensory stimulation are active.

The *cerebellum* lies beneath the cerebrum; it is smaller in size, and mostly governs our balance and muscle coordination.

The *medulla oblongata* links the brain with the spinal cord, and is involved in maintaining our heart rate, respiration, and digestion—the functions that keep the body alive.

Other smaller brain structures include the *pituitary gland* at the base of the skull, which controls hormone levels.

• The **spinal cord** passes down the spine through the vertebrae themselves; from bony projections on each vertebra, spinal nerves radiate out to all parts of the body, dividing down farther and farther, all the way to the toes and fingers.

• **Nerves** are bundles of fibers that conduct sensory impressions to the brain and pass impulses back—for example, to muscles, making us move. Each nerve has a receiving body called the dendrite, and a transmitting end called the axon.

As well as sensory and motor nerves, over which we have conscious control, the *autonomic nerves* control structures of which we are unaware. There are two types of autonomic nerves: *sympathetic nerves* excite us and increase blood flow to the muscles under the influence of the neuro-chemical adrenaline—this is sometimes called the "fight or flight" response; *parasympathetic nerves* link to the digestive system, to the intestines, and to internal organs, slowing down activity and assisting the recovery of the body from stress, thanks to the neurochemical noradrenaline. If the body spends too much time in "fight or flight" mode, it will become severely depleted unless balance is restored through relaxation.

right: top right Using herbs to promote relaxation helps the nervous system to regenerate itself.

right: left Eating a simple, wholesome diet also helps build energy levels and a sense of well-being.

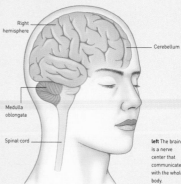

Right hemisphere

Cerebellum

Medulla oblongata

Spinal cord

left The brain is a nerve center that communicates with the whole body.

Types of herbs to help the nervous system are:

- **Nerve restoratives** such as oats and borage, to nourish the nervous system.

- **Sedatives** such as camomile and lemon balm, to help bring relaxation and improve sleep.

- **Stimulants** such as rosemary and peppermint, to uplift low energy and poor concentration (although improving relaxation first is important—we tend to be overstimulated already).

173

Helping the nervous system

Modern life causes the nervous system to be constantly triggered into "fight or flight" mode. Anxieties, pressures, deadlines, traveling from A to B, rushing food intake or skipping meals, plus constant overstimulation of our senses of sight, hearing, taste, touch, and smell, all create a huge challenge for our bodies daily. We need some stress in order to survive and stay healthy, but if there is too much our emotions become overloaded and our immune system can start to show signs of imbalance.

There is no point in using herbs or any other natural method of therapy unless lifestyle issues are addressed as well. Allowing time for meals, eating away from the TV, and taking your supper several hours before going to sleep is a very good start. Plenty of B vitamins and vitamin C from whole grains and fresh fruit and vegetables will help to restore you. Also, building 15 minutes twice a day of yoga, deep breathing, meditation, or visualization into your routine assists the parasympathetic nervous system to rebalance the body.

Headaches

These often occur around the eyes or the forehead as signs of mental stress, tired eyes, or eyestrain. Standard infusion of equal parts of peppermint and camomile helps to relieve pain; essential oil of lavender can be applied neat to the forehead (2 drops maximum) as an analgesic. It can also be beneficial to include liver-tonic herbs, such as dandelion, in infusions to detoxify the body, and warm compresses of peppermint and lavender to soothe the forehead. If you suffer repeatedly from headaches, you should consult your physician. It can also be helpful to get your eyes tested regularly.

Migraine

These are severe one-sided headaches, which can send violent pain down the face, as well as causing visual disturbances and nausea. Feverfew

is a well-known remedy for migraines and can be obtained as a herbal supplement to take orally. Eating fresh feverfew leaves in bread and butter is an old-fashioned but effective way to help. A standard infusion of herbs like peppermint and valerian is pain-killing and helps nausea. Check your diet and exclude migraine-triggering foods like cheese, chocolate, red wine, or high levels of sugar. Managing general stress levels is also important, with relaxing baths and yoga or meditation. If symptoms persist, you should seek medical advice.

Low vitality

Chronic stress can severely deplete general energy levels over time. Passionflower, taken either as a herbal remedy or a tincture, helps restore the nervous system, and St.-John's-wort or borage help feelings of anxiety or depression. A relaxing oat bath with sweet marjoram and myrtle helps relax and restore the system at the end of a long day.

Insomnia

This is very often related to an inability to switch off from daily concerns, or to eating heavy meals late at night, which should definitely be avoided. Standard infusion of lavender flowers and passionflower helps reduce tension before bed, rather than tea or coffee with high levels of caffeine, which is a nervous stimulant.

right Effective herbs for the nervous system ease pain and have a calming effect on the mind.

Feverfew

Borage

Oats

Peppermint

Rosemary

Lemon balm

Herbal first aid

There are a number of very useful items that can be made into a herbal first-aid kit to help in cases of minor accidents and injuries. Herbs can provide very quick and effective first aid if applied immediately, and are safe to use with children. Symptoms like severe shock, burns, bleeding, or respiratory problems should always be medically assessed and treated.

Aloe vera The gel from the leaves of the aloe plant is very soothing and cooling, helpful for minor burns, sunburn, skin rashes, itching, and nettle rash. It can be used as often as needed. It is best sourced from good health food stores.

Arnica This relative of calendula is best used in homeopathic form, either as tiny tablets or as a cream. Taken orally and applied to the skin immediately, it helps minimize bruising, pain, and swelling after local injury. It should be applied to unbroken skin. The pills can also be taken before operations to minimize bruising.

Calendula The flowers, either fresh or dried, are a main standby in herbal first aid. Commercially prepared calendula cream is very useful, or if you grow your own plant you can make your own ointment or herbal oil balm (see pages 130–131). Strong infusion of the flowers is very useful to clean wounds, cuts, and grazes and as a cool compress for minor burns, sunburn, or eczema.

Camomile A standard infusion is excellent as a skin wash, cleanser, and cool compress for itching, inflamed skin or eczema, as well as a soothing herbal tea for insomnia and tension.

Comfrey A standard infusion disinfects and cleanses cuts or scratches; as an ointment, it helps bruising, sprains, and fractures.

Echinacea This is a vital ingredient in the kit; the tincture is most useful, as an antimicrobial cleanser (30 drops in generous ¾ cup water) and as an immune-boosting aid against infection; it can also be taken as a preventive during the wintertime for colds and flu.

Eyebright Fresh or dried leaves and flowers can be made into a standard infusion, which is very soothing as a compress for eye problems such as irritation, soreness, or itching.

Horsetail A strong infusion is very helpful to clean deep cuts and stop bleeding, and can also be used as a compress.

Lavender The essential oil is an excellent treatment for burns, cuts, grazes, insect bites, and headaches (use 2–3 drops neat on absorbent cotton pad applied directly).

Rescue Remedy This combination of 5 Bach flower remedies is a very safe treatment for shock and anxiety (use 4 drops under the tongue, or 4–6 drops in generous ¾ cup water, sipped slowly).

Tea tree The essential oil is powerfully disinfectant and antimicrobial; use 2–3 drops neat on an absorbent cotton pad applied directly to bee and wasp stings, mosquito or other insect bites, spots, boils, warts, or fungal infections. It can be inhaled (use 4 drops in generous 2 cups boiling water) during colds and flu to fight infection and clear the chest.

directory of
herbs

Introduction to **directory**

This section contains profiles of 70 herbs and flowers
selected to be easy to grow and use for cooking
and health. You will also find details of individual
properties and effects of the plants, as well as
individual suggestions for herbal preparations.
Each profile will contain the following key information:

Juniper berries

Angelica

Sage

Calendula

Botanical name

This is the Latin name for a particular plant
species. This name (which appears before the
plant's common name) will help you identify the
plant if you are buying it for the garden or if you
are purchasing a herbal remedy.

Botanical family

All plants belong to family groups, identified
by particular characteristics that are common
to them all. (This name appears after the plant's
common name.) Some examples of common
herb families are:

• *Compositae* family, which contains hundreds of
species with a "daisy"-like flower, including the
common daisy, calendula, arnica, and sunflower.
• *Labiatae* (*Lamiaceae*) family, which contains
all the Mediterranean aromatic herbs like
rosemary, thyme, lavender and peppermint—all
with lance-shape leaves.
• *Umbelliferae* family, which contains plants with
umbels, flat spokes of tiny flowers like an
upturned umbrella, including fennel, dill,
coriander, and angelica.

Part of plant used

This refers to the area of the plant that is used
for cooking or medicine, such as leaves, roots,
wood, flowers, berries, or seeds.

History

This section gives some of the plant's historical
links to medicine and to folklore, often a rich
source of knowledge acquired through hundreds
of years of use.

Plant description and cultivation

These notes apply to growing the plant yourself,
including ideal soil and conditions, propagation
methods, harvesting, and storage.

Active ingredients

These are the ingredients science has identified as
active in the plant, with their names and effects.

Safety information

These are guidelines for the safe use of the
individual plant, particularly medicinally, with
reference to key areas like pregnancy.

Culinary use

Here the plant is linked to cooking and
beverages.

Medicinal use

The use of the plant for general health and
well-being is covered, with ways to use it to ease
common symptoms; where particular methods of
preparation and use are needed, these are shown.

right: top Fresh
basil leaves can
be rubbed onto
insect bites and
stings.

right: center
Borage flowers
are a rich source
of vegetable oil.

right: bottom
Chives give a
delicate onion
flavor to cheese
and egg dishes.

Fenugreek

Black pepper

Other notes about the directory

The herbs are listed in an A–Z format by their common English names for easy reference, so that you will quickly be able to locate the herb you want. You can also use the directory to check on herbs you may like to plant if you are planning a garden, as in pages 24–41.

Aromatic and medicinal herbs and trees make lovely additions to a bed or border, but you will not be able to grow large enough quantities in a garden to extract essential oils such as lavender. With a bush or two, you can easily make a lavender oil balm for a mild fragrance and herb content, but if you want to use essential oils you are advised to purchase them from a specialty supplier or a health food store. This also applies to certain tinctures and herbal remedies, which are best taken orally in commercially prepared doses.

Vitex agnus castus Agnus-castus (Chaste Tree) Verbenaceae

The Latin name of the plant, *agnus* (lamb) and *castus* (chaste), links the plant immediately with a dampening effect on sexuality, an effect called anaphrodisiac. In Ancient Greece, Athenian women would deck their couches with the leaves of the tree during rites sacred to the goddess Ceres. In medieval times, monks would drink ground chasteberry seeds in wine to dampen sexual feelings, and young novices in Italian monasteries would walk over the leaves of this plant on entering the monastic life. Since the Middle Ages, the plant has also been used to deal with female reproductive problems, such as irregular menstruation or low production of breast milk.

Plant description and cultivation

A fragrant deciduous shrub growing to varied heights (3–18 ft, 1–6 m). It is native to southern Europe, western Asia, and also North America. Its young shoots are grayish, becoming sharply toothed lance-shape leaves, dark green above and gray below. It has clusters of blueish-pink scented blooms, which become small, dark-purple aromatic berries. It likes a dry soil and sunny site, and does well in coastal locations.

Part of plant used

Berries.

Active ingredients

Essential oil, flavonoids, bitters.

Safety information

Agnus castus is not recommended in pregnancy or if you are taking hormone replacement therapy (HRT) or the contraceptive pill.

Culinary use

None.

Medicinal use

Modern research shows that agnus castus berries have a progesterone-enhancing effect on women, boosting hormone levels. It is very helpful in the treatment of PMS (pre-menstrual syndrome), especially irritability, mood swings, sore breasts, sweet cravings, and anxiety. It may also help infertility and is useful in early menopause. It is slow to act and has to be taken for at least 25 days continually for noticeable effects, then for a period up to 6 months. The commercial tincture is used (15 drops in generous ¾ cup water once daily, before breakfast).

Aloe vera Aloe Vera Liliaceae

The aloe was known to Dioscorides, one of the Greek fathers of herbal medicine, in about AD 78. In northern Europe, medicinal books from the 10th century or Anglo-Saxon times refer to the plant; it is presumed to have found its way there via trade routes to Egypt and Africa. Originally native to East and South Africa, aloes were successfully introduced in the 17th century to the West Indies, where they are still extensively cultivated and used in Jamaican natural medicine.

Plant description and cultivation

This is a succulent plant with no stem, just thick fleshy leaves containing special sacs full of gel, which oozes out when the leaves are cut. It flowers rarely and grows to 2–3 ft/60–100 cm tall. Aloes require 3 years' growth before their gel can be collected. In northern climates, they need to be grown in greenhouses or conservatories in pots with well-drained soil, at a minimum temperature of 41°F/5°C. In hot climates, they can be grown outside.

Part of plant used

Leaves.

Active ingredients

The gel contains anti-inflammatory saponins and antimicrobial anthraquinones, vitamins C and E, soothing salicylic acid and minerals.

Safety information

There are no contraindications to using the gel on the skin; however, if taking it orally it should be avoided in pregnancy or in breast-feeding mothers. Because of its speedy skin-healing effect, it must be used only on thoroughly clean wounds where there is no infection.

Culinary use

None.

Medicinal use

Aloe vera gel is used on the skin to soothe sunburn, itching, rashes, burns, cuts, eczema, psoriasis, shingles, and any skin inflammation. It is often mixed with cucumber juice, and in this form it can be drunk to help immune function, digestive function, and conditions like irritable bowel syndrome, colitis, or Crohn's disease. It is available in health food stores as both gel and juice. In the Caribbean, fresh leaves are broken and the gel is applied straight on to the skin.

Angelica archangelica Angelica Umbelliferae

Angelica has been revered since ancient times as an anti-infectious and blood-purifying herb. In folklore, it was associated with the archangels Michael and Gabriel. During the great plague in the 17th century, the roots were chewed to protect against infection; and it is used in traditional herbal medicine as a cleansing and detoxifying remedy.

Plant description and cultivation
Aromatic angelica grows to 4–8 ft/1.2–2.4 m in moist rich soil and full sun. It has hollow stems, large pale-green leaves, and globular umbels of yellow-green flowers, followed by flat seeds. It can be sown from ripe seeds, which should be planted in August, or propagated by dividing roots. To harvest, dig up roots in the fall of the first year; wash and dry, then store them in airtight jars. Collect leaves and stems in June. The seed heads should be harvested in late summer and spread on dish towels in a warm dry place; when the seeds drop off, they need to dry fully before airtight storage.

Part of plant used
Roots, leaves, seeds, and stems.

Active ingredients
The roots and seeds contain essential oil, glycosides, organic acids, bitters, tannins, and sugars, which together give the plant digestive tonic, antispasmodic, and expectorant properties.

Safety information
May cause skin sensitivity to UV light, so avoid excessive exposure to sunlight when taking medicinally. Not advised during pregnancy (may cause uterine contractions).

Culinary use
Young stems can be candied in sugar; seeds and roots are used in making liqueurs like Benedictine.

Medicinal use
Infused dry or fresh root helps coughs and catarrh, also lowers fever; it also eases digestive cramps after eating rich food. Fresh or dried root added to a hot bath will help rheumatic pain.

Ocimum basilicum Basil Labiatae (Lamiaceae)

Basil has a long history of use; the herbalist John Parkinson in 1629 said of it, "The ordinary Basill is in a manner wholly spent to make sweete or washing waters among other sweete herbs…" and also "the smell thereof is so excellent that it is fit for a king's house." In India a variety called "tulsi," or holy basil, is grown in gardens to ward off misfortune, and is sacred to the god Vishnu.

Plant description and cultivation

Basil is an annual herb growing to approximately 8–24 in/20–60 cm tall. The stems and leaves are particularly aromatic; to encourage leaf production, nip off flowering stems. There are several varieties: 'Purple Ruffles' is exotically dark with a clovelike aroma; 'Genovese' is compact and highly aromatic; 'Minimum' is very small and good for a little pot; and 'Crispum' has curly leaves with vigorous growth. Sow seed in pots in moist, medium-rich soil in full sun; in more northern climates, it does well on a windowsill or in a greenhouse/conservatory.

Part of plant used

Fresh or dried leaves, essential oil.

Active ingredients

Aromatic essential oil, tannins, glycosides, and saponin give basil antiseptic, stomach-tonic, antispasmodic, and expectorant properties.

Safety information

The essential oil should not be used during pregnancy, but the leaves can be eaten as a food flavoring.

Culinary use

Extensively used in Italian dishes, especially pesto sauce, mozzarella, and fresh tomato salad, and pizza topping.

Medicinal use

Basil essential oil makes a good sinus-clearing inhalation (4 drops in generous 2 cups boiling water). A standard infusion of fresh leaves helps indigestion and constipation; with added honey and lemon, it eases chest congestion and bronchitis. Fresh leaves can be rubbed on insect bites and stings to ease itching. In the bath, fresh leaves invigorate tired muscles.

185

Laurus nobilis Bay (Sweet Laurel) Lauraceae

Bay is originally native to southern Europe and North Africa. The Romans used bay extensively to make laurel wreaths as crowns for generals, and as garlands and sacred offerings. Bay trees were grown to purify the air with their aromatic fragrance. They were introduced to Britain in the 16th century; in ornate gardens, the trees were clipped into very elegant shapes to fit into formal designs.

Plant description and cultivation
Bay trees thrive in pots, provided they are given moderately rich soil and a sunny location; they reach heights of 10 ft/3 m. In the ground they can grow to 50 ft/15 m tall, so pruning is needed if you have a small garden. A popular style is to cut off all the lower branches and encourage a "mop-head," or spherical crown. Leaves are best gathered for drying in high summer for the best essential oil content and flavor; however, fresh leaves can be used all year round, as bay is evergreen. The tree needs protection from frost and cold winds in the winter.

Part of plant used
Aromatic leaves.

Active ingredients
Essential oil, tannic acid, and bitters, giving bay antimicrobial and digestive-stimulating properties.

Safety information
No issues.

Culinary use
Bay is most widely used as a food flavoring for meat-based or vegetable stews, Bolognese sauce, fish dishes, soups, and also sometimes as a flavoring in milk puddings. The leaves release their essential oil particularly well if a dish is simmered slowly for a long time.

Medicinal use
Bay is not widely used as a remedy; however, a standard infusion of dried or fresh leaves is helpful for wind and indigestion, or for influenza as an antimicrobial. A herbal oil balm made with dried or fresh leaves can help muscular aches and bruises.

Borago officinalis Borage Boraginaceae

The herbalist John Gerard said of this wild herb, that, "it maketh a man merrie and joyfull," alluding to its antidepressant qualities. He continues that it helps "to drive away all sadnesse, dullnesse and melancholy." In the early 19th century, the young tops of borage were eaten as early spring greens, and the leaves in salads. The flowers were candied to use as decorations. Nowadays borage seeds are grown commercially to produce a vegetable oil with similar properties to evening primrose oil, taken as a supplement for skin and hormonal support.

Plant description and cultivation
Borage is a shrub that still grows wild in woods and on waste ground. Its height is about 2–3 ft/60–90 cm. It has hollow hairy stems and leaves and blue star-shaped flowers from June onward. It is very attractive to bees. Sow seed in March in moist but well-drained soil in full sun; once established, it will self-seed each year.

Part of plant used
Flowers, leaves, and vegetable oil from the seeds.

Active ingredients
High levels of mucilage in the leaves, as well as tannins, saponin, and minerals, give it restorative and soothing properties; fatty acids in the seeds help hormone fluctuations.

Safety information
No issues.

Culinary use
The young leaves taste rather like cucumber and are good in salads, or added to summer wine cups or punches. Candied flowers are attractive cake decorations, and fresh flowers add unusual color to salads.

Medicinal use
Standard infusion of fresh leaves and flowers helps lower fevers as well as ease indigestion. A strong, fresh flower and leaf infusion can be used as an anti-inflammatory skin wash, mouthwash, or gargle. Taking tincture of borage is helpful for long-term chronic stress. The vegetable oil can be purchased in capsules to take orally for dry skin as well as hormone-balancing effects and to support menopausal changes.

187

Calendula officinalis Calendula (Marigold) Compositae

In Italy, this daisy is called *fiore d'ogni mese*— "flower of every month"—because it blooms so regularly there throughout the year. In the past, looking at the golden flowers was said to strengthen the eyesight, and they were used in soothing eyewashes. In an old 18th-century Herbal, calendula is listed as good for jaundice, headaches, toothache, and strengthening the heart.

Plant description and cultivation

Calendula is a low-growing annual (20 inches/ 50 cm in height), with hairy, slightly sticky leaves and orange flowers blooming from late spring to early fall. For medicinal purposes, it is important to plant this exact species—many members of this botanical family look similar. It is easy to grow in sunny or part-shady places and tolerates most soils. Removing dead flowers ensures a constant supply of new blooms. It self-seeds once established.

Part of plant used

Flowers.

Active ingredients

Saponin, flavonoids, bitters, mucilage, resin, and essential oil give calendula cleansing, antiseptic, astringent, diaphoretic, bitter, diuretic, vulnerary, and alterative properties.

Safety information

Internal use is not advised during pregnancy.

Culinary use

Fresh or dried petals can add attractive natural yellow color to rice, buns, cakes, or cheesecakes.

Medicinal use

A standard infusion of fresh or dried flowers helps the body to sweat out toxins, e.g. in influenza, and also soothes the digestive tract. The saponin and flavonoids make it very useful in an ointment as a vein tonic, either for broken veins, varicose veins, or hemorrhoids; gently massaged into the legs it helps heaviness and cramps. It has a mild estrogenic action and helps PMS and irregular menstruation, used either in infusion or tincture. Calendula is a potent skin healer, staunching bleeding, cleansing wounds, preventing infection, and promoting tissue repair.

Matricaria chamomilla and *Anthemis nobilis* Camomile Compositae

Both these species of camomile are widely used in herbal medicine. The name "camomile" comes from the Greek *kamai melon*, which literally means "ground apple," because the herb grows at soil level and has an apple-like aroma. Culpeper calls camomile the "plant physician," because the plant helps promote the general health of the whole garden, probably by attracting beneficial insects.

Plant description and cultivation
German or wild camomile (*Matricata chamomilla*) grows to 2 ft/60 cm in height and has feathery, aromatic leaves and distinctive pure-white petals around a golden center. Roman camomile (*Anthemis nobilis*) has similar leaves but the flowers have a more feathery appearance and grow very close to the ground. Roman camomile "treneague" is nonflowering and can be used to grow an aromatic lawn.

Part of plant used
Flowers.

Active ingredients
Both species contain essential oil; in German camomile there is more chamazulene, an anti-inflammatory ingredient that turns the oil blue, and in Roman camomile there are more esters, giving a stronger fruity aroma. Other important ingredients in the flowers and leaves are flavonoids, fatty acids, amino acids, bitters, and tannin; the properties are anti-inflammatory, antispasmodic, and sedative.

Safety information
No issues.

Culinary use
As a refreshing tea, camomile helps the digestion; the flowers of German camomile tend to be sold commercially as a herbal infusion.

Medicinal use
Either species can be used; fresh or dried flowers in a strong infusion, cooled, make a soothing skin wash for irritation, nettlerash, eczema, heat rash, cuts, and sunburn. Its infusion helps indigestion of a nervous origin, insomnia, mood swings, and irritability; it also soothes the membrane of the digestive tract. The bitters help to stimulate digestive juices. Both essential oils are used in aromatherapy for skin and digestive issues.

189

Elettaria cardamomum Cardamom 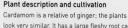 Zingiberaceae

In India, where the plant originates, the name is *elattari*; it has been used in Ayurvedic medicine for centuries as a respiratory tonic, circulatory stimulant, and adrenal tonic. It has been known as cardamom since Ancient Greek times; in the first century AD, Dioscorides included it in his *Herbal*, which contained many exotic spices.

Plant description and cultivation
Cardamom is a relative of ginger; the plants look very similar. It has a large fleshy root called a rhizome, which produces long stems and elegant lance-shape leaves, growing quite tall (6–9 ft/2–3 m); it produces small yellow and violet flowers from the base of the plant. These become small green pods containing shiny black aromatic seeds. It will grow in a greenhouse/conservatory in a minimum temperature of 64°F/18°C, in well-drained rich soil and partial shade. It can be propagated by seed or by dividing the roots. The spice is traded extensively from India and the Far East, either as whole pods or ground seeds.

Part of plant used
Seeds.

Active ingredients
Essential oil, mucilage, and resin give cardamom antispasmodic, warming, circulatory-stimulating, and digestive-tonic properties.

Safety information
No issues.

Culinary use
Cardamom is a key ingredient in Indian cooking as a sweetly aromatic curry spice, combined with others like ginger, coriander seeds, black pepper, and cumin. It is also drunk as a spicy tea, and used to flavor Indian ice creams and sweets.

Medicinal use
In Ayurvedic medicine, cardamom infusion helps colds, influenza, coughs, and sinusitis. 1 teaspoon pods boiled in 1 cup of milk is a soothing aromatic drink at bedtime during the winter months. Cardamom essential oil is used in aromatherapy massage to help respiratory problems and poor circulation and to boost immunity.

Daucus carota Carrot Umbelliferae

This vegetable was mentioned in the writings of the Roman Pliny the Elder in the first century AD and featured in cook books from the second century AD. Carrots were cultivated throughout known history in Europe, and were introduced to Britain in the reign of Queen Elizabeth I. Originally, carrots were white and very pungent; extensive cultivation produced the sweeter, orange varieties that we know today. Wild carrots are more useful medicinally, though the herb and seeds of the cultivated variety can also be used.

Plant description and cultivation
The plant is a biennial herb up to 3 ft/1 m tall, with feathery, fine leaves, dense umbels of whitish-pink flowers that become flat seeds, and thick white or orange taproots. It requires sandy, well-drained soil and full sun. The leaves and top part of the plant can be picked in late spring for infusions and the seeds can be collected and dried at the end of the summer.

Part of plant used
Leaves, seeds, and roots.

Active ingredients
In the leaves and seeds: essential oil, alkaloids with antispasmodic and digestive-tonic properties; in the root vegetable: nutrients like vitamin C, carotene, sugars, and minerals.

Safety information
No issues.

Culinary use
Carrots are a popular vegetable, eaten either raw or cooked. Fresh carrot juice is packed with vitamin C and provitamin A as well as minerals; equal parts of carrot and fresh apple juice is an excellent all-round tonic.

Medicinal use
Standard infusion of leaves, stems, and flowers helps to generally detoxify the system, especially where there is water retention, cystitis, or prostatitis. A ½ cup (4 fl oz/125 ml) morning and night is recommended. Infusion of the seeds (1 tsp in generous ¾ cup water) is excellent for indigestion, wind, and bloating.

Anthriscus cerefolium Chervil Umbelliferae

In the Middle Ages, chervil was valued as a medicinal plant useful for cleansing the kidneys and liver. It was also used to bathe the eyes. It is a vital ingredient in traditional French herb blends for *bouquets garnis* or *fines herbes*, used to flavor savory dishes, and is better known these days for its culinary than its medicinal uses. Although this herb can be found in the wild, there are several poisonous species that resemble it, so it is best to buy seeds from a reputable supplier and grow your own.

Plant description and cultivation
Chervil is a hardy annual plant 1–2 ft/30–60 cm tall, with bright green feathery leaves and flat umbels of tiny white flowers in early summer. It prefers light, moist soil and a sunny location, and is easily grown from seed in the garden, in pots or on a windowsill. Cut away flowering stems to maximize leaf production.

Part of plant used
Fresh leaves.

Active ingredients
Aromatic essential oil with digestive-tonic. properties.

Safety information
No issues.

Culinary use
Fresh chervil leaves are used extensively in French cooking in soups, flavored butters, sauces, salad dressings, and especially in omelet or egg dishes; they are also very good with chicken. They need to be added at the end of cooking or as a garnish to prevent the flavor getting lost through overheating. The flavor is slightly more anise-like than parsley; the two work together well as combined flavors and can be added to salad-green combinations.

Medicinal use
None.

Allium schoenoprasum Chives Liliaceae/Alliaceae

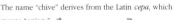

The chive is the smallest member of the onion family, closely related to garlic, leek, and shallot. It originated in Europe, and is found from northern latitudes all the way to Corsica and Greece. It is likely that the Romans brought it to Britain. The Latin *schoenas* means rushes or sedge; chive does have a grasslike appearance. The name "chive" derives from the Latin *cepa*, which means "onion."

Plant description and cultivation

The plant is a hardy perennial that grows from bulbs. The slender aromatic leaves are about 12 in/30 cm tall; pinkish-purple globular flowers appear in early summer and are very attractive to bees and hover-flies. Once it is established, it can be propagated by dividing clumps of bulbs in early spring or fall. The fresh leaves can be constantly cut for kitchen use, even until the first frosts. It is an ideal herb for a kitchen garden or border, and also does well in a pot; it will tolerate most soils but needs regular watering and nutrients.

Part of plant used
Leaves.

Active ingredients
Essential oil with sulfur compounds, which has a digestive-tonic and stimulating effect.

Safety information
No issues.

Culinary use
Chives are a marvellous flavoring to add to egg or cheese dishes like omelets. They are also very tasty added to mashed potatoes, or to melted butter poured over new potatoes. They add a delicate onion flavor to soups, sauces, and salad dressings, and can be used freely in salad-green combinations. They are also good with cucumber or tomato salad.

Medicinal use
Chives are not used medicinally, but like all the onion family they have a beneficial effect on circulation and digestion, thanks to the sulfur compounds in their powerful flavor.

Cinnamomum zeylanicum Cinnamon Lauraceae

Cinnamon has been an important spice since biblical times, in incense, medicine, and cooking. In Eastern medicine it is a traditional remedy for respiratory, immune, digestive, and menstrual problems. Originally native to Sri Lanka, the spice trade was monopolized there first by the Portuguese in the 16th century and then by the Dutch in the 17th century. It also thrives in southern India and Malaysia, and is now cultivated in the Caribbean.

Plant description and cultivation
Cinnamon is a tree growing to 30 ft/9 m in height with brown papery bark, shiny tough green leaves, creamy white flowers, and blue oval berries. It needs sandy soil, a tropical climate with plenty of rain, hot sunshine, and a minimum temperature of 59°F/15°C. The commercial spice is the dried inner bark of young shoots. The trees are cut back close to the ground to encourage re-sprouting.

Part of plant used
Inner bark.

Active ingredients
Aromatic essential oil extracted by distillation, rich in eugenol (clovelike aroma), as well other aroma-chemicals like pinene and cineol (medicinal aromas), creating a warming, antiseptic, and digestive tonic effect.

Safety information
The essential oil should not be used on sensitive or allergy-prone skin, or inhaled by individuals with asthma. The dried spice is very mild with no contraindications.

Culinary use
The sticks or ground dried spice are very soft, sweet, and pungent; the flavor complements cooked apples or pears, or mulled wine. It is also very tasty in spicy cakes and cookies.

Medicinal use
A standard infusion of dried powder/sticks with added slice of lemon and 1 tsp honey is excellent for sore throats, colds, or early stages of influenza; it also eases indigestion after eating rich food. The essential oil is used in aromatherapy massage for muscular aches and digestive problems.

Salvia sclarea Clary Sage Labiatae (Lamiaceae)

The old French name for this herb is *toute bonne* ("all good"), and the name "clary" is a corruption of "clear eye," referring to the use of the herb as a soothing eyewash. It originates from southern Europe, particularly France and Italy, and was introduced to Britain in the 16th century. In the 19th century, clary sage was used as an alternative to hops, making beers that were extremely heady thanks to the strong aroma!

Plant description and cultivation

Clary sage is a stunning plant, growing to 4 ft/ 1.2 m tall with very large downy leaves and tall spikes of pinkish-blue flowers in late summer. The whole plant has a very distinctive fragrance. It likes moist, fertile soil in full sun and can be grown from seed sown in the spring. It will die off in the second year, but will have produced plenty of seed for re-sowing. The leaves can be used throughout the season; the flowering tops are harvested in early summer and the seeds in late summer.

Part of plant used

Leaves (herbalism); flowering tops (essential oil).

Active ingredients

Tannins, bitters, and essential oil extracted by steam distillation. Clary sage has warming, antispasmodic, tonic, and hormone-balancing properties.

Safety information

Clary sage is not recommended in pregnancy.

Culinary use

The leaves, flowers, and essential oil are used to flavor liqueurs and vermouth; in the past, the young leaves were fried in batter and eaten as a side vegetable.

Medicinal use

A strong infusion of young leaves is a useful cleanser for cuts, grazes, and wounds; a poultice of the leaves helps draw out splinters and infection from cuts or boils. Soaking ½ tsp seeds in generous ¾ cup hot water for a few minutes releases a mucilage which, when strained, makes an excellent wash for sore, tired eyes. The essential oil is used in aromatherapy massage to help hormonal imbalance, depression, and exhaustion.

Eugenia caryophyllus Clove Myrtaceae

Pungent aromatic cloves were probably brought to Europe by Persian and Arab traders from the Indonesian islands where they originated. The Latin name *caryophyllus* dates back to the first-century AD Roman writer Pliny the Elder, who knew them as *caryophyllon*. In the 16th century, they were a popular protection against the plague, included in the scented pomanders carried on the person. The name "clove" comes from the French *clou*, meaning "nail," which they resemble.

Plant description and cultivation
The clove tree grows to 65 ft/20 m in height with gray bark and dark green shiny leaves. Aromatic green buds appear and if they are not picked, they will turn into dark-red flowers; dried, the buds are the cloves sold commercially as spice. The tree has to be at least 6 years old before the cloves can be harvested. The tree requires tropical conditions—fertile soil, high humidity, and hot temperatures.

Part of plant used
Dried, unripe flower buds.

Active ingredients
Essential oil (extracted by steam distillation) in the dried buds rich in eugenol, an aroma-chemical with highly antiseptic, expectorant, and antiviral properties.

Safety information
Clove bud essential oil should not be used on mucus membrane or on individuals with sensitive or allergy-prone skin. Whole cloves are safe to use medicinally; no more than 5 or 6 per application.

Culinary use
Cloves are delicious in cooked apples, stewed fruit, pickles, and chutneys; they complement cooked ham or pork dishes and are vital in mulled wine.

Medicinal use
Infuse 5 cloves in generous ¾ cup boiling water for stomach ache, indigestion, wind, and nausea, or colds and influenza. Soften 1 clove by soaking in 4 tbsp boiling water for 10 minutes, then place between the teeth to numb toothache; use the liquid as a mouthwash to tone the gums.

Symphytum officinale Comfrey Boraginaceae

The name comes from the Greek *sympho* ("combined together") and *phyto* ("plant"), referring to the long-established skin and bone-healing properties of the plant. The herbalist Gerard said of it, "A salve concocted from the fresh herb will certainly tend to promote the healing of bruised and broken parts." Culpeper later added, "The root boiled in water or wine and the decoction drunk helps all inward hurts, bruises, wounds and causes the phlegm to be easily spit forth."

Plant description and cultivation

The plant is a perennial with vigorous growth up to 4 ft/1.2 m, and about 3 ft/1 m spread. The leaves are large, fleshy, and hairy and small violet or pink flowers appear in early summer. It needs damp soil and some shade. It is best propagated by dividing roots in the spring. It makes a wonderful garden fertilizer and compost activator (see pages 52–53). Young leaves are best for medicinal use, and the roots are made into a tincture.

Part of plant used

Leaves and roots.

Active ingredients

Alkaloids, abundant mucilage, tannin, allantoin, starch, and essential oil with anti-inflammatory, wound-healing, antiseptic, and scar-healing properties.

Safety information

Internal use of comfrey is not advised for self-medication, as it contains some alkaloids, which may cause liver damage.

Culinary use

None.

Medicinal use

Ointment made from comfrey leaves is excellent for bruises, wounds, cuts, scars, varicose veins, and muscular aches, as well as helping recovery from fractures. A poultice of comfrey leaves helps boils, abscesses, and large areas of acne on the skin by reducing inflammation and drawing out infection. The allantoin content helps the skin to heal and repair itself.

197

Coriandrum sativum Coriander Umbelliferae

Seeds of the plant were found in the tomb of Tutankhamun, dating back to around 1300 BC. In Egypt, the seeds and leaves are still extensively used in soups and in making bread. In the Bible (Exodus 16:31), the seeds are likened to God-given manna from heaven. The plant was brought to Britain by the Romans; in the first century AD, Pliny the Elder used the name *coriandrum* and writes that the best-quality spice comes from Egypt. The Chinese believed the seeds conferred longevity and used the whole plant to treat hemorrhoids, nausea, and toothache.

Plant description and cultivation
An annual up to 2 ft/60 cm tall with pungent, divided feathery leaves and umbels of whitish-pink flowers, followed by ridged seeds. It can easily be grown from seed and needs to be planted straight into the garden in late spring; it requires well-drained fertile soil and full sun. Pinch out flowering stems to maximize leaf production; harvest seeds at the end of the summer by tying paper bags over flower heads and hanging them upside down in a warm place.

Part of plant used
Leaves and seeds.

Active ingredients
Leaves and seeds contain tannins, sugar, and vitamin C; the seeds are particularly rich in essential oil extracted by steam distillation. Coriander has antispasmodic and digestive tonic properties.

Safety information
No issues.

Culinary use
Chopped fresh leaves (cilantro) are a delicious garnish on curries, in salads, or in dressings. The seeds are used in curries, pickles, chutneys, breads, and cakes. To make a simple curry powder, mix together 1 oz/30 g dried ginger, 1 oz/30 g coriander seeds, 1 oz/30 g cardamom seeds, 1 tsp/5 g cayenne pepper, and 1 oz/30 g turmeric powder; grind to a fine blend in a pestle and mortar and store in an airtight jar.

Medicinal use
The seeds are most potent medicinally; a standard infusion calms the cramping pains of indigestion or wind and helps digest fatty foods. The essential oil is used in aromatherapy massage for muscular aches and pains, and stress-related indigestion.

Centaurea cyanus Cornflower Compositae

The name *centaurea* refers to the famous Chiron, half-man, half-horse, the centaur of Greek myth who taught the healing powers of plants, and *cyanus* means "blue." As the common name "cornflower" implies, they were once to be found growing widely in fields of cereal crops but are not seen today due to the use of chemical herbicides on crops. In the days of hand-reaping, the tough stems of cornflower gave it the name "hurt sickle" because it tended to dull the blade of the sickle used to cut the crop. In the past, the flowers were used as a blue dye and as ink.

Plant description and cultivation
The beautiful blue star-shaped flowers are very striking in a border; they are annuals, growing to 32 in/80 cm tall with feathery leaves and tough stems. The flowers grow on long stems to raise them above the corn, and have daisy-shape heads with striking blue petals around a purple center. They can easily be grown from seed straight into the garden in late spring after the last frost, and also do well in pots. Plant them in well-drained soil and full sun. Flowers can be used fresh or dried.

Part of plant used
Flowers.

Active ingredients
The flowers contain blue pigments, saponins, mucilage, and tannins, giving the plant diuretic, cleansing, and anti-inflammatory properties.

Safety information
No issues.

Culinary use
None.

Medicinal use
A strong infusion of the flowers can be used as an eyebath and eyewash for sore tired eyes or styes, and also as a mouthwash for mouth ulcers. In equal parts with peppermint and camomile, it makes a soothing standard infusion for indigestion and constipation. In blends of herbs for the bath, the flowers cleanse and gently soothe the skin.

Curcumis sativa Cucumber Curcurbitaceae

Cucumbers have been cultivated for at least 3,000 years. The Romans liked them both raw and cooked; the writer Pliny the Elder noted that the Emperor Tiberius would not eat a meal without them. They were very popular in Egypt as food and medicine, valued for their cooling properties. In Britain, they were known at the court of King Edward III in the 14th century, and were widely cultivated by the 17th century. Gerard writes of them as cooling "to all manner of ... pimples, rubies and such like...".

Plant description and cultivation
Cucumber is a member of the same botanical family as large zucchini, melons, and pumpkins; a trailing annual with triangular leaves and yellow flowers, followed by the long fruit with green skin, moist whitish flesh, and white seeds. It must be grown under glass if temperatures fall below 50°F/10°C. It can be grown from seed and needs rich, moist soil, ample water, and humidity. Small cucumbers can be grown in pots, encouraged to climb up canes.

Part of plant used
The whole fruit.

Active ingredients
Cucumber is over 90 percent water, giving it moisturizing and cooling properties. It also contains vitamins C and B complex, calcium, phosphorus, and iron.

Safety information
No issues.

Culinary use
Cucumber is delicious raw in salads or mixed with natural yogurt as a mouth-cooling relish with curries. Fresh cucumber juice mixed with fresh celery, carrot, and apple juices makes a nutrient-rich vegetable tonic. Drink half a glass of mixed juice topped with spring water.

Medicinal use
Applying fresh cucumber slices directly to sunburn, cuts, or skin irritation is very soothing. Fresh cucumber slices straight from the refrigerator are a treat for tired, red eyes. Cucumber soap, creams, and lotions were once used to whiten and refine the skin. Try this old recipe: 1/2 cup fresh cucumber juice mixed with 1/2 cup glycerin and rose water; use twice daily to cleanse and soften the skin. Keep refrigerated.

Taraxacum officinale Dandelion Compositae

The name *taraxacum* seems to be derived from two Greek words, *taraxos*, meaning disorder, and *akos* meaning remedy. The plant has been in use since Ancient Greek times as a cleansing and diuretic medicine. In Britain, dandelion leaves were used to make a type of beer in the 19th century, a country cordial called "dandelion and burdock." Dandelion wine was made from the flowers.

Plant description and cultivation
There is usually no need to plant dandelion specifically—gardeners are all too familiar with it as a weed. It grows on a stout taproot, producing lush green leaves and a single flower stems, which matures into a yellow, daisy-like head, followed by spherical fluffy seed heads. What is less known these days is how useful it actually is!

Part of plant used
Leaves and roots.

Active ingredients
Leaves and roots contain bitters, sterols, tannin, glycosides, resin, essential oil, vitamins A and C; these give digestive stimulant, bitter tonic, strong diuretic, and liver-supportive properties.

Safety information
Because of its strong diuretic properties, it is not recommended for individuals with severe kidney conditions.

Culinary use
Young dandelion leaves are delicious in salads, giving a pungent bitter taste; try them in a combination of lettuce leaves, fresh chopped shallot, and chives. Dried, roasted, and ground dandelion roots make a caffeine-free coffee substitute.

Medicinal use
Dandelion root is most commonly used medicinally as a bitter tonic for digestive complaints; a decoction of the root helps to stimulate the appetite as well as the digestion of rich foods. The roots also contain inulin, which helps the pancreas to control blood-sugar levels (it is not related to the similarly-named insulin).

Anethum graveolens Dill Umbelliferae

In the first century AD, the Greek herbalist Dioscorides wrote of *anethon*, which is considered to be this herb. It has been used as a remedy since early medieval times, and the name "dill" is derived from the Norse *dilla*—to calm—alluding to the digestive soothing properties of the plant. It was used in charms against witches, supposedly rendering their spells impotent. Culpeper says of it, "… to be sure it strengthens the brain … the seed is of more use than the leaves and more effectual to digest raw and vicious humours…"

Plant description and cultivation

Dill is very similar-looking to fennel, except that it is an annual and is not so tall. It grows to 3 ft/ 1 m with a single stem and aromatic feathery leaves.It has umbels of tiny yellow flowers and flat oval seeds. It can be grown from seed in the late spring, and requires nutrient-rich, well-drained soil and plenty of moisture. It is best planted away from fennel to avoid cross-pollination. The leaves can be used fresh and the seeds harvested in late summer by tying paper bags around flower heads and hanging them upside down in a warm place.

Part of plant used

Leaves and seeds.

Active ingredients

Essential oil rich in carvone and limonene, as well as fatty oil, tannins, and mucilage. The essential oil is extracted by steam distillation and used in the pharmaceutical industry. Dill has digestive-tonic and antispasmodic properties, as well as being slightly sedative.

Safety information

No issues.

Culinary use

The fresh leaves give a delicate anise flavor to soups, sauces, and fish dishes, and are also used in pickles and chutneys. They are also good in cucumber salad and egg or cheese dishes.

Medicinal use

Standard infusion of the leaves is extremely mild and gentle on the digestion, even suitable for children aged 5 onward. It helps indigestion (especially stress-related), stomach cramps, and wind; it also eases constipation. In Indian medicine, ground seeds are used to help diarrhea, and fresh seeds are chewed to sweeten the breath.

Echinacea purpurea Echinacea (Coneflower) Compositae

Echinacea is native to the USA, where it was extensively used by the Native Americans to heal wounds, treat snakebite, ease toothache, and as a general disinfectant. This practice was adopted by early settlers, who used the plant to help immune infections. Modern research has confirmed echinacea's immune-boosting properties and it is extensively used in medical herbal practice as an antiviral.

Plant description and cultivation
It is a perennial, 4 ft/1.2 m tall, with a thick root called a rhizome and pointed, lance-shape leaves. It produces deep-pink, daisy-like flowers with a raised golden conical center (there are also paler pink and white-flowered species). It grows wild in grassland and prairie locations, and requires well-drained, nutrient-rich soil in sun or part shade. Cutting back the flowers as they fade encourages new blooms. It can be grown from seed in the spring, or propagated by dividing roots.

Plant part used
Roots: dried and powdered.

Active ingredients
The roots contain inulin, polysaccharides, essential oil, resin, plant sterols, and fatty acids. Echinacea has been proved to increase body resistance to infection.

Safety information
No issues.

Culinary use
None.

Medicinal use
Echinacea's immune-boosting properties make it essential in the treatment of colds and influenza, as well as more chronic conditions like glandular fever or ME/post-viral fatigue. It stimulates the production of white blood cells, which fight infection, and is therefore being used as a support for HIV/AIDS. It is best taken in capsule form or as a commercially prepared tincture. A decoction of the fresh roots can be used to make an ointment, or applied directly to clean and disinfected cuts or wounds. It is also useful taken in small amounts over a longer period as a blood purifier; however, this should be under the supervision of a qualified herbal practitioner.

Sambucus nigra Elder Caprifoliaceae

The Romans knew this tree as *sambucus*. "Elder" comes from the Anglo-Saxon word *aeld*, meaning "fire," because the hollow twigs were used to blow sparks into flame. In old English tradition, it was believed to be the wood of Christ's cross, and in northern Europe superstition still forbids cutting elder branches or wood without first asking permission of the "Hlyde-Moer," the "elder mother" spirit who lives in the tree.

Plant description and cultivation

The elder tree grows up to 30 ft/10 m in height, with dull green leaves and flat heads of creamy white flowers in early summer, followed by small black berries. It still grows wild in woods and hedgerows. Although there are some ornamental varieties available, only the true wild species is of medicinal value. It requires moist, well-drained soil, in sun or part-shade.

Part of plant used

Flowers and berries.

Active ingredients

The flowers contain glycosides, mucilage, tannins, and organic acids, which give them soothing and diaphoretic (sweat-inducing) properties. The berries contain pigments, sugar, and large amounts of vitamin C.

Safety information

Elder leaves are toxic and should not be used. Berries should not be eaten raw, but can be boiled into syrups and made into wine.

Culinary use

Fresh elderflowers dipped in batter and fried make a delicious treat; added to stewed gooseberries or other acid fruits, they give a delicate flavor. The flowers can also be used to make a cordial, teas, or aromatic vinegar.

Medicinal use

Equal parts of elderflower, yarrow, and mint leaves is a key herbal blend for colds and influenza, coughs, sinusitis, and catarrh. The berries can be made into a nutritious syrup, which also soothes sore throats and supports the immune system (see pages 152–153). Standard infusion of elderflowers, cooled, is a soothing skin toner and can be added to face creams or masks.

Eucalyptus globulus Eucalyptus Myrtaceae

Eucalyptus is native to Australia, where there are some 300 species. Trees can reach heights of up to 300 ft/100 m. They are very efficient at absorbing water, even in desert conditions; in North Africa and southern Europe, they have been planted in marshy areas to reclaim land and reduce the mosquito population. Eucalyptus essential oil has been produced on a large commercial scale since the 19th century.

Plant description and cultivation
Eucalyptus is a tall tree with whitish bark that peels away. The wood is aromatic as well as the leaves, which are usually slightly darker on the upper surface and very pale beneath. They contain sacs with essential oil. The flowers are whitish, followed by round berries. Trees can be planted in hot climates and even temperate gardens, provided the temperature does not fall below 23°F/–5°C. They require well-drained soil, lots of moisture, and full sun.

Part of plant used
Leaves.

Active ingredients
Essential oil in the leaves, mostly cineol and pinene, extracted by steam distillation, giving expectorant, antiseptic, and wound-healing properties.

Safety information
The essential oil should not be used on sensitive or allergy-prone skin. Infusion of fresh leaves should be used with caution on sensitive skin.

Culinary use
None.

Medicinal use
Strong infusion of fresh eucalyptus leaves is useful for cleaning cuts and grazes. Combined infusion of fresh eucalyptus, lavender, and red clover flowers can also be used to make a skin-healing ointment. Essential oil of eucalyptus can be inhaled for sinusitis, colds, influenza, and chest infections (4 drops in generous 2 cups boiling water); 4 drops eucalyptus and 4 drops lavender essential oils in 4 tsp vegetable carrier oil can be massaged into aching muscles, cold hands and feet, or the chest for coughs.

Oenothera biennis Evening Primrose Onagraceae

The plant is originally native to North America and was imported into Italy in the 17th century; it then spread throughout Europe. Originally the leaves were eaten in salads and the roots cooked like a vegetable. In the early 1980s, research identified significant amounts of gamma-linolenic acid (GLA) in the seeds; this compound has a significant effect on levels of prostaglandins (hormone-like substances) and therefore hormone balance. Evening primrose is now farmed commercially for the extraction of the fatty oil.

Plant description and cultivation
It is a tall biennial that grows up to 5ft/1.5m in height, with a thick yellow taproot and a rosette of leaves at the base from which the flower stems rise. The leaves are narrow and dark green, and the flowers are in yellow clusters, opening at night to attract moths, followed by downy pods filled with seeds. It will do well in most soils, as it is hardy, though it likes a warm, sunny position. Once established, it will self-seed freely.

Plant part used
Seeds (pressed to release fatty oil).

Active ingredients
Vegetable oil in the seeds rich in gamma-linolenic acid (GLA) and other fatty acids, with hormone-balancing and skin-rejuvenating properties.

Safety information
No issues.

Culinary use
None.

Medicinal use
The oil taken in capsules as a supplement helps PMS, period pain, dry skin, acne, eczema, and menopausal symptoms. It needs to be taken regularly for at least 3 months to see an effect, because the levels of GLA need to build up in the body to rebalance the prostaglandins. Clinical research has shown evening primrose supplementation to be beneficial for eczema and hyperactivity in children.

Euphrasia officinalis Eyebright Scrophulariaceae

The name *euphrasia* is of Greek origin, derived from Euphrosyne, the name of one of the Three Graces known for her joy and laughter. It is believed the name was given to the plant because it gave such relief to sufferers of eye problems. In the 14th century, its sight-restoring properties were famous; in the 16th century, people drank eyebright tea, eyebright wine, and eyebright ale as tonics. Culpeper the herbalist said of it, "Eyebright taken inwardly … dropped into the eyes for several days together helpeth all infirmities of the eyes that cause dimness of sight … it strengthens the weak brain or memory."

Plant description and cultivation
It is an annual herb with a parasitic habit, because it attaches itself with suckers to the roots of other plants, particularly grass, to obtain nutrients. It therefore needs to be sown near or in grass; it does no harm as it dies back in the fall. Eyebright has tiny-toothed round leaves and a small wiry stem up to 12 inches/30 cm in height. The delicate flowers are whitish with veinlike streaks of purple around a yellow center. The flowering tops are best harvested in July or August, when it is in full flower, used fresh or carefully dried and stored.

Part of plant used
Flowering tops.

Active ingredients
Glycosides, tannins, essential oil, saponins, and resin give soothing, anti-inflammatory properties.

Safety information
No issues.

Culinary use
None.

Medicinal use
Standard infusion of the fresh flowering tops is helpful for hay fever and allergic rhinitis. It is also said to help ease catarrh and chest infections. A strong infusion helps eye inflammation, soreness, tiredness, and itching; use it as an eyewash or as a cool compress. The herbal tincture can be taken as an eye remedy and there is also a homeopathic tincture and remedy of eyebright for similar complaints.

Foeniculum vulgare Fennel Umbelliferae

In her 12th-century *Physica*, the German abbess, physician, and mystic Hildegard of Bingen recommends fennel above all other herbs for eye strain, stomach complaints, coughs, runny nose, toning the heart, improving the skin, bad breath, and general detoxification; she used it either as an infusion or boiled the seeds in red wine. Even earlier, in the first century AD, Pliny the Elder recommended it for as many as 20 complaints, including weight loss owing to its diuretic action.

Plant description and cultivation
A biennial up to 6 ft/2 m tall, with long stems and mid-green feathery aromatic foliage. Umbels of yellow flowers bloom in high summer, attracting bees and hover-flies. The seeds are ridged and yellow-green. It can be grown from seed and requires sandy soil and full sun. Clip back flowering stems to encourage more leaves for culinary use. The seeds can be harvested in September; tie paper bags around flower heads, then hang them upside down in a warm place.

Part of plant used
Leaves and seeds.

Active ingredients
The seeds contain essential oil, fatty oil, proteins, sugars, and mucilage; the essential oil is extracted by steam distillation. Fennel seeds have antispasmodic, carminative, stomach-tonic, diuretic, and galactogogue properties.

Safety information
The essential oil or the seeds should not be taken orally or used during pregnancy. Using the leaves as food seasoning is safe.

Culinary use
The leaves give a strong anise flavour to oily fish dishes, and are an aromatic garnish to soups, meat, and vegetable stews. The seeds can be chewed after a meal to sweeten the breath.

Medicinal use
Standard infusion of the seeds is recommended for stomachache, indigestion, wind, and after eating rich foods; it is also diuretic, reducing fluid retention. It increases breast milk in nursing mothers and can ease colic in babies. Strong infusion of the seeds is a good antiseptic mouthwash and gargle for sore throats.

Trigonella foenum-graecum Fenugreek Leguminosae

The name *foenum graecum* means "greek hay," alluding to the mixing of the plant with hay in horse fodder. *Trigonella* refers to the trifoliate arrangement of the leaves, resembling clover. Fenugreek seeds have been used in Europe and Asia since antiquity in medicine and cooking. In China and India, they are used to cleanse the body and skin of impurities.

Plant description and cultivation
A hardy annual herb up to 2 ft/60 cm tall, with an erect branching stem and leaves arranged in 3 lobes. It has pale-yellow flowers in summer followed by curved pods containing aromatic seeds, which can be collected and dried. The leaves can be used fresh. It can be grown from seed in well-drained, nutrient-rich soil in full sun.

Plant part used
Leaves and seeds.

Active ingredients
Fenugreek seeds contain alkaloids, steroidal saponins with hormone-balancing properties, as well as flavonoids, soothing mucilage, and vitamins A, B, and C.

Safety information
Fenugreek leaves and seeds should not be used medicinally during pregnancy; using the herb as a food flavoring is safe.

Culinary use
Fresh leaves are cooked and eaten as a vegetable; the dried ground seeds are used in blends for Indian curries and in North African, Egyptian, and Middle Eastern cookery. Seeds can also be sprouted to eat fresh in salads.

Medicinal use
Drinking standard infusion of the seeds releases mucilage, soothing inflammation in the digestive tract, lowering fever, and detoxifying the body. The herb also has a reputation for balancing the hormones and improving breast milk flow, again taken as infusion. Applied externally, it will soothe inflamed skin, acne, and boils.

Tanacetum parthenium Feverfew Compositae

The name "feverfew" comes from the Latin *febris* (fever) and *fugure* (to chase away), accurately describing the traditional use of this herb to lower fever. It originated in south-eastern Europe and Asia Minor, and has spread via the Mediterranean to many other parts of the world. In the 17th century, the herbalist Culpeper said of it, "It is very effectual for all pains in the head ... Venus has commended this herb to succour her sisters, to be a general strengthener of their wombs ... it is chiefly used for diseases of the mother..."

Plant description and cultivation
A bushy hardy perennial up to 3 ft/1 m tall, with divided, downy, dark-green aromatic leaves. The flowers have white petals and yellow centers. Although there are some ornamental varieties such as Aureum, with golden leaves, they do not have medicinal properties. Feverfew grows in any type of soil, even surviving drought; seeds can be planted in spring, or cuttings taken from mature plants. The leaves and flowers can be used fresh or picked in summer, carefully dried and stored.

Part of plant used
Flowering tops.

Active ingredients
Essential oil with strong camphoraceous aroma, bitters, tannins, and mucilage, sesquiterpenes that may have a pain-relieving effect.

Safety information
Chewing leaves in excess may cause mouth ulcers.

Culinary use
None.

Medicinal use
Feverfew has been scientifically shown to be effective for headaches and migraines, to ease the pain of arthritis and improve sleep. Commercially prepared capsules of dried herb or a tincture are effective; a traditional approach is to eat 2 or 3 fresh leaves in bread and butter once a day for 4–5 days. An infusion of 30 drops of feverfew tincture diluted in $^1/_2$ cup water helps protect against and heal insect bites. Standard infusion of the fresh flowering tops helps relieve PMS, mood swings, and irregular periods.

Allium sativum Garlic Liliaceae

Originally from India and central Asia, garlic is now cultivated all over the world. It was probably introduced to Britain by the Romans. The Greek writer Herodotus tells that the builders of the Egyptian pyramids ate large quantities of it. The name "garlic" derives from Anglo-Saxon *gar* (spear) and *leac* (leek), probably because the leaves look like leek and the cloves like spearheads.

Plant description and cultivation
A perennial herb with a bulb divided into cloves, tall dark-green leaves, and greenish-white flowers. The bulbs need to be planted in fall in rich soil and a sunny position; they should be dug up the following summer and dried in the sun before storage.

Part of plant used
Garlic cloves.

Active ingredients
Essential oil containing allicin, which breaks down when the surface is cut to produce the active ingredient allicin and other sulfur compounds, all antibacterial, antimicrobial, and antiviral; vitamins A and C, amino acids, fatty oil.

Safety information
Eating more than 2 fresh garlic cloves daily can cause loose bowels in some people.

Culinary use
Extensive in European, Middle Eastern, Indian, and Far Eastern cookery as a pungent flavor; in meat and vegetable stews, garlic bread, garlic butter, sauces, and soups.

Medicinal use
Two fresh crushed cloves daily in bread and butter or mashed potato is an effective antiviral during colds and flu. It can be taken in commercial capsules if the taste is not liked; it is thoroughly recommended during the winter months for influenza, coughs, chest infections, bronchitis, and general low immunity. It is also helpful in the diet or as a supplement for high blood pressure, high cholesterol, and as a blood-thinning remedy for circulatory disease (if you have one or more of these conditions, consult your physician if you wish to use it medicinally).

Zingiber officinale Ginger Zingiberaceae

Ginger has been used for millennia in China and India as a remedy for diarrhea, malaria, colds, and stomach disorders, an aphrodisiac, and a vital culinary spice. In Europe, it is mentioned in leech books from Anglo-Saxon times (10th century AD) and was popular in sweet and savory cooking from medieval times onward. In the 16th century, the Spaniards imported it into the East Indies and Americas for cultivation, where it now flourishes.

Plant description and cultivation
A perennial plant with a fleshy root (rhizome), tall elegant pairs of lancelike leaves on stems up to 4 ft/1.2 m tall, and very aromatic flowers on cones separate to the leaves. It requires fertile, moist soil, very rich in nutrients, and a humid tropical climate. If grown in a greenhouse or hot location, it will need regular spraying with water to stop the leaves from drying out.

Part of plant used
Root, fresh or dried.

Active ingredients
Essential oil with antispasmodic properties, also resin, fats, starch, vitamins A and B, minerals, and amino acids, warming and tonic to digestion and circulation. The essential oil is extracted by steam distillation.

Safety information
No issues.

Culinary use
Dried gingerroot is an ingredient in curry-powder blends as well as a sweet spice used in baking gingerbread and cakes. Fresh root is used in Indian, Chinese, and Thai cookery for a pungent flavor. Candied ginger in sugar is used in confectionery.

Medicinal use
In Chinese medicine, fresh root is used to treat colds, flu, and respiratory infections by increasing sweating; standard infusion with 1 tsp honey and a slice of lemon can be taken 3 times daily. One cup of infusion daily can help morning sickness in pregnancy. In tablets or tincture, ginger can be used for nausea, travel sickness, and indigestion. The essential oil is used in aromatherapy massage for muscular and digestive discomfort and poor circulation.

Calluna vulgaris/Erica vulgaris Heather Ericaceae

Wild heather has a long history of use in herbal tradition as a sedative remedy and also to detoxify the kidneys and urinary tract. It is native to northern Europe, North Africa, and eastern North America. The name *calluna* derives from the Greek word, meaning "to clean," referring to its detoxifying action. The flowers were sometimes used to release an orange-yellow color for dyeing cloth.

Plant description and cultivation
A tough shrub with stems up to 2 ft/60 cm, tiny, overlapping triangular leaves and spikes of deep-pink flowers blooming from July to September. There are many ornamental varieties, but only the wild species is used medicinally. It grows extensively on bogs, moors, hillsides, and heathland. It can be planted from seed and it requires very moist acidic soil in full sun. The flowers can be picked in late summer and used fresh, or hung upside down in bunches to dry before storing for use during the winter. Heather is excellent in the garden for attracting bees, butterflies, and other beneficial insects. Honey from the flowers has an exquisite taste.

Part of plant used
Fresh flowering tops.

Active ingredients
The flowering stems contain glycosides, arbutin (a known diuretic ingredient), tannins, citric acid, and resin, giving anti-inflammatory, detoxifying, and sedative properties.

Safety information
No issues.

Culinary use
None.

Medicinal use
Heather is a traditional remedy in hot baths to ease rheumatic pain and poor circulation, or it can also be added to an ointment for massaging into the joints or affected areas. It is also helpful as a diuretic and urinary antiseptic for fluid retention, gout, cystitis, and prostatitis, taken as a standard infusion twice a day. A sedative and muscle-relieving herbal bath blend could be fresh heather, lavender, and sweet marjoram in a cheesecloth bag tied over the faucets.

Marrubium vulgare Horehound (White) Labiatae

Horehound has been esteemed since Roman times, and its name *marrubium* derives from the Hebrew *marrob*, a bitter herb used by Jews during the Passover feast. The herbalist Gerard said of it, "Syrup made of the greene fresh leaves and sugar is a most singular remedie against the cough and wheezing of the lungs…," and Culpeper wrote "it helpeth to bring tough phlegm from the chest… and cold rheum from the lungs of aged persons, especially those who are asthmatic and short-winded."

Plant description and cultivation
A tufted perennial herb with a short root, 4-sided stems, and wrinkled, toothed, hairy, pointed leaves. In summertime, clusters of tiny white flowers appear in the joints between the leaves and the stems. It has a very pleasant, apple-like smell. White horehound is easily grown even in poor soil. It can be propagated by seed in spring, or by taking cuttings or dividing roots. It does not flower until it is 2 years old. The flowers, stems, and leaves can be cut in late summer and made into syrup, used fresh or dried.

Part of plant used
Flowering tops.

Active ingredients
Bitters, alcohols, alkaloids, tannin, saponin, and resin, giving antispasmodic, expectorant, sedative, liver-supportive, emmenagogue, and sedative properties.

Safety information
Not advised during pregnancy.

Culinary use
None.

Medicinal use
Exceptional for helping coughs, particularly where there is phlegm on the chest, asthma, or bronchitis; it is best to make the fresh herb into a syrup for use during the wintertime. It is a pleasant-tasting and useful remedy for children. An ointment made with the leaves is helpful for healing wounds, and hot compresses or poultices can heal inflamed or infected skin. Standard infusion of the herb can be drunk as a cold and influenza remedy, to help coughs, and also for menstrual imbalance.

Armoracia rusticana Horseradish Cruciferae/Brassicaceae

Since the Middle Ages, both roots and leaves were extensively used in herbal medicine and cooking throughout mainland Europe. The 16th-century herbalist Gerard shows in his writing that in England at that time, it was still regarded only as a condiment to accompany food. In 1640, Parkinson described it as a strong-tasting sauce enjoyed by "laboring men"; by the 18th century, it was finally listed in London as a medicinal remedy.

Plant description and cultivation
It is a perennial with a deep fleshy taproot and thick, large leaves, which sprout from the base of the stem. It has a flower head made up of many tiny white blooms, which appear in summer. It prefers moist soil and grows vigorously, so that once established it is almost impossible to eradicate. Roots can be dug up in the fall and used fresh, and leaves used throughout the season.

Part of plant used
Leaves and roots.

Active ingredients
Essential oil with mustard glycosides, resin, enzymes, and vitamin C, giving digestive-stimulant, laxative, and expectorant properties.

Safety information
Do not use on individuals with sensitive or allergy-prone skin. Do not eat if suffering from stomach ulcers. Do not use as a remedy if you have low thyroid function or are taking thyroxine.

Culinary use
Horseradish sauce made with cream and vinegar is traditionally eaten with roast beef, other strong meats, or oily fish to assist digestion. The young leaves can be added to salad-green combinations for a slightly pungent flavor.

Medicinal use
Horseradish is an extremely powerful circulatory stimulant and antiseptic, similar to mustard. The fresh root of the plant can be made into a syrup to help with coughs, catarrh, and chest infections and as a general tonic. A poultice of grated root is helpful for rheumatic pains, but observe safety guidelines above.

Equisetum arvense Horsetail Fern Equisetaceae

Horsetails belong to their own plant family, closely allied to ferns. During the carboniferous period, the ancestors of these plants were as huge as palm trees; they have been on the earth for at least 200 million years. This species is found growing wild on waste ground, in woods and wet meadows, mostly regarded as a weed; yet the plant has some profound healing abilities. In the 17th century, Culpeper said of it, "It solders together fresh wounds … the juice or distilled water is of service in inflammations, pustules or red weals….," alluding to its skin-healing effects.

Plant description and cultivation
A tough perennial that grows to 20 inches/50 cm in height. It has brown stems that produce cones, releasing spores; this method of reproduction is similar to ferns. The mass of green stems are sterile. It grows best in moist conditions in sun or part shade. It can be propagated by division of roots, but once established in the garden it will be impossible to eradicate. It may be best to find a regular wild source away from traffic, harvesting in June or July and drying for winter use.

Part of plant used
Fresh or dried stems.

Active ingredients
Silica is found in large quantities (up to 70%), saponins, alkaloids, flavonoids, and minerals giving diuretic, nutrient, and astringent properties.

Safety information
Use with caution on sensitive, allergy-prone skin.

Culinary use
None.

Medicinal use
A standard infusion of the herb, drunk twice daily, is indicated for low energy and anemia, as well as dull skin and lifeless hair. The infusion can also be used to clean cuts and wounds and promote skin healing, to help bronchitis and chest complaints and to improve elimination in cystitis, prostatitis, and other urinary infections. The herb can be used to make a skin-healing ointment.

Hyssopus officinalis Hyssop Labiatae

In the first century AD, Dioscorides called this plant *hyssopus*, from the Hebrew *azob*, or "holy herb," used to cleanse sacred spaces; it may not be the herb mentioned by that name in the Bible. Hippocrates and Dioscorides both recommended this plant for respiratory complaints, as did Culpeper in the 17th century: "… it expectorates tough phlegm and is effectual in all cold griefs or diseases of the chest and lungs when taken as a syrup…"

Plant description and cultivation

A bushy perennial, semievergreen because it can lose foliage in heavy frosts. It grows to 3 ft/1 m high with woody stems at the base, small dark-green leaves, and spikes of deep, purple-blue flowers from June to August. It is very attractive to bees and butterflies. Native to the Mediterranean, it thrives in rocky dry soils, and needs a very sunny position. Propagate by seed in spring or softwood cuttings taken from a parent plant in summer. Prune back hard in early spring to prevent the bush becoming straggly.

Part of plant used

Flowering tops, fresh or dried.

Active ingredients

Essential oil with pinene and pinocamphone, glycosides, bitters, and tannins—giving tonic, expectorant, astringent, diuretic, and emmenagogue properties.

Safety information

Hyssop is not recommended for epileptics; do not use in pregnancy.

Culinary use

None.

Medicinal use

As a syrup or standard infusion, hyssop is beneficial for coughs, colds, influenza, and chest infections; it will encourage sweating and elimination of phlegm. Sweeten the infusion with honey if desired. It also works well combined with horehound, which also has expectorant qualities. Using fresh flowering tops in the bath is an old country remedy for rheumatism. Cooled infusion can be used to bathe sore eyes and soothe insect bites and stings. It is available commercially as a tincture.

Juniperus communis Juniper Cupressaceae

Juniper berries have been used since biblical times as a protection against any kind of infection, whether it be snakes, plague, or poison. Juniper twigs were burned in Europe as a kind of incense. The name "juniper" is a corruption of the Dutch name *genever*, the original name of gin, which is flavored with the berries. Culpeper says of it: "The berries are good for coughs, shortness of breath … they strengthen the brain, fortify the sight by strengthening the nerves, are good for agues, gout, and sciatica and strengthen the limbs."

Plant description and cultivation

A coniferous evergreen shrub up to 13 ft/4 m tall, with reddish-brown twigs and blue-green needles; the berries are borne on female plants and stay green for over 2 years before they ripen and turn blue-black; then they can be harvested. Juniper requires a sunny position and will tolerate most soils, though it does best in lime-rich ground. It grows naturally on the edges of woods or heathland, and requires plenty of moisture. It can be grown from seed or from cuttings taken in spring.

Part of plant used

Ripe berries.

Active ingredients

In the berries: resin, essential oil rich in pinene, sugars, tannins, flavonoids, and vitamin C, giving them strong diuretic, rubefacient, carminative, and antiseptic properties. The essential oil is extracted by distillation.

Safety information

Juniper berries should not be used medicinally in pregnancy or if there is any kind of kidney disease.

Culinary use

In northern Europe, a jelly with the berries is sometimes eaten as a tonic during the winter; the berries are also cooked with ham or *sauerkraut* (salted cabbage).

Medicinal use

A standard infusion of the crushed dried berries is helpful for rheumatism, gout, or sluggish digestion. A strong infusion of the berries can be used as an antiseptic mouthwash for the gums. The essential oil is used in aromatherapy massage and in sports liniments for muscular pain, poor circulation, and rheumatic pain.

Alchemilla vulgaris Lady's-Mantle Rosaceae

The name "lady's-mantle" was first officially given to the plant in the 16th century by the botanist Tragus. It had been associated with the Virgin Mary since the Middle Ages, and the name actually means "the mantle of Our Lady." It was also given because the leaf shape looks like a cloak. The name *alchemilla* links to the Arabic word *alkemelych* (alchemy); the perfect diamond-bright drops of dew that collect on its leaves were believed to have magical powers.

Plant description and cultivation
A perennial herb up to 20 inches/50 cm high with branching hairy stems and velvety leaves with toothed edges; it has many tiny yellow flowers from June until September. It will grow in most soils; in the wild it is found in mountain regions, on hillsides and even on rocky ledges. It likes full sun but will tolerate some shade. It is best to harvest flowers and leaves in June or July, when they are at their best; they need to be carefully dried and stored in the dark for winter use.

Part of plant used
Flowers and leaves.

Active ingredients
Tannins, essential oils, saponins, bitter compounds, and salicylic acid, giving it astringent, diuretic, antispasmodic, emmenagogue, and anti-inflammatory properties.

Safety information
Do not use in pregnancy.

Culinary use
The roots used to be eaten as a vegetable.

Medicinal use
A standard infusion, particularly in the late menstrual cycle, helps PMS and menstrual cramps; it is also useful for diarrhea, digestive spasms, and indigestion. It can be taken as a commercially prepared supplement to help harmonize menstruation and ease menopausal symptoms. A strong infusion applied to the skin helps to stop bleeding, clean wounds, ease sore skin, and calm insect bites; the herb can also be used in an ointment for healing wounds. Tincture of the herb is used in northern Europe to help ease insomnia.

219

Lavandula angustifolia Lavender Labiatae/Lamiaceae

Lavender is originally native to the southern Mediterranean and was probably brought to Britain by the Romans. The name "lavender" comes from the Latin *lavare*, to wash. In the 16th century, Gerard said, "it profiteth them much that have the palsy [paralysis] if they be washed with the distilled water from the lavender flowers…" and Culpeper later wrote: "It is of especial use for pains in the head and brain … cramps, convulsions and faintings … applied to the temples and nostrils it reduces the tremblings and passions of the heart…"

Plant description and cultivation
There are at least 80 known species and countless varieties of lavender grown all over the world. The most commonly used medicinally is the *Lavandula angustifolia*; strongly pungent spike lavender (*Lavandula spica*) and the more medicinal-smelling hybrid lavender (*Lavandula x intermedia*) are used in the pharmaceutical industry. Lavender is an aromatic shrub up to 3 ft/1 m high, with compact, woody stems at the base covered with gray-green leaves, and tall spikes of purple flowers in midsummer. It needs pruning back hard in late summer or early spring to keep in shape; it is best propagated by cuttings in late spring. Flowers should be harvested around the end of July. It requires full sun and light sandy soil.

Part of plant used
Flowering tops.

Active ingredients
Essential oil with linalyl acetate and tannins, giving it antispasmodic, sedative, rubefacient, and tonic properties. The essential oil is extracted by steam distillation.

Safety information
In pregnancy, use under practitioner supervision.

Culinary use
Lavender flowers can be used to decorate cakes, or in biscuits or buns for an unusual taste.

Medicinal use
A standard infusion of flowers and stems helps headaches, migraines, PMS, general stress, anxiety, and insomnia. Externally, the infusion can be used as a skin-soothing wash. Infused lavender oil balm is very useful for aching muscles, and with rosemary it improves the circulation. The essential oil is widely used in aromatherapy massage for muscular pain and stress.

Melissa officinalis Lemon Balm Labiatae/Lamiaceae

Other common names for this herb are "bee balm" or "sweet balm," for it is extremely attractive to beneficial insects. The name "melissa" comes from the Greek word for bee, and the honey from the bush is delicious. In the first century AD, Roman writers Pliny the Elder and Dioscorides used it for slowing blood flow and healing wounds without infection. A 17th-century book of pharmacists' formulae says, "An essence of Balm, given in Canary wine every morning, will renew youth, strengthen the brain, relieve a languishing nature and prevent baldness."

Plant description and cultivation

A vigorous perennial that dies back each year and re-shoots from the base, up to 3 ft/1 m tall, with tough 4-sided stems and strongly lemon-scented, rough-textured toothed leaves with a sharp point. To maximize leaf production, pinch out flowering stems; these have tiny whitish flowers in late summer. The aromatic leaves wilt and lose their fragrance quickly when picked, so are best used fresh. It grows in most soils, preferring sun or part shade. It self-seeds easily once established.

Part of plant used

Fresh leaves.

Active ingredients

Essential oil (containing citral, limonene, and other sweet aroma-chemicals, though in a tiny amount), tannin, and flavonoids, giving antispasmodic, sedative, antihistamine, and antiseptic properties.

Safety information

No issues.

Culinary use

Fresh leaves can be chopped into summer salad combinations and mixed with fresh orange slices for a citrus tang; it can also be added to summer cups, sauces, and desserts as a garnish.

Medicinal use

The standard infusion of the fresh leaves is used for digestive headaches, indigestion, stress-related stomach issues, and wind. It soothes the nerves and calms fraught emotions. It can also be used to bathe cuts and grazes, insect bites, stings, and nettlerash, and is reputed to be helpful in reducing hay-fever symptoms. The essential oil is very expensive and difficult to source, but is used in aromatherapy massage to help shingles, chickenpox, and cold sores as well as stress.

221

Cymbopogon citratus Lemongrass Gramineae

Aromatic lemongrass is widely cultivated in India and China, where it is used medicinally to help lower fever, especially malarial, as well as treating stress-related symptoms. It is grown in tropical gardens in countries like Sri Lanka and the Seychelles, and has only relatively recently become well-known in the West, thanks to the rising popularity of Thai and Indian recipes, where fresh lemongrass adds a particular and delicate flavor.

Plant description and cultivation
It is a tall, clump-forming grass up to 5 ft/1.5 m tall, with linear, strongly lemon-scented leaves. It is a tender plant, but can easily be grown in pots in a conservatory or greenhouse provided the temperature does not go below 45°F/7°C. It requires moist, very well-drained soil with generous levels of nutrients and high humidity—leaves may need spraying to keep them moist.

Part of plant used
Leaves (grass).

Active ingredients
Essential oil rich in citral, limonene, and other citrus-scented aroma-chemicals; the oil is extracted by steam distillation and used in the perfumery and aromatherapy industries. It has antispasmodic, rubefacient, and digestive-tonic properties.

Safety information
The essential oil should not be used on individuals with sensitive or allergy-prone skin, or on infants.

Culinary use
The fresh, chopped lower stems are used as a flavoring in Thai, Malaysian, and Indian cookery.

Medicinal use
The essential oil is used in aromatherapy massage to the stomach for indigestion or stomach cramps and to the muscles for aches and pains, injuries, or poor circulation. Combined with lavender and rosemary, it makes a wonderful tonic for weak, stressed limbs and sports massage (3 drops rosemary, 3 drops lavender, and 2 drops lemongrass essential oils in 4 tsp vegetable carrier oil). Combined with patchouli essential oil, lemongrass makes an effective insect repellent, applied to the skin (2 drops lemongrass, 6 drops patchouli essential oils in 4 tsp vegetable carrier oil).

Lippia citriodora/Aloysia citriodora Lemon Verbena Verbenaceae

This herb is originally native to South America, particularly Peru and the Andes, where it is still used extensively in teas, as a skin wash and as a natural cosmetic ingredient. It was introduced to Europe in the late 18th century and spread throughout the continent, becoming particularly popular in Victorian dried-flower envelopes and pillows. In France it has become one of the most popular herbal teas, "verveine," regularly served in cafés and restaurants.

Plant description and cultivation
A hardy perennial climbing on a tough wooden stem up to 26 ft/8 m if left unpruned. It has deeply lobed dark leaves and clings to support with tendrils. Its flowers are pale pink or yellowish in base color, with fringes of purple and white. It needs well-drained sandy soil and a very sunny position, with a wall, fence, or trellis for support. It needs shelter in very northern latitudes. It can be propagated using cuttings in the late summer and is best started from a plant purchased at a garden center.

Part of plant used
Flowers and vine.

Active ingredients
Several alkaloids, flavonoids, sugar, and gum, giving mild sedative, tranquilizing, and relaxant properties.

Safety information
Do not use if you are taking tranquilizing drugs.

Culinary use
None.

Medicinal use
A standard infusion of the fresh flowers and leaves helps insomnia, nervous stress and exhaustion, nervous indigestion, and PMS; it relaxes the nervous system thanks to the alkaloids it contains, and fortunately it is nonaddictive. It can also be used to lower high blood pressure, but should only be taken for this condition under professional supervision. A commercial herbal tincture is available as well as a homeopathic remedy, and passionflowers are often included in commercial herbal tea blends for relaxation.

Levisticum officinale Lovage Umbelliferae

This is an old English cottage herb, in use for hundreds of years as a seasoning and digestive tonic. Culpeper said of it in the 17th century, "It eases all inward gripings and pains, dissolves wind and resists poison and infection. A decoction of the herb is a cure for ague [fever] and pains of the body and bowel due to cold." In early recipes, lovage seeds were crushed rather like pepper to give flavor to dishes, as they have a hot taste; they were also used in the bath as a warming treatment for rheumatism and as an aphrodisiac—"lovage" is from the old English word meaning "love-ache."

Plant description and cultivation
A very hardy herbaceous perennial with deep fleshy roots, and stems up to 6 ft/3 m tall. It has divided, glossy green leaves with a spicy aroma and umbels of yellowish flowers in summer, followed by small seeds. It likes well-nourished moist soil in sun or part shade. It is best propagated by dividing roots in the fall, although it can be grown from seeds. Leaves can be harvested fresh throughout spring and summer, and the root is dug up and dried in the fall for decoctions.

Part of plant used
Leaves and roots.

Active ingredients
Roots need to be 3 years old before harvesting; they contain essential oil as well as coumarins, sugars, esters, and resin, giving stomach tonic, liver-supportive, diuretic, expectorant, and antirheumatic properties.

Safety information
Do not use in pregnancy or in kidney conditions.

Culinary use
Young lovage leaves can be made into soups, as well as added to salad-green combinations, and the seeds can be added to bread.

Medicinal use
A standard infusion of the leaves helps nervous exhaustion, rheumatism, and digestion of rich foods. A decoction or tincture of the root helps indigestion, colic, wind, and urinary disorders like cystitis. Added to the bath, a strong infusion of the leaves is cleansing and detoxifying to the skin.

Origanum majorana Marjoram Labiatae/Lamiaceae

The name *origanum* comes from the Greek words *oros ganos*—meaning "joy of the mountain." Marjoram is related to *Origanum vulgare*, the oregano herb used in Italian cooking, but is slightly lower-growing and has darker-colored leaves. It has been grown as a medicinal and culinary herb since Ancient Egyptian times and was known to the Greeks and Romans. It was probably introduced to Britain in the Middle Ages.

Plant description and cultivation
A half-hardy perennial with small, oval green leaves with points, and tiny stems of pinkish flowers in late summer. Pinch out flower stems to maximize leaf production for culinary use. It requires well-drained but moist soil with plenty of nutrients, positioned in full sun. It is best sown from seed in the spring but will not resist frost, so cover and protect in late fall. Leaves can be harvested throughout the growing season.

Part of plant used
Leaves.

Active ingredients
Essential oil and tannins, bitters, carotenes, and vitamin C, giving stomach tonic, antispasmodic, and sedative properties. The essential oil is extracted by steam distillation.

Safety information
No issues.

Culinary use
Fresh leaves give a light and delicious flavor to pasta sauce, pizza, herb vinegars, herb oils, and herb breads, as well as chicken dishes.

Medicinal use
A standard infusion of fresh leaves helps indigestion or digestion of rich foods as well as PMS and menstrual cramps. A strong infusion or leaves scattered in the bath helps muscular aches and pains as well as rheumatism. The essential oil is used in aromatherapy massage to help aches and pains, stress-related stomach disorders, and menstrual pain as well as anxiety and insomnia; it combines well with lavender for a relaxing massage (5 drops sweet marjoram, 5 drops lavender essential oils in 4 tsp vegetable carrier oil).

Myrtus communis Myrtle Myrtaceae

This beautiful sweet-smelling bush, originally from the southern Mediterranean, was dedicated to Aphrodite, the goddess of love, and has a long tradition of use as a female medicine and natural cosmetic. Myrtle was traditionally included in bridal bouquets and afterward the wedding sprigs were planted by the new couple's home to ensure fertility and good fortune. In Ancient Greece, the dried berries were used in cooking as a spice, as well as for dyeing hair!

Plant description and cultivation

A lovely aromatic evergreen shrub up to 10 ft/3 m tall, with tiny oval, glossy dark-green leaves with a sharp point, fragrant creamy white flowers with a golden center in July/August, and small blue-black berries in late summer. It requires light, well-drained soil and plenty of nutrients; it will survive frosts if placed by a wall. It needs full sun and warmth. The leaves are aromatic all year round but particularly strong-smelling in July and August; they dry well and contain their aroma.

Part of plant used

Leaves.

Active ingredients

Essential oil in the leaves with camphoraceous, sweet, and citrus aroma-chemicals (extracted by steam distillation), giving expectorant, antiseptic, immune-stimulant, and cleansing properties.

Safety information

No issues.

Culinary use

In the Middle East, the leaves and sometimes the berries are used to flavor strong meats.

Medicinal use

A standard infusion of fresh or dried leaves is taken as an early morning tea in the Mediterranean regions, particularly as a tonic to the urinary and reproductive organs. Myrtle is very pleasant combined with peppermint or lemon balm for a hot or cold infusion mixed with slices of fresh lemon and honey to taste. The infusion is also helpful for chesty coughs, colds, sore throats, and sinus infections; the leaves or the essential oil can be used for steam inhalations (see pages 132–133). Added to the bath, a strong myrtle infusion cleanses and deodorizes the skin.

Tropaeolum majus Nasturtium (Indian Cress) Tropaeolaceae

The name *nasturtium* comes from the Latin "nasturcium," which was given to various types of cress; the plant is closely related to watercress (*Nasturtium officinale*). The plant is originally native to South America, introduced to Spain from Peru in the 16th century. It soon became a very popular garden ornamental, and by the 17th century it was appreciated as a salad ingredient. The pickled seeds were used as a seasoning, rather like capers.

Plant description and cultivation
Nasturtium can grow as high as 10 ft/3 m, climbing on trailing stems. It has circular-shape leaves with radiating veins, and brightly colored orange or yellow flowers, followed by round seeds. It will grow in most soils, even poor, in full sun or part-shade; however, it needs regular watering, especially in hot weather. There are many ornamental varieties; for medicinal purposes, obtain seeds from a herbal supplier. It is easy to grow from seed planted in late spring directly into the ground.

Part of plant used
Leaves, flowers, and seeds (all used fresh).

Active ingredients
In the seeds, essential oil similar to mustard, fatty oil, and proteins, giving powerful antibacterial and antimicrobial effects. The leaves are rich in vitamin C, iron, and essential oil, giving a peppery taste.

Safety information
Medicinal use in pregnancy should be under the supervision of a practitioner.

Culinary use
The fresh green seeds can be pickled like capers; the leaves add a pungent taste to green salad combinations and the flowers are also edible, adding bright contrasting color.

Medicinal use
A standard infusion of crushed, fresh green seeds is a powerful antiseptic in cases of sore throats, sinusitis, and bronchitis, as well as urinary infections like cystitis and prostatitis. In France, baths of nasturtium leaves are used to regulate the menstrual cycle. Cooled infusion can be used as a skin-soothing and cleansing wash, especially for oily or problem skin. Tincture of nasturtium leaves and seeds is said to help baldness.

Urtica dioica Nettle Urticaceae

Nettles tend to be regarded as a troublesome weed, and yet they are invaluable medicinally and horticulturally. When they originally landed in Britain, Roman soldiers planted nettle seeds so they could rub the plants on their skin to relieve the damp and cold. The name "nettle" is from the Anglo-Saxon word for the plant, *netele*, which is related to the word for needle—nettle stems yield long fibers, once used for sewing.

Plant description and cultivation

This plant spreads very efficiently as a weed on long, creeping roots. It prefers moist, nitrogen-rich soil in sun or shade. Its stems can grow to 5 ft/1.5 m tall. The dull-green toothed leaves are covered in stinging hairs; in late summer, small yellowish flowers appear. The young spring stems are used for culinary purposes and medicinally. Nettles can also be used to return nitrogen to the soil as a liquid plant food; combined with comfrey leaves, they also make a liquid compost activator (see pages 52–53). The smaller species *Urtica urens* is used to prepare the homeopathic remedy Urtica.

Part of plant used

Young leaves.

Active ingredients

Formic acid, tannins, histamine, chlorophyll, minerals (iron, potassium, manganese, and sulfur), and vitamins A and C, giving astringent, tonic, antirheumatic, and blood-purifying properties.

Safety information

If stung by nettles, try rubbing on fresh sage, rosemary, or peppermint leaves. In the wild, rubbing with dock leaves will also help.

Culinary use

Cooked young leaves and stems used to be eaten as early spring greens, or nettle soup.

Medicinal use

A standard infusion of fresh leaves helps gout, rheumatism, and arthritis. Eating cooked nettles is a very good source of iron because the vitamin C helps absorption. The infusion also balances excessive menstrual bleeding, or irregular periods in puberty or the menopause. Strong nettle infusion can be used as a hair rinse to tone the scalp and help dandruff.

Avena sativa Oat Graminaceae

In the 12th century, the German abbess, mystic, and physician Hildegard of Bingen regarded oat as a valuable nutrient, second only to spelt (*Triticum vulgare*). She recommended it as a porridge or as cookies to be eaten to build reserves of strength, particularly in periods of weakness or illness. In the 16th century, Gerard mentions the widespread use of oats in baking throughout northern England, especially for "oaten cakes," also a staple in Scotland, of course. In the 17th century, Culpeper writes "the meal of oats boiled with vinegar takes away the freckles and spots in the face"; they have long been used to soothe the skin.

Plant description and cultivation
A tall grass up to 4 ft/1.2 m tall, with hollow jointed stems bearing the flower heads that become the seeds, harvested as oatmeal. Oats are an important commercial grain crop grown all over the world. For medicinal purposes, try to obtain organically grown oats to avoid ingesting any herbicides or chemical residues.

Part of plant used
Seeds (oatmeal).

Active ingredients
Saponins (rich source), alkaloids, flavonoid, starch, protein, fat, minerals including silica, iron, calcium, copper, magnesium, and zinc, giving cleansing, digestive-soothing, tonic, nerve-restorative, and appetite-stimulating properties.

Safety information
Oats are not recommended for individuals sensitive to gluten.

Culinary use
As porridge or baked in cookies, bread, or cakes.

Medicinal use
A bath with 3 tbsp oatmeal in a cheesecloth bag tied over the tap is very skin-soothing; fine oatmeal also cleanses the skin in face masks (see pages 162–163). Standard infusion of oats soothes the throat and eases chesty coughs, as well as being a nerve tonic for stress or emotional anxiety. A hot compress made from the infusion will help draw infection out of boils or abscesses, and also eases itching skin. Tincture of oat can be taken to help high levels of stress and insomnia.

229

Olea europea Olive Olaceae

Olives have been cultivated in the Middle East for at least 3,000 years. In Ancient Egypt, olive growers were exempt from military service. The name "olive" comes from the Latin *oleum*, meaning oil; it was burned in sacred lamps in temples and its leaves were made into victory wreaths for athletes. In the Bible, the story of Noah tells of the dove that returned with a sprig of olive in its beak; this has led to the idea of the "olive branch," or the peace offering.

Plant description and cultivation
An evergreen tree up to 40-ft/12-m tall, with a pale-gray bark, long, smooth, leathery green leaves, and creamy white flowers followed by the fruit—the olives—which ripen to dark purple. The olives are picked green for pressing because they are less acid, which improves the quality of the olive oil. First pressed "extra virgin" olive oil has the finest flavor and highest vitamin and mineral content. The trees require well-drained soil and full sun; although they are frost-hardy, they will not produce fruit at more northern latitudes.

Part of plant used
Fruit (olives crushed to yield olive oil).

Active ingredients
High levels of vitamin E (antioxidant) and oleic acid, an omega-9 fatty acid, which can lower harmful cholesterol in the blood.

Safety information
No issues.

Culinary use
Vital in Mediterranean recipes for salad dressings, sauces, breads, pizzas, pasta, mayonnaise, and meat or fish dishes.

Medicinal use
In a recent clinical study, patients with high blood pressure who used 6–8 tsp olive oil in their cooking and diet daily for a 6-month period, halved their use of blood-pressure medication. In older people, keeping up this intake of olive oil has been shown to link to better memory recall; there is also a low instance of bowel cancer in southern Mediterranean populations, where olive oil is a major part of the diet. The oil is an excellent skin and hair tonic and is used in shampoos and cosmetics.

Origanum vulgare Oregano (Wild Marjoram) Labiatae (Lamiaceae)

In Ancient Greece, oregano was used as a remedy for narcotic poisons and convulsions, and as a poultice for deep wounds. The Romans believed oregano brought joy to the dead, so they often planted it on tombs; it was also believed to bring happiness at weddings and was made into bridal wreaths. Because of its powerful aroma, it was used in medieval times as a "strewing herb," mixed into the straw that formed a floor covering.

Plant description and cultivation
It is a bushy perennial up to 2 ft/60 cm tall, with highly aromatic oval leaves with pointed ends. It produces stems of tiny, pinkish-purple flowers in late summer and is very attractive to bees, butterflies, and other beneficial insects. Its leaves contain more thymol than sweet marjoram (*Origanum majorana*), making it much more pungent and stronger-flavored, especially if it is grown in a warm location in full sun. It will thrive in a well-drained sandy soil and in the wild grows well even in coastal locations. It is best propagated by cuttings. Gather the flowering tops in August or September to dry for winter use.

Part of plant used
Leaves.

Active ingredients
Essential oil in the leaves with pungent camphoraceous aroma thanks to the thymol content, as well as tannins and bitters giving antispasmodic, stomach-tonic, astringent, expectorant, sedative, and carminative properties.

Safety information
Do not use medicinally in pregnancy; food flavoring is safe.

Culinary use
Adds a strong flavor to pizzas and Italian recipes, as well as to green salad combinations.

Medicinal use
Infusion of the fresh leaves helps headaches, menstrual cramps, insomnia, and the digestion of rich foods. The leaves added to the bath will help rheumatic pain and aching muscles; a herbal oil balm made with oregano and lavender will also ease pain and stiffness when massaged into the limbs. Hot compresses of a strong infusion will help clean and reduce swelling of cuts and wounds.

231

Petroselinum crispum Parsley Umbelliferae

Originally native to the Mediterranean, parsley is now widely cultivated in many varieties. The name *petroselinum* was given to the plant by Dioscorides in the first century AD, from the Greek *petra* (rock) and *selinon* (celery). It was sacred to the goddess Persephone, the Queen of the Underworld, and wreaths of it were placed on tombs. In the 16th century, Gerard said of garden parsley, "It is delightful to the taste and agreeable to the stomache," and went on to say that it could neutralize poison; this may be because it has a strong aroma—even able to quench garlic!

Plant description and cultivation
A biennial growing on a stout root up to 2 ft/60 cm tall, with triangular 3-lobed leaves that curl at the ends and give a ruffled appearance. Umbels of yellow flowers bloom in the second year, followed by oval seed pods containing sickle-shaped seeds. It requires rich, moist but well-drained soil in part sun, part shade; if you have the wrong sort of soil, you could try it in a pot. It is propagated from seed sown in the late spring. There is a flat-leaf French variety, which has a lovely aromatic flavor.

Part of plant used
Leaves and seeds.

Active ingredients
The seeds are most potent medicinally, with an essential oil (up to 7%), flavonoids, glycosides, vitamins A and C, and minerals, giving strong diuretic, emmenagogue, carminative, and stomach-tonic properties. The leaves are very rich in vitamin C and iron.

Safety information
Do not use seeds medicinally in pregnancy or in cases of kidney disease. Use of fresh leaves as food flavoring is safe.

Culinary use
Extensively as a flavoring in soups, sauces, egg and cheese dishes, salad dressings, meat and fish dishes.

Medicinal use
Standard infusion of the leaves is excellent for helping indigestion, especially after rich foods, as well as fluid retention and gout; it stimulates the appetite and improves assimilation of nutrients. Although the seeds are used in professional herbalism, they are not recommended for self-dosage.

Passiflora incarnata Passionflower Passifloraceae

This is a beautifully shaped flower with an amazing inner geometry, which gets its name because it reminded early missionaries of the crucifixion of Christ (known as his Passion). Another name associated with Christ, *incarnata* (incarnate), is also included in the name. The internal structures of the flower look like nails and the crown of thorns. It originates from North and South America and is now widely grown in gardens at fairly cool latitudes, where it thrives provided it is in a sheltered spot. In Native American medicine, it was used to calm the nerves.

Plant description and cultivation

A hardy perennial climbing on a tough wooden stem up to 26/8 m ft if left unpruned. It has deeply lobed dark leaves and clings to support with tendrils. Its flowers are pale pink or yellowish in base color, with fringes of purple and white. It needs well-drained sandy soil and a very sunny position, with a wall, fence, or trellis for support. It needs shelter in very northern latitudes. It can be propagated using cuttings in the late summer and is best started from a plant purchased at a garden center.

Part of plant used

Flowers and vine.

Active ingredients

Several alkaloids, flavonoids, sugar, and gum, giving mild sedative, tranquilizing, and relaxant properties.

Safety information

Do not use if you are taking tranquilizing drugs.

Culinary use

None.

Medicinal use

A standard infusion of the fresh flowers and leaves helps insomnia, nervous stress and exhaustion, nervous indigestion, and PMS; it relaxes the nervous system thanks to the alkaloids it contains, and fortunately it is nonaddictive. It can also be used to lower high blood pressure, but should only be taken for this condition under professional supervision. A commercial herbal tincture is available as well as a homeopathic remedy, and passionflowers are often included in commercial herbal tea blends for relaxation.

Piper nigrum Black Pepper Piperaceae

Back in the fifth century AD, ransoms of hundreds of pounds in weight of peppercorns were demanded for cities like Rome; the berries were considered as valuable as gold. Pepper was available more widely in Europe during the Middle Ages thanks to trade routes to India and later Malaysia, and by the 17th century it was a very popular spice in Britain, although heavily taxed by the government. In Indian Ayurvedic medicine, it is used for fevers, respiratory and chest infections, and to improve circulation.

Plant description and cultivation
A vine that if left unpruned can reach heights of over 24 ft/8 m. It has a very tough, woody stem and heart-shape shiny dark-green leaves. Small drooping clusters of tiny white flowers become the peppercorns, which are red as they mature; left in the sun, they turn black. White pepper is produced from the ripe dried berries with the black husk removed. Black peppercorns contain the most essential oil and give the sharpest flavor. The pepper plant requires deep, rich, well-manured soil, full sun, and a humid tropical atmosphere. It will grow in greenhouses or conservatories in cooler latitudes, but will not flower; it also needs regular spraying with water to keep the leaves moist.

Part of plant used
Fruits (peppercorns).

Active ingredients
Essential oil with sabinene, pinene, and other spicy pungent aroma-chemicals, giving stomach-tonic, digestive, circulation-stimulant, analgesic, and antiseptic properties.

Safety information
No issues.

Culinary use
Used to enhance flavors of savory dishes.

Medicinal use
In Ayurvedic medicine, an infusion made with 6 lightly crushed peppercorns, 1 tsp honey, and 1 cup boiling water is used as a digestive tonic and liver-supportive remedy, as well as a good tonic during episodes of influenza, colds, or sore throats. Other spices like clove or cinnamon can be combined with black pepper to boost immunity. In aromatherapy massage, the essential oil is used to help aches and pains, poor circulation, and indigestion.

Mentha x piperita Peppermint Labiatae/Lamiaceae

In the first century AD, Romans would deck themselves with wreaths of peppermint during feasts and eat it in flavored sauces. Oddly, the herb did not become popular in Britain until its medicinal properties were acknowledged in the 17th century. In the 18th century, it was cultivated in England as a commercial crop in Mitcham, Surrey, producing an essential oil that was then considered to be the best in the world. Germany and France have continued as major producers, and now most essential oil is produced in the USA.

Plant description and cultivation
Peppermint is a hybrid of two species, *Mentha aquatica* (water mint) and *Mentha spicata* (spearmint) and occurs in two varieties, called black or white. It is a tough, invasive plant with creeping roots, strong, 4-sided, reddish stems up to 3 ft/1 m tall and lance-shape, slightly toothed aromatic leaves. In the summertime, it will produce tall spikes of pinkish flowers. It thrives in damp, heavy soil and also likes shade. Once introduced, it is difficult to eradicate; try containing it by planting in large pots sunk deep into the soil with their bases removed, to restrict the roots but allow for drainage. Pick leaves fresh throughout the season, in high summer for drying.

Part of plant used
Leaves.

Active ingredients
Essential oil rich in menthol (extracted by steam distillation) as well as bitters and tannins, giving digestive-tonic, antispasmodic, analgesic, carminative, and expectorant properties.

Safety information
Use essential oil with caution on sensitive or allergy-prone skin.

Culinary use
Fresh leaves as garnishes for summer desserts, punches, or summer drinks.

Medicinal use
Standard infusion of fresh or dried leaves eases stomachaches due to indigestion or sluggish digestion. Peppermint combines well with lemon balm or lemon verbena for digestive upsets or with German camomile for stress-related indigestion. The menthol content is analgesic; and in aromatherapy it is used for massage for poor circulation and abdominal tension.

235

Rubus idaeus Raspberry Rosaceae

In traditional Chinese Medicine, the fruits are used to help kidney complaints; in Ancient Greece, the fruits and leaves were regarded as urinary tonics and decongestants. The name *rubus* means "thorny shrub" and *idaeus* is said to refer to Mount Ida in Greece, where raspberries grew wild in abundance. Culpeper said of it, "Venus owns this shrub ... the fruit has a pleasant grateful smell and taste, is cordial, strengthens the stomach and stays [prevents] vomiting..."

Plant description and cultivation
A deciduous shrub with prickly biennial stems up to 5 ft/1.4 m high, with alternate leaves that are deeply veined and toothed at the edges; they are green and hairy above and white and velvety below. The white flowers bloom in May or June, followed by the fragrant, compound red berries. It grows wild in woodland and on hillsides; in a garden it needs full sun and well-drained, slightly acid soil. It is very fast-growing, so one shrub will be ideal in a small space. The leaves are best picked just before the flowers open, and used fresh or dried; the fruit is picked when ripe and eaten fresh or frozen for wintertime.

Part of plant used
Leaves and fruits.

Active ingredients
In the leaves, tannins, pectin, vitamin C, organic acids, and fragarin, giving uterine-tonic, galactogogue, diuretic, astringent, and expectorant properties. The fruits are rich in vitamin C, organic acids, and sugars.

Safety information
The leaves should not be used medicinally during early pregnancy but can be used in the last month and during labor.

Culinary use
The fruits in desserts, wine, or vinegar.

Medicinal use
A standard infusion of the leaves is excellent for menstrual cramps and childbirth pains, toning uterine and pelvic muscles. It can be drunk during the last month of pregnancy to prepare for the birth and stimulate milk flow. It can also be given to children to ease cramps from indigestion or diarrhea. A strong infusion makes a good mouthwash or gargle for sore throats.

Trifolium pratense Red Clover Legumininosae

This plant is native to Europe, growing wild in pastures, on hillsides and in meadows; it has been cultivated as animal fodder since prehistoric times. The name *trifolium* refers to the 3-lobed (trefoil) leaves, and the common name "clover" comes from the Anglo-Saxon name for the plant, *claefre*. It is extremely attractive to bees, bumble bees, and butterflies; the honey from the flowers is one of the finest. It has long been used in Europe as a wound-healing herb and is now naturalized in North America and Australia as a field crop.

Plant description and cultivation
A short-lived perennial up to 2 ft/60 cm tall; it can grow close to the ground or erect. The soft green leaves are trifoliate and the flowers are deep pink, densely packed in compact flowerheads. It needs moist, well-drained soil and full sun, and can easily be grown from seed. The flowers need to be harvested when they are in full bloom, any time from May through to September.

Part of plant used
Flowers.

Active ingredients
In the flowers: tannins, glycosides, organic acids, pigments, flavonoids, and coumarins, giving astringent, expectorant, vulnerary, and antispasmodic properties.

Safety information
No issues.

Culinary use
Fresh young shoots can be added to salads or soups, or cooked like spinach.

Medicinal use
A standard infusion of the flowers is very pleasant-tasting and helps bronchitis, hoarseness, chest infections, and coughs as well as indigestion. It is useful given to children with whooping cough; try preparing it as a syrup. It can be used to clean and disinfect cuts and wounds, as well as to soothe skin conditions like eczema or psoriasis. Red clover is useful in a skin-healing ointment with calendula. Compresses or poultices of the flowers speed up the healing of burns, sunburn, or sore, inflamed skin. Regular herbal supplementation with red clover can help PMS symptoms like acne, as well as regulate the hormones.

Rosa damascena, Rosa centifolia and *Rosa gallica* Rose Rosaceae

Roses originated in China and spread via trade routes through India to Persia, and into the Middle East and Europe. They are one of the most celebrated species of flower across many cultures and are grown in countless modern species and varieties. The three species named above—the damask rose, the cabbage rose, and the apothecary's rose—are the three most important "old" roses for medicinal and perfumery use. The finest damask roses grow in Bulgaria and Morocco, cabbage roses in France and North Africa, and the apothecary's rose in France. They are highly scented and not as regular in shape as modern roses.

Plant description and cultivation
These roses grow up to 6 ft/2 m in height with trailing prickly stems and leaflets arranged in groups of 5 or 7. They produce fragrant, many-petalled flowers in a range of colors; the "old" damasks are soft pink, the centifolias slightly deeper pink, and the gallicas deep pink or red. They need shelter and full sun for at least part of the day, and are extremely hungry for nutrients; feeding regularly helps avoid pests. They should be purchased from specialist suppliers to ensure the correct species is planted.

Part of plant used
Petals.

Active ingredients
In all three rose flowers, essential oil with various floral aroma-chemicals (as many as 300), as well as tannins, glycosides, and pigments, giving anti-inflammatory, astringent, liver-tonic, digestive-tonic properties. Essential oils and floral waters are extracted by distillation and solvent extraction, and are very costly.

Safety information
No issues.

Culinary use
Rose water is used in frosting, and candied petals can be used as cake decorations.

Medicinal use
Rose water can be drunk to help diarrhea and the digestion of fatty foods, and can also be used to cleanse and soothe sore inflamed skin, eczema or acne. The essential oil is used in perfumery and also in aromatherapy massage to ease stress, anxiety, and emotional trauma.

Rosmarinus officinalis Rosemary Labiatae/Lamiaceae

The name *rosmarinus* means "dew of the sea"; it originates from the rocky coastlines of the southern Mediterranean. It was a symbol of fidelity and was used in bridal wreaths and bouquets; it was burned as incense in Ancient Greece, sacred to the goddess Artemis, the huntress. During the 16th century, branches of rosemary were gilded and tied with ribbons, then given to guests at weddings or as New Year tokens of good fortune; they were also frequently used as fragrant Christmas decorations, along with holly and yew.

Plant description and cultivation
Rosemary is an evergreen shrub up to 4 ft/2 m high, with woody stems and strongly aromatic narrow leaves. In early spring, it produces pale-blue or pink flowers, which are an important source of food for bees. It thrives in sandy, well-drained soil in full sun; it needs shelter in cooler climates. The leaves can be used fresh all year round, but are most aromatic in July or August, and best picked then for drying. Propagate from cuttings or by layering, and prune back after flowering.

Part of plant used
Leaves.

Active ingredients
In the leaves—essential oil with pinene and other fresh aroma-chemicals, (extracted by steam distillation), also tannins, saponin, and organic acids, giving circulation-stimulant, digestive-tonic, antispasmodic, and analgesic properties.

Safety information
Do not use medicinally with epileptics or during pregnancy; food flavoring is safe.

Culinary use
With lamb, pork, and other meat dishes, in vinegars, marinades, and salad dressings.

Medicinal use
A standard infusion of fresh or dried leaves helps headaches, migraine, and general fatigue as well as indigestion and wind. A herbal oil balm made with equal parts of myrtle, rosemary, and lavender rubbed into the skin helps rheumatism. The leaves or the essential oil (4 drops) added to a warm morning bath are invigorating. The essential oil is used in muscle balms and sports rubs, as well as in aromatherapy massage for aches and pains and poor circulation.

Salvia officinalis Sage (Common) Labiatae/Lamiaceae

The name "sage" is from the Latin *salvere*, meaning to save or to be in good health; an old English saying runs: "He that would live for aye [ever] should eat Sage in May"; an old name for it is *Salvia salvatrix*—meaning Sage the Savior. Gerard said of it in the 16th century: "Sage is singularly good for the head and brain, it quickeneth the senses and memory, strengtheneth the sinews, restoreth health to those that have the palsy…" In Italy, an old country health tonic is to eat fresh sage leaves in bread and butter.

Plant description and cultivation
An evergreen, highly aromatic shrub up to 2 ft/ 60 cm tall with woody stems and velvety aromatic gray-green leaves. In early summer, it produces spikes of purple-blue flowers, which are very attractive to bees and butterflies. It requires light, well-drained soil in full sun and does not like too much water. Leaves can be harvested all year round but are most aromatic in August; pick them then for drying. Propagate by cuttings or by layering.

Part of plant used
Leaves.

Active ingredients
Essential oil rich in thujone and other pungent aroma-chemicals, also bitters, estrogenic compounds, phenolic acids, resin, and tannins, giving antiseptic, antifungal, antispasmodic, diuretic, and estrogen-balancing properties.

Safety information
Due to the thujone content, the leaves are not to be used medicinally during pregnancy, though they can be used as food flavoring.

Culinary use
Sparingly with pork, lamb, and other strong meats, also in cheese dishes; with apple sauce.

Medicinal use
A standard infusion of fresh/dried leaves helps colds, coughs, chest infections, and influenza. It can also stop excess sweating, which—along with the estrogenic effect—makes it an excellent remedy during the menopause. (Note: a standard infusion should not be drunk continually for more than 4 days, as it is a powerful herb.) A strong infusion makes a good gargle for sore throats and an antiseptic mouthwash for ulcers and sore gums.

Satureja hortensis Savory (Summer) Labiatae/Lamiaceae

The name *satureja* was first used by Pliny the Elder in the first century AD, and is thought to be linked to Satyr, the mythical part-man, part-goat—the herb was said to be an aphrodisiac. Virgil, another famous Roman writer, praised the fragrance of the plant and said it should be placed near beehives. It actually has a peppery taste, and was used in Roman recipes as a pungent seasoning. Culpeper prized it and advised the use of dried leaves in syrups for winter use "to expel tough phlegm from the chest."

Plant description and cultivation
A small bushy annual with erect woody stems up to 15 in/38 cm tall, and small lance-shape dark-green leaves; tiny white flowers appear in summer. It needs well-drained soil in full sun and can be planted in pots. It works well planted between rows of beans to keep away blackfly. Propagate from seed in the garden in late spring and harvest the leaves in August when they are most aromatic.

Part of plant used
Leaves, young stems.

Active ingredients
In the leaves and young stems, essential oil with carvacrol and cymene as well as resins, phenolic compounds, tannins, and mucilage, giving it antispasmodic, carminative, astringent, stomach-tonic, and expectorant properties.

Safety information
Do not use medicinally in pregnancy; as a food flavoring it is safe to use sparingly.

Culinary use
This is the bean herb, improving the taste and avoiding wind! It is also used in stuffings, nut loaves, vegetarian pâtés, and egg, poultry, or meat dishes.

Medicinal use
A standard infusion helps indigestion and excess wind, stimulates the appetite and eases diarrhea. It is also reputed to destroy intestinal parasites. A syrup of the dried leaves is an excellent expectorant for coughs and phlegm. Fresh savory leaves rubbed directly onto wasp or bee stings bring instant relief.

Rumex acetosa Sorrel Polygonaceae

Garden sorrel is common all over Europe. It is generally found growing wild in pastureland, where the soil is iron and nitrogen-rich. Various species were used in cookery from the 14th century onward, and in the 16th century, during the reign of Henry VIII, it was held in great esteem as a nourishing salad. In the 18th century, John Evelyn wrote that it gives "… so great a quickness [vitality] to the salad that it should never be left out." Culpeper added, "Sorrel … cools any inflammation and heat of the blood in agues [fevers] pestilential … or sickness in fainting…," and recommended it as a poultice for plague sores. It was also used as a green dye, and mashed up with vinegar and sugar as an old-fashioned relish with cold meat, called "greensauce."

Plant description and cultivation
A hardy perennial up to 4 ft/1.2 m tall with large green oblong-based leaves with a distinctive point, and large spikes of reddish-brown flowers in mid-summer. Once established, it self-seeds quickly, in rich moist soil with sun or part shade. The young leaves are best as they are more tender.

Part of plant used
Fresh leaves.

Active ingredients
In the leaves: tannins, vitamin C, and oxalic acid, which is toxic in excess, because it can interfere with iron absorption. This is why young leaves are used, and only sparingly. Sorrel has diuretic and blood-cleansing properties.

Safety information
Not advised in the diet or medicinally during pregnancy or if you are anemic.

Culinary use
Young leaves sparingly in salad-green combinations and in soup.

Medicinal use
A standard infusion of the young leaves, cooled, is a soothing drink during fevers, a gargle for sore throats, and a tonic for indigestion. As a poultice, the young leaves draw out poison from boils and infected wounds.

Hypericum perforatum St.-John's-Wort Hypericaceae

The herb has many ancient associations; in medieval times, it was hung in doorways and windows to drive away evil spirits, and the name *hypericum* is derived from a Greek phrase meaning "over an apparition," linking to the herb's supernatural powers. In the Middle Ages, the knights of St. John used it extensively to heal sword wounds in crusaders. It is in full flower around the summer solstice of 21 June, which is a time sacred to St. John; at that time, the flowers were gathered still covered in dew and used to aid conception.

Plant description and cultivation
A hardy perennial up to 2 ft/60 cm tall, with erect, partly woody stems and opposite pairs of oval leaves, which show tiny oil glands when held up to the light. The golden-yellow flowers have 5 petals. It requires well-drained soil in sun or part-shade and spreads rapidly once established; it can be propagated by dividing roots. There are many ornamental varieties—the species *Hypericum perforatum* is required for medicinal use. The flowering stems can be picked from July onward and used fresh.

Part of plant used
Flowering stems.

Active ingredients
Tannins, flavonoid gycosides including the red-pigmented hypericin, essential oil, and resin, giving sedative, anti-inflammatory, antiseptic, and astringent properties.

Safety information
Prolonged exposure to strong sunlight after using the herb medicinally can cause skin allergies in some people.

Culinary use
None.

Medicinal use
Herbal oil balm made with the fresh flowering tops turns red because of the hypericin and is used to relieve the pain of neuralgia or sciatica, as well as burns, wounds, bruises, and hemorrhoids (piles). Commercially prepared St.-John's-wort is available as a tincture and capsules, and is recommended for depression and mood swings, for example around the menopause. A standard infusion of the fresh flowering tops helps ease menstrual cramps.

Helianthus annuus Sunflower Compositae/Asteraceae

Sunflower is originally native to south-western North America and Mexico, where it was cultivated by the Native Americans as far back as 1000 BC. It was introduced to Europe in the 16th century, but was not grown as a crop until it reached Russia, where large-scale cultivation was extremely successful. Today it is produced in many countries worldwide, used as cattle fodder and also grown for the seeds, which are pressed to yield a vegetable oil. The name *helianthus* is from the Greek words *helios* (sun) and *anthos* (flower).

Plant description and cultivation
A very tall annual up to 10 ft/3 m, with large golden daisy flowerheads, some of which can be as wide as 16 in/40 cm. It has long, bright-yellow petals and brown tubular disk florets in its center where the seeds form. The seeds are striped black and white and the average flower produces approximately 1,000. It needs well-drained soil in full sun, but will need watering in hot weather. There are numerous ornamental varieties, with colors ranging from orange to deep reddish-brown, and they are very easy to grow in pots.

Part of plant used
Seeds.

Active ingredients
The seeds are an important source of vegetable oil, containing unsaturated linolenic and oleic fatty acids (up to 45%), as well as palmitic and arachic acid and vitamin E; this combination is extremely beneficial to the skin, helping to soften and rebuild the upper layers. Taken in the diet, it maintains cell structure and reduces blood cholesterol.

Safety information
No issues.

Culinary use
Extensively in salad dressings, mayonnaise, as a light cooking oil; the seeds can be roasted and used as toppings, or added to breads.

Medicinal use
An excellent base for a herbal oil balm, sunflower is easy to work into the skin and does not leave a fatty residue. Combined with cocoa butter, it makes a very effective ointment (see pages 130–131) for dry skin, eczema, and for healing damaged skin.

Artemisia dracunculus Tarragon (French) Compositae/Asteraceae

The name in French is *estragon* or *herbe au dragon*, dragon's herb, possibly because the roots have a coiled appearance somewhat like snakes, and also because of the ancient reputation of the plant as curing all sorts of bites and poisons. It first appeared in English gardens in Tudor times, during the 15th and 16th centuries. John Evelyn in the 17th century recommended it in salads, and Culpeper advised it as a menstrual tonic.

Plant description and cultivation
A perennial herb up to 3 ft/1 m tall, with branching stems and narrow, pointed aromatic green leaves. It does produce greenish-white flowers, but in northern climates it does not produce seeds, so it has to be propagated by root division or taking cuttings in spring. It needs moist but well-drained soil and full sun. The stems are best harvested just before the flowers bloom, on a dry day. Hang them upside down to dry and then gently pull the leaves off the twigs. This is also the best time to harvest if you want to make aromatic vinegar.

Part of plant used
Flowering stems.

Active ingredients
As well as bitters and tannins in the leaves, there is also a powerful essential oil with very pungent aroma-chemicals including estragole, which is abortifacient; it also has cleansing and liver-supportive properties.

Safety information
Due to the estragole content, do not use medicinally during pregnancy and only sparingly in food.

Culinary use
Tarragon is mainly used in cooking; in egg, cheese, meat and fish dishes, pâtés, salad-green mixtures and salad dressings, aromatic vinegars and oils, and herb butters; it also enhances root vegetables like parsnips and carrots. It is a classic herb in French cuisine. Generally, just 3 or 4 fresh leaves are enough to flavor a dish, or 1/2 tsp dried tarragon.

Medicinal use
A standard infusion of the fresh or dried leaves can be used as a mouthwash for toothache, sore gums, or mouth ulcers.

Thymus vulgaris Thyme Labiatae/Lamiaceae

The Greeks used thyme as a purifying incense to cleanse temples and homes. The name "thyme" may link to the Greek word *thumus*, meaning courage; the warm, powerful aroma has long been appreciated for its uplifting qualities. Roman commentators praised it as a fumigator and antiseptic, and it may well have been introduced into Britain by the Romans. It was very popular by the 16th century, when Gerard noted that it "helpeth the bitings of any venomous beast, either taken in drinke or outwardly applied."

Plant description and cultivation
A low-growing perennial up to 18 inches/46 cm tall, with woody stems forming a dense mat, covered with tiny dark-green aromatic leaves and spikes of pinkish flowers in summer. The whole plant is very attractive to bees, butterflies, and other beneficial insects. It requires well-drained, preferably sandy soil in a warm and very sunny position. Propagate using cuttings in summer or layering in spring. Although the leaves can be harvested for much of the year, the flavor is most pungent in summer, when thyme should be picked for drying.

Part of plant used
Leaves.

Active ingredients
In the flowering stems and leaves: essential oil rich in thymol and other pungent aroma-chemicals, also bitters, tannins, flavonoids, and saponins, giving antiseptic, expectorant, uterine-stimulant, antimicrobial, and vulnerary properties.

Safety information
Do not use medicinally in pregnancy; used sparingly as a food flavoring, it is safe.

Culinary use
With meat and fish, in casseroles and stews, and with root vegetables like carrots; also in herbal vinegars and oils.

Medicinal use
Standard infusion of fresh/dried leaves with 1tsp honey is an excellent tonic for sore throats, coughs and colds, shortness of breath, and hoarseness. Thyme can also be made into a syrup for use in the wintertime as an antiseptic. Thyme essential oil is used in commercial liniments, chest rubs, and medicines for respiratory and muscular complaints.

Curcuma longa Turmeric Zingiberaceae

Turmeric is a vital cooking spice and traditional remedy in India, where it originates. In Ayurvedic medicine, it is used as a blood-purifier, an anti-inflammatory, and an antiparasitic remedy; recent scientific research has confirmed its beneficial effects on the intestines, suggesting that turmeric in the diet may account for the low incidence of bowel cancer in India. It is also used in Ayurvedic practice to treat digestive and skin problems, as well as wounds and damaged skin. The root is also used as a yellow dye in place of saffron, which is more expensive.

Plant description and cultivation

A close relative of ginger, it is a perennial up to 4 ft/1.2 m tall with shiny, pointed pairs of lance-shape leaves and dense spikes of yellow flowers. It has a yellow-colored, fleshy tuberous root, which is boiled, dried, and powdered before being used as spice. It requires well-drained, moist, and well-nourished soil, a humid atmosphere, and minimum temperature of 45°F/7°C; it can be grown in pots in greenhouses or conservatories provided the leaves are kept moist. Propagation is by division of roots.

Part of plant used

Roots.

Active ingredients

Essential oil in the roots rich in turmerone and other spicy aroma-chemicals, with cleansing, diuretic, anti-inflammatory, antiparasitic, and potentially antitumoral properties. The fragrance is musky and bitter-sweet.

Safety information

No issues.

Culinary use

In Indian curry powders for meat and vegetable dishes; also to color rice yellow.

Medicinal use

An infusion of $\frac{1}{2}$ tsp turmeric powder in generous $\frac{3}{4}$ cup milk helps intestinal parasites, diarrhea, and sluggish digestion as well as coughs, colds, or sore throats. In India, it is also used as a tonic for anemia because it is rich in iron. Turmeric powder mixed to a paste with a little chickpea flour and water is applied externally to cuts and wounds to speed up healing, as well as a skin-smoothing paste to improve and brighten the complexion.

Valeriana officinalis Valerian Valerianaceae

In Ancient Greek times this remedy was known as *phu* (a reference to its strong odor); however, by medieval times it had acquired the name "all heal," and was employed particularly for its effect on the nervous system. The name *valeriana* is possibly derived from the Latin *valere* (to be healthy). Culpeper said of it in the 17th century, "It is an excellent medicine for loosening the bowels when other medicines fail. It is excellent for headaches, tremblings, palpitations, hysteric complaints and the vapours [depression]."

Plant description and cultivation

A tall hardy perennial up to 5 ft/1.5 m, with an extensive root system that produces angular, erect, furrowed stems. The opposite leaves have between 7 and 13 leaflets, and the small flowers are pinkish-white and densely packed. It grows wild in damp meadows and ditches or near streams; in the garden, it needs moist, fertile soil in a sunny position. It can be sown from seed in spring or propagated by root division in fall. Once established, it can be invasive. There is a red ornamental valerian, *Centranthus ruber*, which has no medicinal value.

Part of plant used

Two-year-old roots are dried and used.

Active ingredients

Essential oil with pungent valeranone and other aroma-chemicals (extracted by steam distillation), as well as valepotriates (sedative ingredients), alkaloids, bitters, and tannins, giving strongly sedative, antispasmodic, and hypnotic properties.

Safety information

Do not use if you are taking sedative drugs; do not use over a long period as it can cause headaches.

Culinary use

None.

Medicinal use

Commercially prepared capsules or a tincture can be taken for insomnia, depression, and nervous tension; research indicates a beneficial effect on the heart and a lowering of high blood pressure. Valerian also helps stress-related conditions of the bowel, such as irritable bowel syndrome or spastic colon. However, you are best advised to consult a professional herbal practitioner for guidance and use, especially if your condition is more chronic or long-term.

Fragaria vesca Wild Strawberry Rosaceae

The earliest mention of the strawberry is in a 10th-century Anglo-Saxon plant list; the name is probably derived from the Anglo-Saxon *streauberige*, linked to the word "strewn"—thrown about and haphazard in appearance—as the long trailing stems and untidy habits of the plant show well. It was an extremely popular fruit by the 17th century—the playwright Ben Jonson speaks of "A pot of strawberries gathered in the wood to mingle with your cream," long before the teatime treat at Wimbledon tennis tournament!

Plant description and cultivation

Only the wild strawberry is used medicinally; the common domestic variety *Fragaria ananassa* is a large-fruited hybrid of American origin and its leaves have no medicinal value. *Fragaria vesca* is a perennial herb with a short rhizome, rosettes of trifoliate leaves, and long runners at root level, which spread beyond the parent, then take root and become new plants. The flowers arise directly from root level on long stems and swell up to become the red fruit; wild strawberries are very small and tart as well as sweet. The plant requires fertile, well-drained soil in sun or part-shade. The leaves are picked and dried in midsummer for medicinal use.

Part of plant used

Leaves and fruit.

Active ingredients

In the leaves, mainly tannins, bitters, vitamin C, and essential oil, giving astringent, diuretic, and tonic properties.

Safety information

No issues.

Culinary use

Also rich in vitamin C, the fruits can be eaten as dessert or made into jelly.

Medicinal use

A standard infusion of fresh or dried leaves helps gout or cystitis, as well as digestive problems and bad breath; it also soothes and calms the nerves. Cooled leaf infusion is an astringent, skin-toning lotion and the fruits can be added to face packs or simple cleansers to tone the pores and clear the complexion. A poultice of mashed fruit quickly cools burns or sunburn.

Hamamelis virginiana Witch Hazel Hamamelidaceae

Originally a native American remedy for swellings, bruises, pulled muscles, and sore eyes, the plant was first collected from the damp woods of Virginia, hence the second part of the botanical name. The name *hamamelis* links to the Greek words *hama* (at the same time) and *melis* (fruit), because the new flowers appear as the previous year's fruit is ripening. The association with witches seems to link to the use of young twigs as divining rods in the search for water. An old name for the tree is "snapping hazelnut" because the seeds are actually ejected over some distance when they are ripe.

Plant description and cultivation

A deciduous tree or shrub up to 16 ft/5 m tall with smooth bark and alternate oval leaves with deep veins. Clusters of fragrant yellow flowers appear in early February or March. The tree needs moderately fertile, well-drained soil in a sunny or part-shady position. Propagation is best from seed sown first in containers and then transported to the garden site. The twigs are cut after flowering to make distilled witch hazel water, and the bark is used to make a tincture.

Part of plant used

Leaves and bark.

Active ingredients

The bark and leaves contain coumarin glycosides, saponins, tannins, and bitters, giving astringent, anti-inflammatory, and antiseptic properties.

Safety information

No issues.

Culinary use

None.

Medicinal use

Ointment of witch hazel made with a strong infusion of the leaves is helpful for hemorrhoids (piles) and varicose veins. Distilled witch hazel is astringent and cleansing to open or blocked pores, blackheads, and acne, as well as bruising and as a first-aid remedy for bleeding, burns, nose bleeds, or sore eyes; it can also be applied to varicose veins as a compress. There is a commercial tincture available, which should be used under professional guidance. A standard infusion of the leaves can be drunk to ease bowel irregularity.

Achillea millefolium Yarrow (Milfoil) Compositae

Yarrow has an amazing number of evocative old names, showing its long history of use; "old man's pepper" refers to its use as snuff, "soldier's woundwort," "bloodwort" and "staunchweed" to its ability to slow bleeding. The name "yarrow" is a corruption of the Anglo-Saxon name of the plant, *gearwe*. In the 17th century, Culpeper said that it "… restrains violent bleedings and is excellent for piles; a strong tea is made of the leaves and drunk frequently. The ointment made from the leaves is applied to ulcers … and all such runnings as abound with moisture."

Plant description and cultivation
A perennial up to 12 in/30 cm tall with finely divided, feathery gray-green leaves and tall stems with flat clusters of small creamy-pink flowers, at their best in July. It spreads rapidly through creeping roots or by self-seeding. It thrives in most soils, in sun or part-shade. In a garden, it is best cultivated in a pot to avoid its spreading too much. There are ornamental varieties with red or yellow flowers, but these have no medicinal value.

Part of plant used
Flowering heads.

Active ingredients
In the flowering tops, essential oil with azulene, formed during distillation, which turns the oil blue; also alkaloids, saponins, amino acids, salycilic acid, and sugars, giving analgesic, anti-inflammatory, astringent, diaphoretic, and stomach-tonic properties.

Safety information
Prolonged overuse can lead to headaches and skin sensitivity in direct sunlight.

Culinary use
None.

Medicinal use
A standard infusion of the dried or fresh leaves helps severe head colds or influenza, especially in combination with equal parts of peppermint and elderflower. Like the latter, yarrow encourages sweating and helps to reduce fever. Cooled infusion can be used to clean and disinfect cuts and grazes and stop bleeding. In the bath or in an ointment, yarrow has an analgesic effect on rheumatism, thanks to the azulene and the salycilic acid it contains (similar to aspirin). A poultice of fresh leaves is excellent for healing wounds.

glossary

ABORTIFACIENT—a substance that causes abortion.

ACTIVE INGREDIENT—a medicinally active substance.

ACUTE—a condition that comes on rapidly and intensively and is of short duration.

ALKALOID—a strong-acting plant ingredient.

ANAEMIA—deficiency of iron.

ANALGESIC—reduces pain.

ANAPHRODISIAC—reduces sexual desire.

ANTIBIOTIC—kills microorganisms.

ANTIDIAPHORETIC—stops excessive perspiration.

ANTI-INFLAMMATORY—reduces inflammation.

ANTIRHEUMATIC—eases rheumatism.

ANTISPASMODIC—relieves spasm of involuntary muscles (e.g. colon).

ANTISEPTIC—kills bacterial microorganisms.

ANNUAL—a plant with a single-year life cycle, requiring fresh sowing each year.

APHRODISIAC—increases sexual desire.

AROMATIC—a substance with a fragrant scent.

AROMA-CHEMICAL—a fragrant ingredient in an essential oil.

ASTRINGENT—contracts tissue and stops bleeding.

BALM—a preparation made by soaking plant material in a fatty oil.

BARK—the outer covering of a woody stem or trunk.

BIENNIAL—a plant that completes its life cycle in 2 years, growing in year 1 and flowering or fruiting in year 2.

BITTER—a substance that is usually antibacterial and bitter tasting.

BULB—a plant's underground storage organ with fleshy leaves and a short stem around the next year's shoot.

CARMINATIVE—relieves intestinal gas.

CHRONIC—a condition with milder symptoms but persisting over a long period.

COMPRESS—a wet pad of material applied to the body, usually to prevent bleeding and relieve inflammation.

COMPOUND—of leaves or flowers, meaning a cluster with branches.

DECOCTION—a preparation of roots or tough plant material boiled in water.

DECIDUOUS—a tree or shrub that drops its leaves each fall and regrows them in the spring.

DEMULCENT—a soothing substance that protects mucus membranes.

DIAPHORETIC—increases perspiration.

DIGESTIVE TONIC—helps digestive processes.

DIURETIC—increases elimination of water via the kidneys and bladder.

EDEMA—buildup of fluid in the tissues.

EMMENAGOGUE—stimulates menstruation.

ESSENTIAL OIL—a concentrated, fragrant volatile extract from a single plant.

EVERGREEN—a tree or shrub that stays green all year round.

EXPECTORANT—helps the chest expel excess phlegm.

FATTY OIL—a natural vegetable oil, e.g. evening primrose.

FEATHERY—of leaves, divided into many fine segments.

FLAVONOID—a group of organic pigments in plants.

GALACTOGOGUE—stimulates breast-milk flow.

GLYCOSIDE—a substance containing sugar.

HERBAL—a book with descriptions of herbs and their preparations.

HYBRID—a plant produced by crossing two species (shown with an "x" in the Latin name).

HYPERTENSIVE—a substance that increases blood pressure.

HYPOTENSIVE—a substance that reduces blood pressure.

INDIGENOUS—a plant native to the place where it grows.

INFUSION—plant material steeped in boiling water.

INTRODUCED—a plant species brought to an area by man.

MUCILAGE—a gel-like substance secreted by certain plants.

NARCOTIC—a substance that gives feelings of stupor, and also relieves pain.

NEEDLE—a very narrow leaf, e.g. that of a pine tree.

OINTMENT—an oil and fat-based emulsion used to heal the skin.

PERENNIAL—a plant that lives for more than 2 years, flowering each summer; some die down to root stock over the winter and regrow in spring (e.g. lemon balm).

POULTICE—a pad of moist material normally applied directly to the body to relieve soreness and inflammation.

RHIZOME—a fleshy root, (e.g. ginger).

RUBEFACIENT—has a localized reddening effect on the skin.

RUNNERS—a creeping root system.

SAPONINS—plant ingredients that foam in water.

SEDATIVE—a calming substance that relieves tension and causes drowsiness.

STIMULANT—a substance that increases physiological activity.

TANNINS—a group of plant ingredients with astringent and antibacterial effects.

TAPROOT—a thick, main root growing straight downward (e.g. carrot).

TINCTURE—a plant remedy made by soaking material in alcohol.

TONIC—an invigorating action on the body.

TRIFOLIATE—3-lobed leaves (e.g. clover).

UMBEL—an umbrella-shape flower head with stems of equal length radiating out from one point (e.g. angelica).

VULNERARY—wound-healing action.

resources

USA

Professional herbal associations:

American Herbalists Guild
1931 Gaddis Road
Canton
GA 30115
Tel: 770 751 6021
Email: ahgoffice.earthlink.net
Website: americanherbalistsguild.com

American Holistic Medical Association
12101 Menaul Blvd., NE, Suite C
Albuquerque
NM 87112
Tel: 505 292 7788
Website: www.holisticmedicine.org

Other useful US websites:
www.herbnet.com
www.herbworld.com
www.herbalgram.org

UK

For general information on herbs including medicinal, culinary, and horticultural aspects, contact:

The Herb Society
Sulgrave Manor
Sulgrave
Banbury
OX17 2SD
Tel: 01295 768899
Email: email@herbsociety.co.uk
Website: www.herbsociety.org.uk

Suppliers of herbs:

G Baldwin & Co
171/173 Walworth Rd
London SE17 1RW
Tel: 020 7703 5550
Email: sales@baldwins.co.uk
Website: www.baldwins.co.uk

Neal's Yard Remedies
8–10 Ingate Place
London SW8 3NS
Tel: 020 7498 1686
Email: mail@nealsyardremedies.com
Website: www.nealsyardremedies.com

For a list of qualified professional herbal practitioners, contact:

National Institute of Medical Herbalists
56 Longbrook St.
Exeter
Devon EX4 6AH
Tel: 01392 426022
Email: nimh@ukexeter.freeserve.co.uk
Website: www.nimh.org.uk

Useful UK websites:
www.herbcentre.co.uk
www.botanical.com

AUSTRALIA

Information on herbs:

Focus on Herbs
Consultancy and information service
PO Box 203
Launceston
Tasmania 7250
Tel: 03 6330 1493
Email: admin@focusonherbs.com.au
Website: www.focusonherbs.com.au

Queensland Herb Society
PO Box 1114
Kenmore
Queensland 4069
Tel. 07 5426 8299
Website: homepage.powerup.com.au
/~sage/index.htm

index

index

picture acknowledgments

The Bridgewater Book Company would like to thank Corbis for the permission to reproduce copyright material: pp. 2, 4, 12, 14, 21, 23, 32, 33, 37, 41, 45, 46, 47, 49, 53, 64, 120, 155, 207, 214.